Aho-Girl

\\'ahô͵gərl\\ *Japanese, noun.*
A clueless girl.

12 | Hiroyuki

CHARACTER PROFILES

AHO-GIRL's Cast of Characters

Name **Akuru Akutsu (Akkun)**

Memo

Childhood friend of Yoshiko, who lives next door. Plays the aggravated straight man to Yoshiko's absurdity. Tries to cure Yoshiko of her stupidity, but despite all his effort, it's not going very well.

Name **Yoshiko Hanabatake**

Memo

An inexpressibly clueless high school girl. Favorite food: bananas. Has been friends with Akkun since they were kids and is in love with him. Lives entirely by impulse. Tends to enjoy life too much.

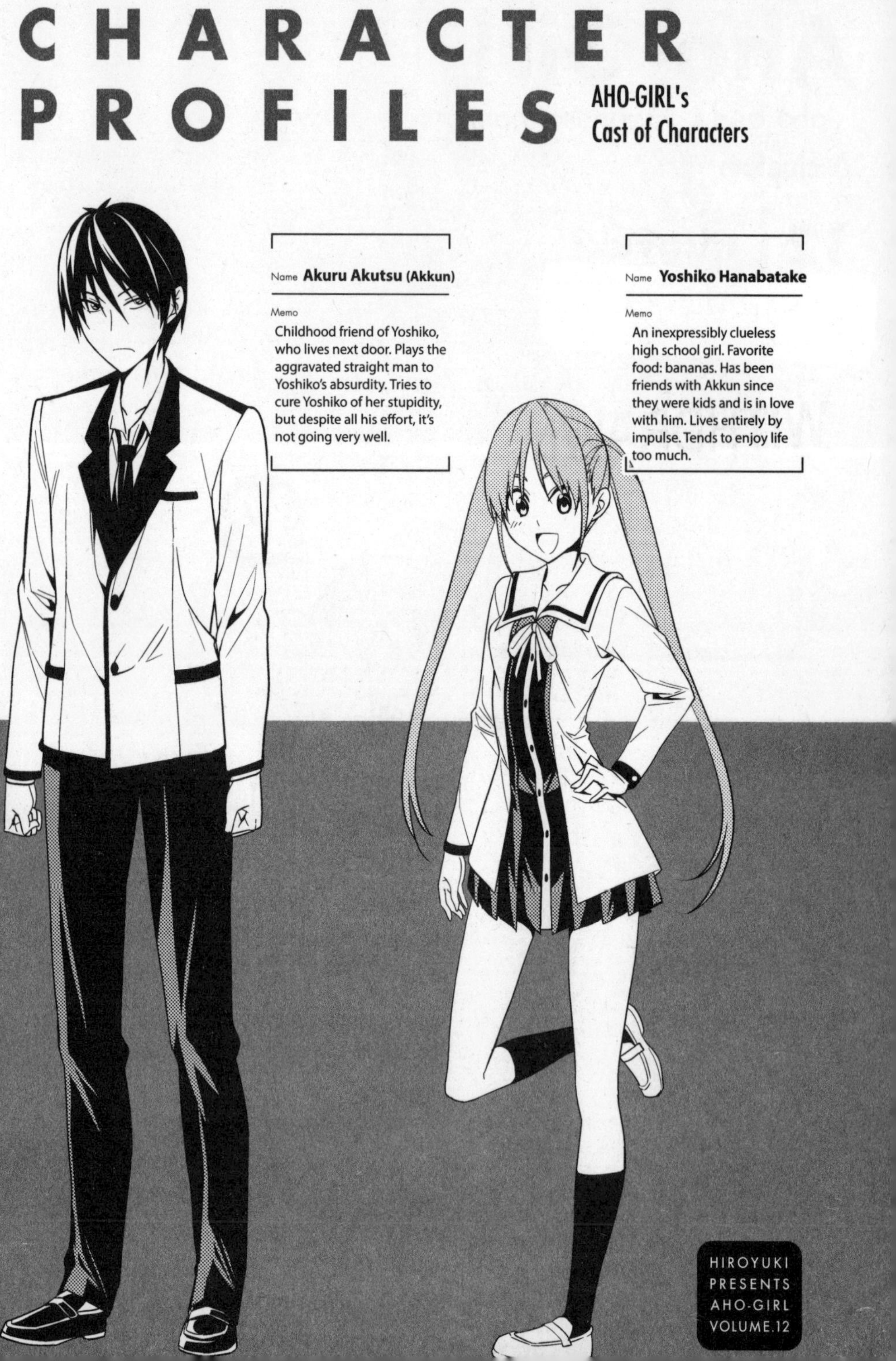

HIROYUKI PRESENTS AHO-GIRL VOLUME.12

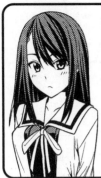

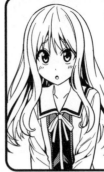

Name **Sayaka Sumino**

Memo

Yoshiko's friend. She's a very kind girl. She knows her kindness lands her in all sorts of trouble, yet she remains kind. Worries about being boring.

Name **Head Monitor**

Memo

An upperclassman at Yoshiko's school. Has fallen head over heels for Akkun and begun to stray from the moral path, but she doesn't realize it. G cup.

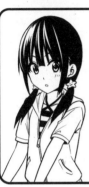

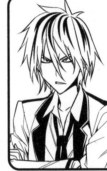

Name **Ryuichi Kurosaki**

Memo

An unfortunate hooligan who knows nothing of human kindness and therefore was easily won over by Yoshiko. Seems to want to be friends with Akkun, but there's not much hope for that.

Name **Ruri Akutsu**

Memo

Her brother Akkun is outstanding, but she's not quite so fortunate. She is dismayed by her terrible grades. Perhaps the day will come when all her hard work pays off… She hates Yoshiko.

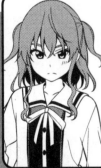

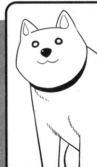

Name **Dog**

Memo

A ridiculously big dog Yoshiko found at the park. Started out vicious, but once vanquished by Yoshiko, has become docile. Is quite clever and tries to stop Yoshiko from her wilder impulses.

Name **Akane Eimura**

Memo

A gal in Yoshiko's class. An impulsive person, she is easy to get on board with just about anything. She'd like to have a boyfriend, but then her friend Kii asked her out and now she's panicking over that. She's a pretty lonely person, actually.

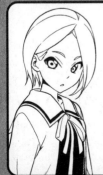

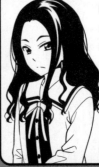

Name **Kuroko Shiina**

Memo

Akane's friend. A gal who looks very grown-up at first glance. Has a very pure, ongoing relationship with her boyfriend, who she's known since they were little. She's actually very private and sucks at talking about romance.

Name **Kii Hiiragi**

Memo

Akane's friend. It's hard to tell what this gal is thinking. Of the three, she's the most sedate. Her relationship status isn't very clear…

AHO-GIRL

12 CONTENTS

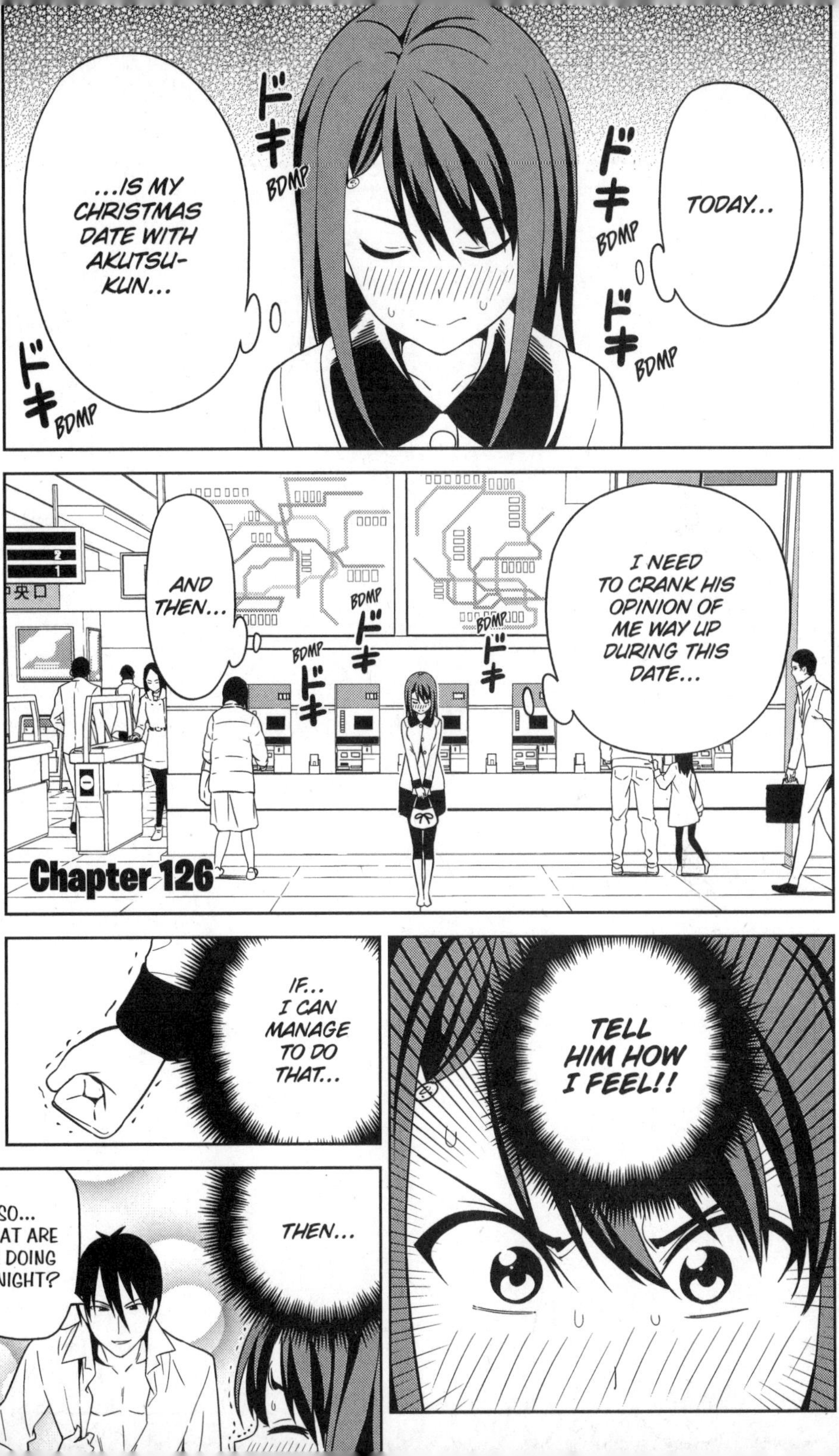

TODAY...
ドキ BDMP
ドキ BDMP
ドキ BDMP
...IS MY CHRISTMAS DATE WITH AKUTSU-KUN...
ドキ BDMP
I NEED TO CRANK HIS OPINION OF ME WAY UP DURING THIS DATE...
ドキ BDMP
ドキ BDMP
ドキ BDMP
AND THEN...
中央口
Chapter 126
TELL HIM HOW I FEEL!!
IF... I CAN MANAGE TO DO THAT...
THEN...
SO... WHAT ARE WE DOING TONIGHT?

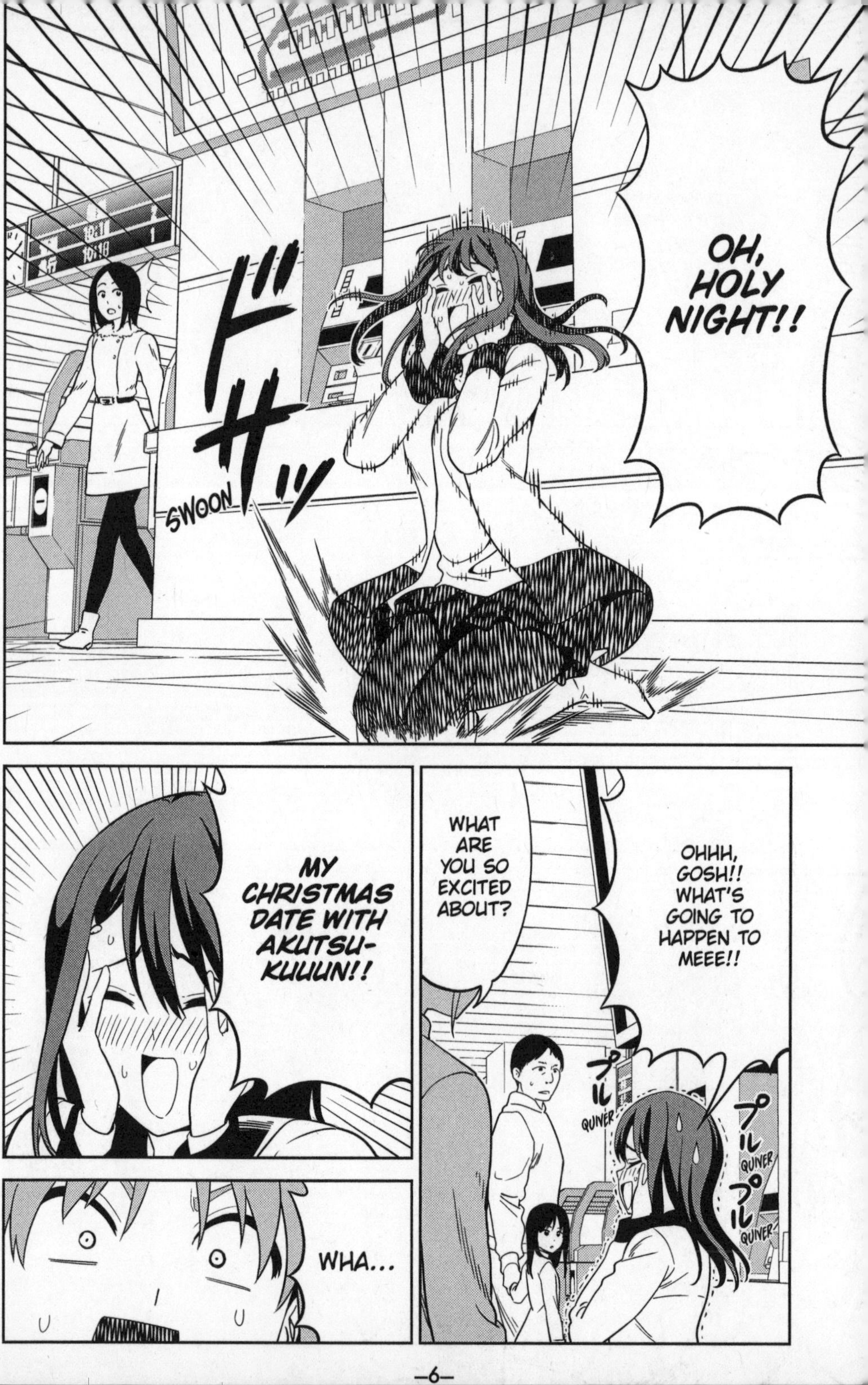
OH, HOLY NIGHT!!
ドサッ
SWOON
OHHH, GOSH!! WHAT'S GOING TO HAPPEN TO MEEE!!
WHAT ARE YOU SO EXCITED ABOUT?
プル
QUIVER
プル
QUIVER
プル
QUIVER
MY CHRISTMAS DATE WITH AKUTSU-KUUUN!!
WHA...

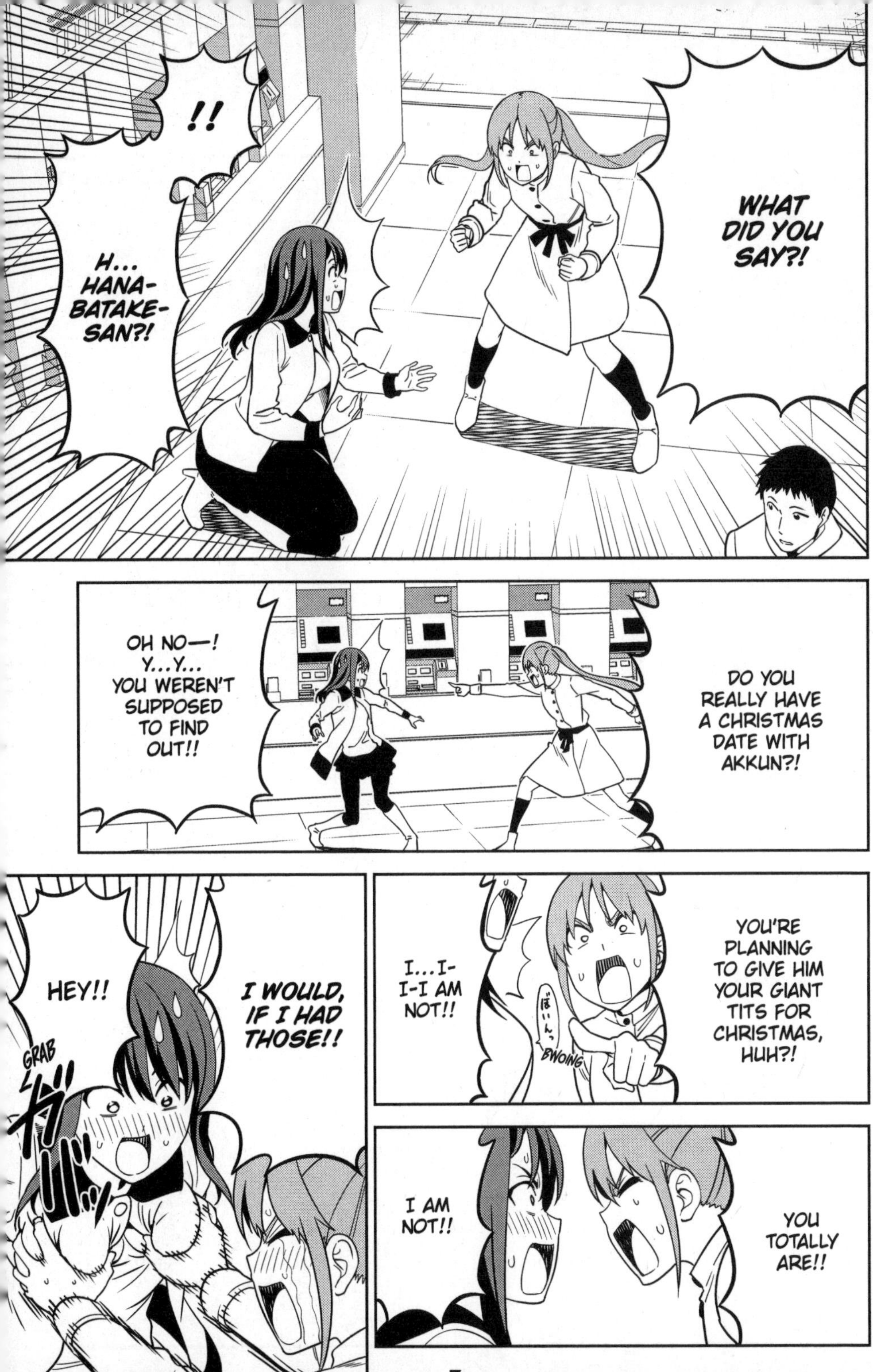
WHAT DID YOU SAY?!
!!
H... HANA-BATAKE-SAN?!
DO YOU REALLY HAVE A CHRISTMAS DATE WITH AKKUN?!
OH NO—! Y...Y... YOU WEREN'T SUPPOSED TO FIND OUT!!
YOU'RE PLANNING TO GIVE HIM YOUR GIANT TITS FOR CHRISTMAS, HUH?!
ばいんっ
BWOING
I... I- I-I AM NOT!!
YOU TOTALLY ARE!!
I AM NOT!!
I WOULD, IF I HAD THOSE!!
HEY!!
GRAB

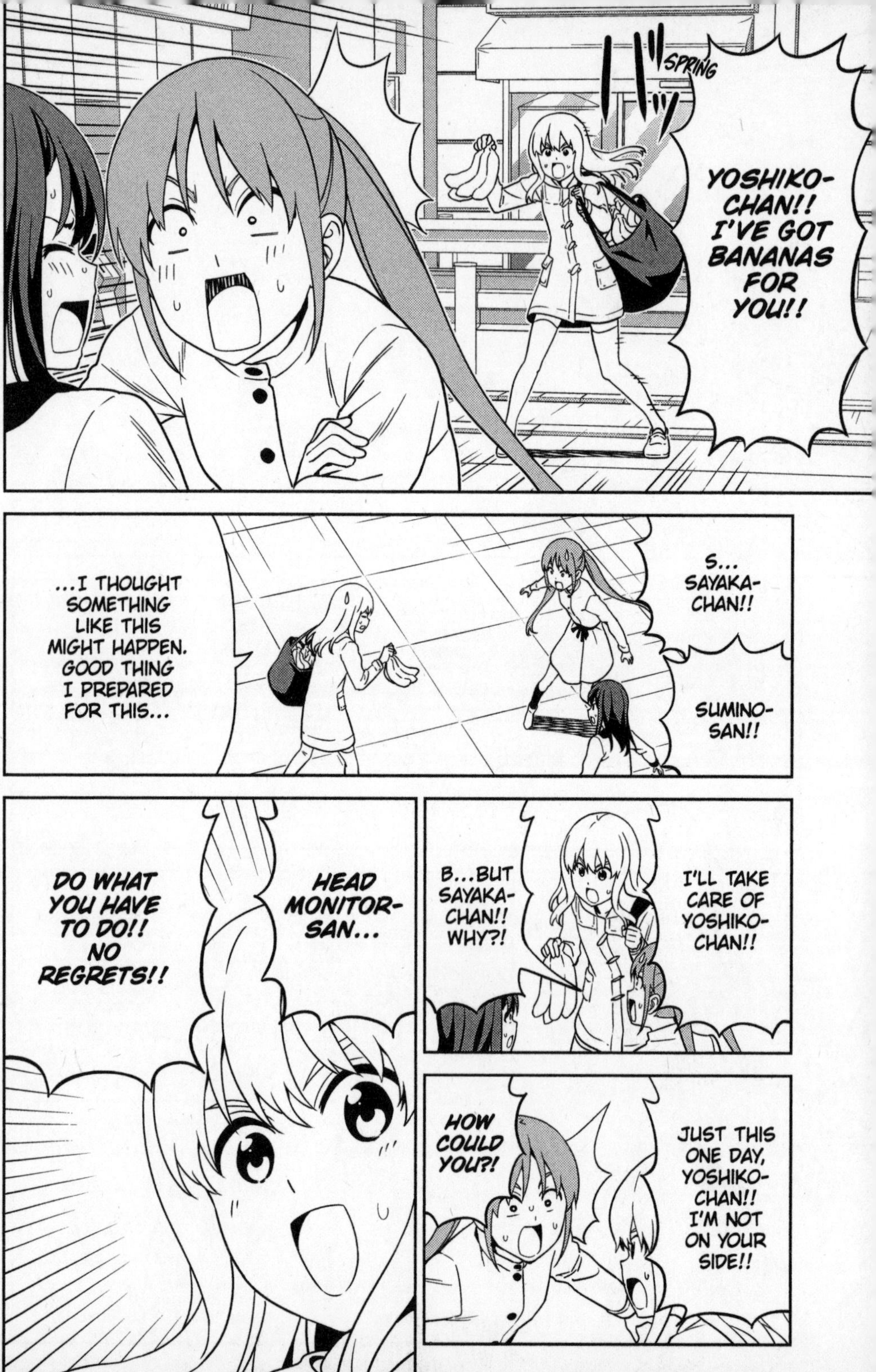
SPRING
YOSHIKO-CHAN!! I'VE GOT BANANAS FOR YOU!!
S... SAYAKA-CHAN!!
SUMINO-SAN!!
...I THOUGHT SOMETHING LIKE THIS MIGHT HAPPEN. GOOD THING I PREPARED FOR THIS...
I'LL TAKE CARE OF YOSHIKO-CHAN!!
B...BUT SAYAKA-CHAN!! WHY?!
JUST THIS ONE DAY, YOSHIKO-CHAN!! I'M NOT ON YOUR SIDE!!
HOW COULD YOU?!
HEAD MONITOR-SAN...
DO WHAT YOU HAVE TO DO!! NO REGRETS!!

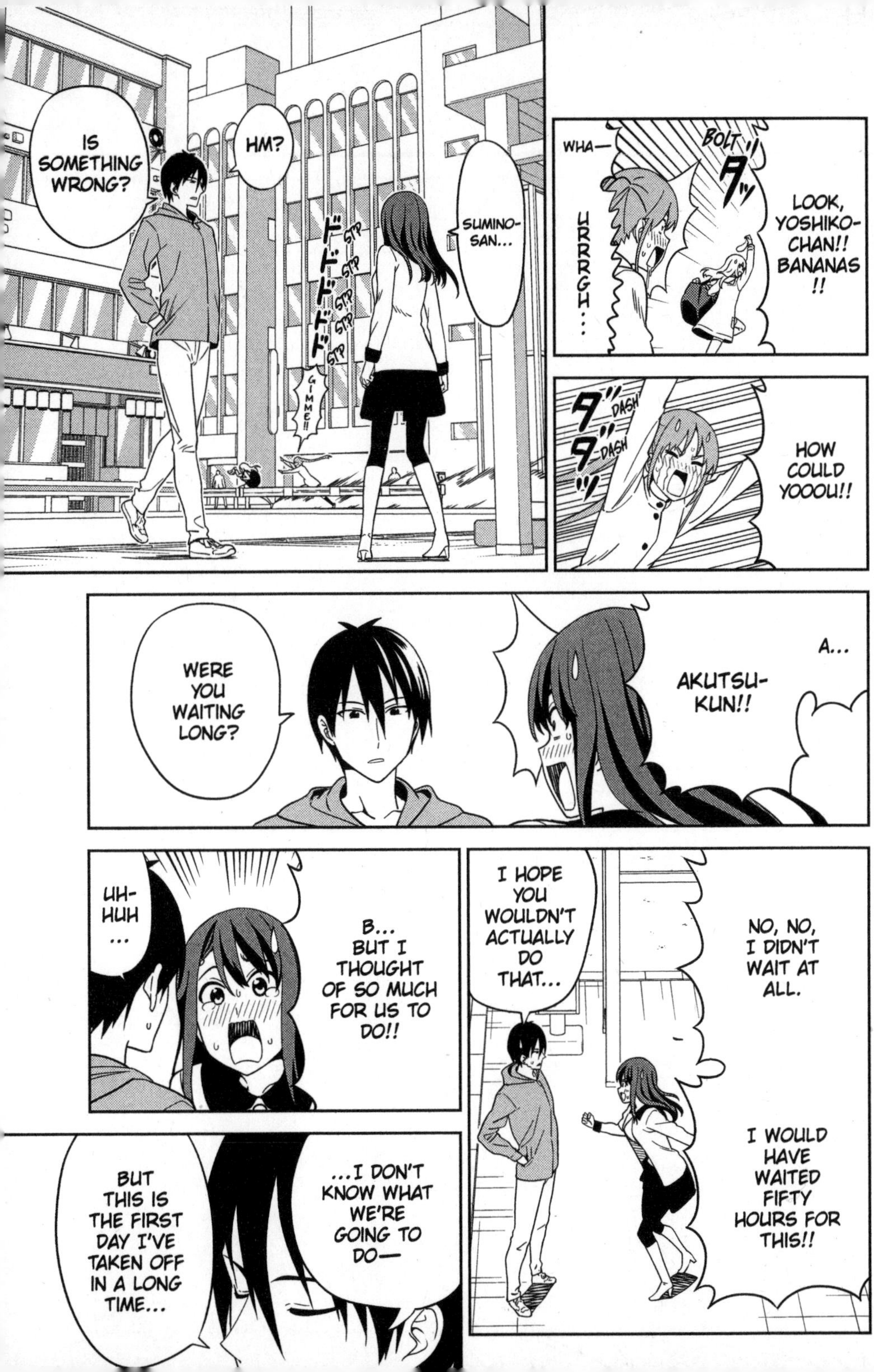
WHA—
BOLT
LOOK, YOSHIKO-CHAN!! BANANAS!!
URRRGH...
DASH
DASH
HOW COULD YOOOU!!
SUMINO-SAN...
STP STP STP STP STP
GIMME!!
HM?
IS SOMETHING WRONG?
A...
AKUTSU-KUN!!
WERE YOU WAITING LONG?
NO, NO, I DIDN'T WAIT AT ALL.
I WOULD HAVE WAITED FIFTY HOURS FOR THIS!!
I HOPE YOU WOULDN'T ACTUALLY DO THAT...
B... BUT I THOUGHT OF SO MUCH FOR US TO DO!!
UH-HUH...
...I DON'T KNOW WHAT WE'RE GOING TO DO—
BUT THIS IS THE FIRST DAY I'VE TAKEN OFF IN A LONG TIME...

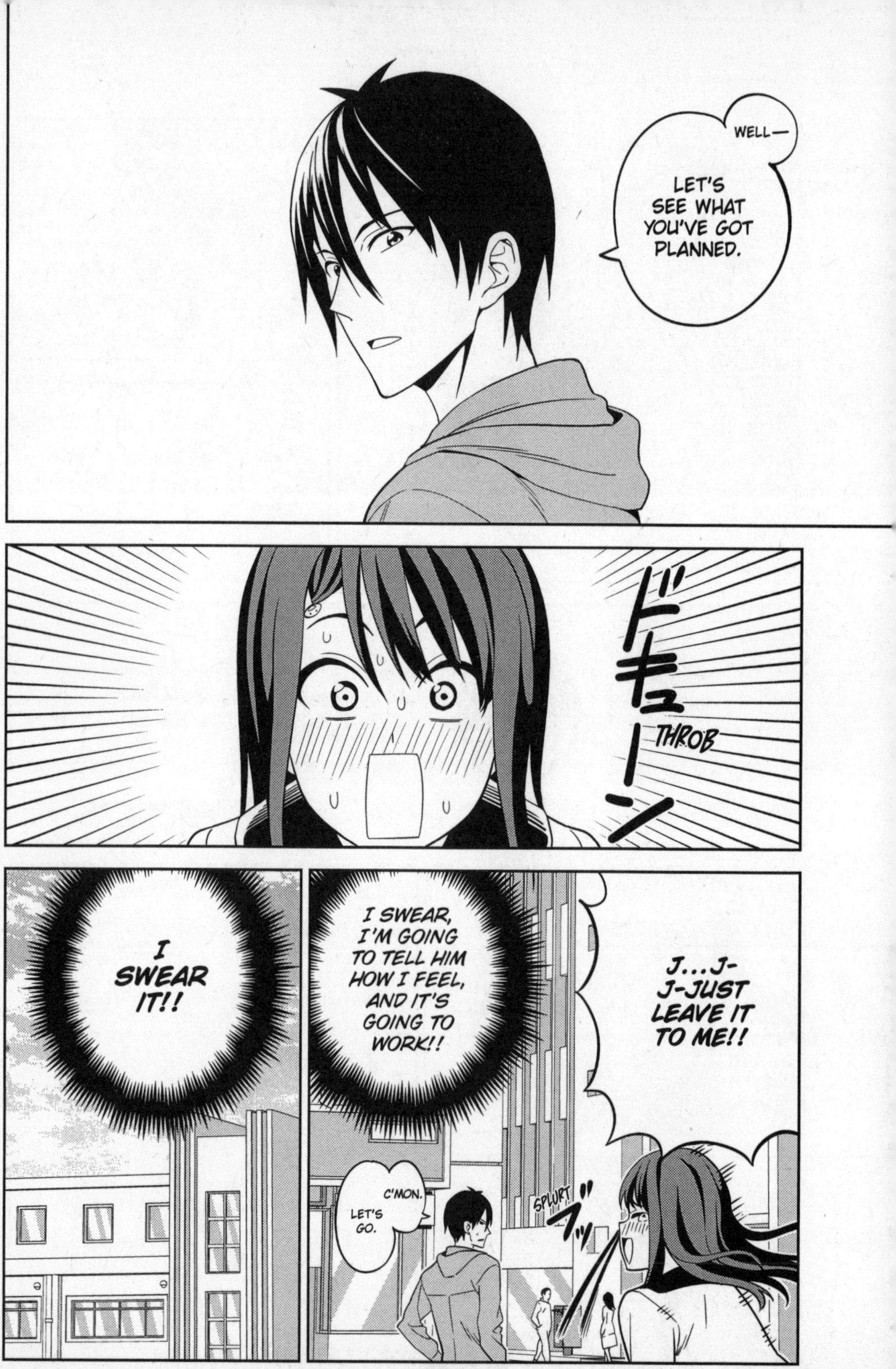
WELL—
LET'S SEE WHAT YOU'VE GOT PLANNED.
ドキューン
THROB
J...J-J-JUST LEAVE IT TO ME!!
I SWEAR, I'M GOING TO TELL HIM HOW I FEEL, AND IT'S GOING TO WORK!!
SPLURT
ブッ
C'MON.
LET'S GO.
I SWEAR IT!!

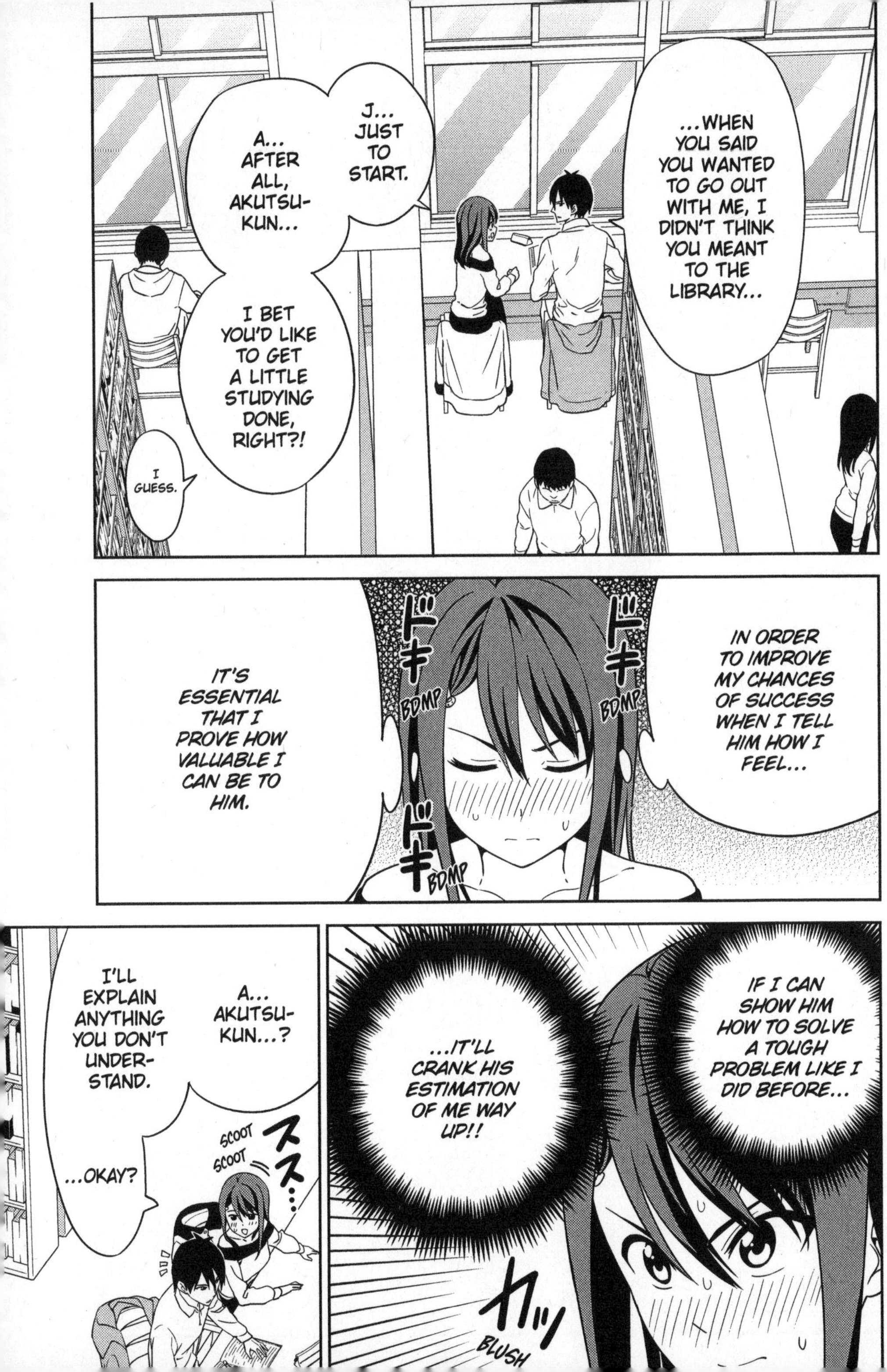
...WHEN YOU SAID YOU WANTED TO GO OUT WITH ME, I DIDN'T THINK YOU MEANT TO THE LIBRARY...
J... JUST TO START.
A... AFTER ALL, AKUTSU-KUN...
I BET YOU'D LIKE TO GET A LITTLE STUDYING DONE, RIGHT?!
I GUESS.
IN ORDER TO IMPROVE MY CHANCES OF SUCCESS WHEN I TELL HIM HOW I FEEL...
ドキ BDMP
ドキ BDMP
ドキ BDMP
IT'S ESSENTIAL THAT I PROVE HOW VALUABLE I CAN BE TO HIM.
IF I CAN SHOW HIM HOW TO SOLVE A TOUGH PROBLEM LIKE I DID BEFORE...
...IT'LL CRANK HIS ESTIMATION OF ME WAY UP!!
カッ BLUSH
A... AKUTSU-KUN...?
I'LL EXPLAIN ANYTHING YOU DON'T UNDER-STAND.
...OKAY?
スス... SCOOT SCOOT

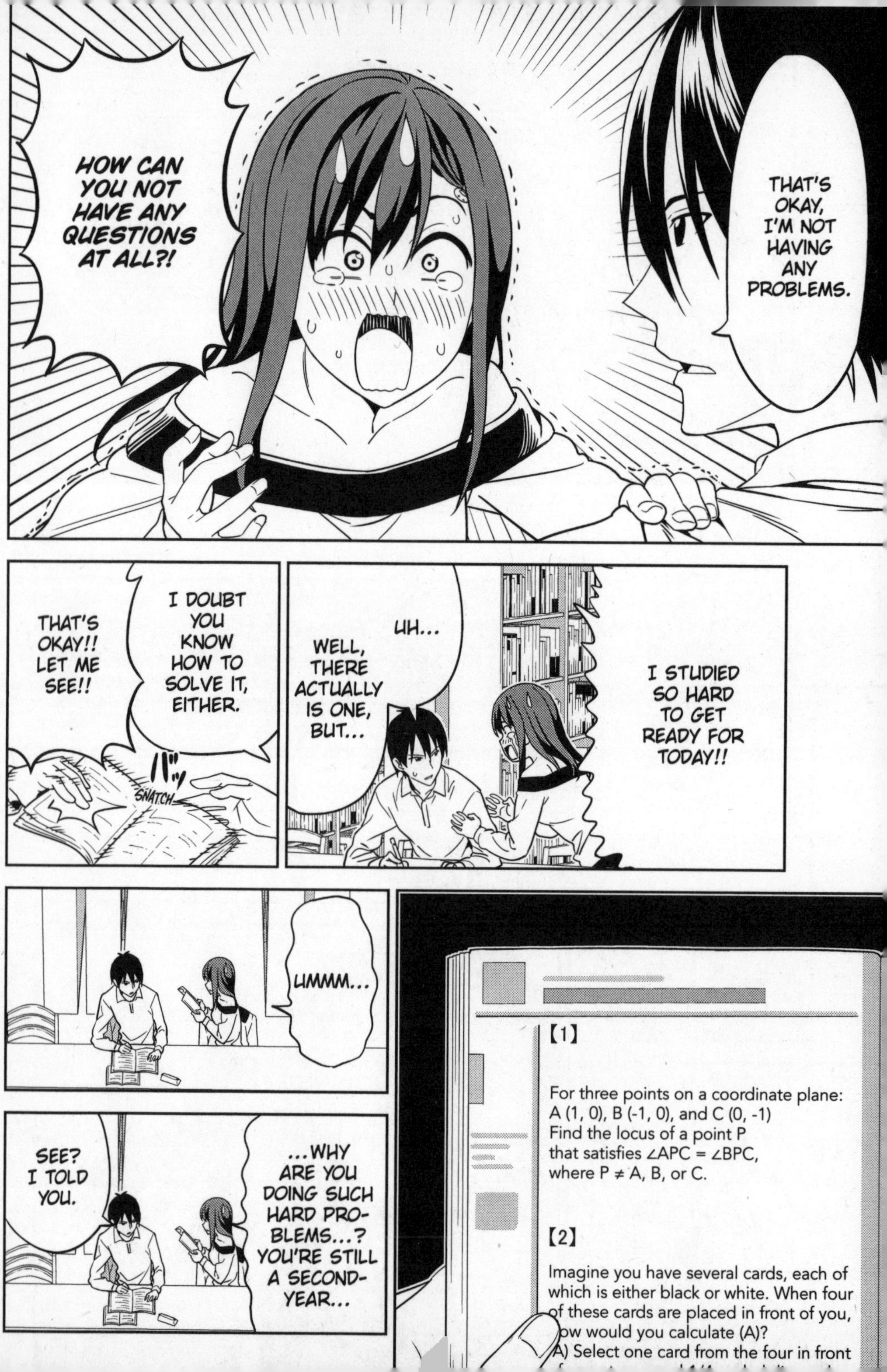
THAT'S OKAY, I'M NOT HAVING ANY PROBLEMS.
HOW CAN YOU NOT HAVE ANY QUESTIONS AT ALL?!
I STUDIED SO HARD TO GET READY FOR TODAY!!
UH...
WELL, THERE ACTUALLY IS ONE, BUT...
I DOUBT YOU KNOW HOW TO SOLVE IT, EITHER.
THAT'S OKAY!! LET ME SEE!!
SNATCH
【1】
For three points on a coordinate plane:
A (1, 0), B (-1, 0), and C (0, -1)
Find the locus of a point P
that satisfies ∠APC = ∠BPC,
where P ≠ A, B, or C.
【2】
Imagine you have several cards, each of which is either black or white. When four of these cards are placed in front of you,
ow would you calculate (A)?
A) Select one card from the four in front
UMMM...
...WHY ARE YOU DOING SUCH HARD PROBLEMS...? YOU'RE STILL A SECOND-YEAR...
SEE? I TOLD YOU.

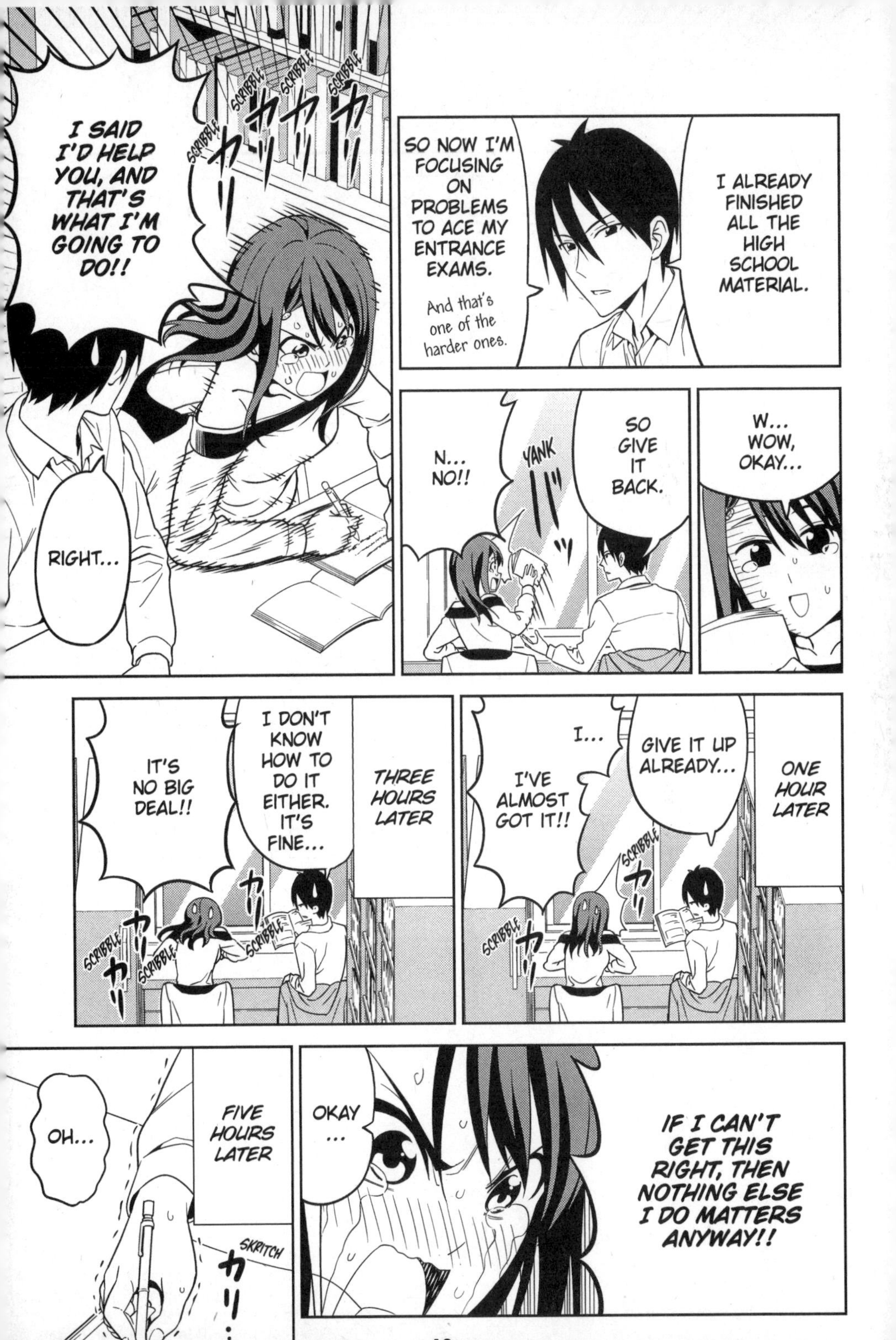
I ALREADY FINISHED ALL THE HIGH SCHOOL MATERIAL.
SO NOW I'M FOCUSING ON PROBLEMS TO ACE MY ENTRANCE EXAMS.
And that's one of the harder ones.
W... WOW, OKAY...
SO GIVE IT BACK.
YANK
N... NO!!
SCRIBBLE
SCRIBBLE
SCRIBBLE
SCRIBBLE
I SAID I'D HELP YOU, AND THAT'S WHAT I'M GOING TO DO!!
RIGHT...
ONE HOUR LATER
GIVE IT UP ALREADY...
I...
I'VE ALMOST GOT IT!!
SCRIBBLE
SCRIBBLE
THREE HOURS LATER
I DON'T KNOW HOW TO DO IT EITHER. IT'S FINE...
IT'S NO BIG DEAL!!
SCRIBBLE
SCRIBBLE
SCRIBBLE
IF I CAN'T GET THIS RIGHT, THEN NOTHING ELSE I DO MATTERS ANYWAY!!
OKAY...
FIVE HOURS LATER
OH...
SKRITCH

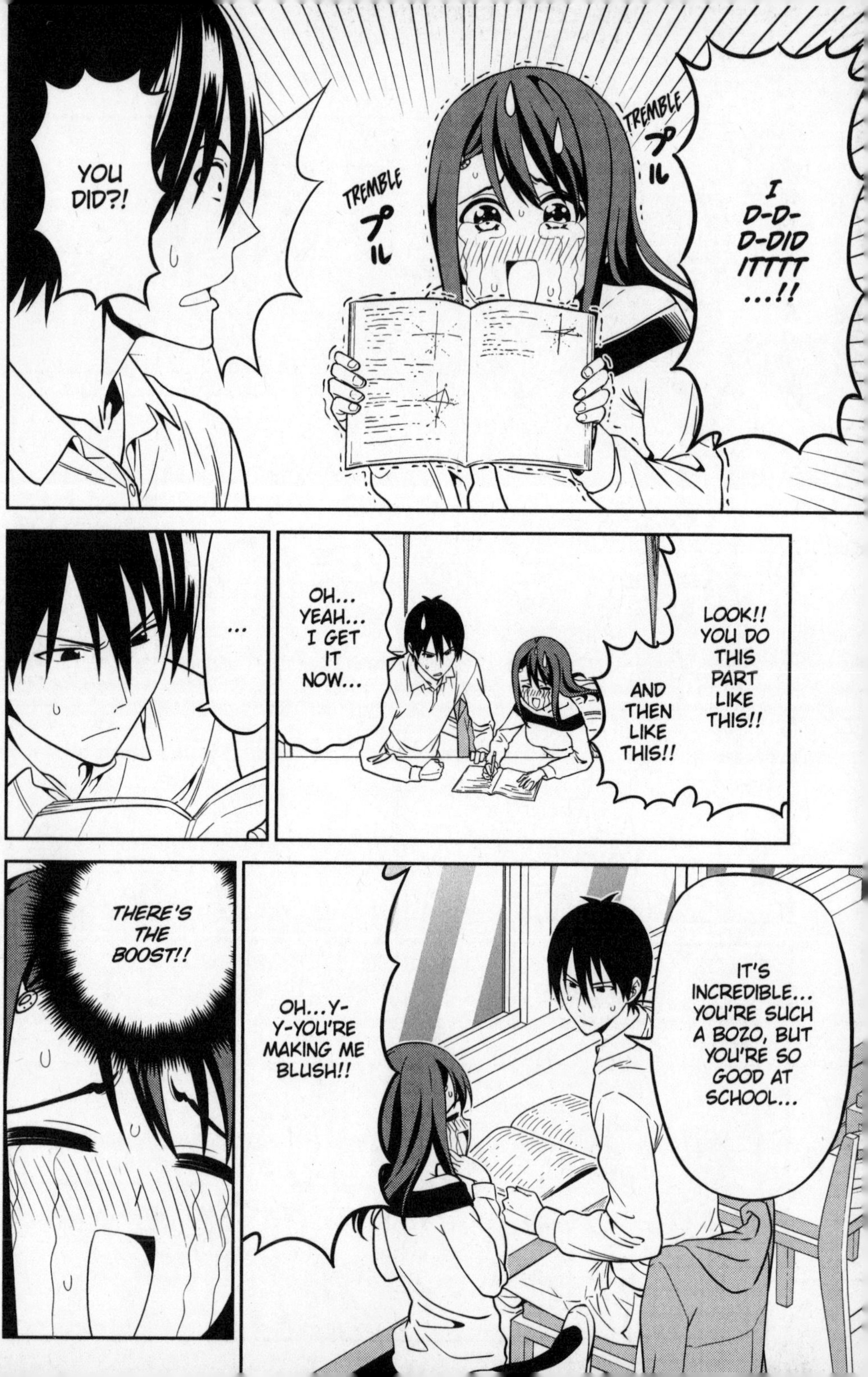
I D-D-D-DID ITTTT...!!
TREMBLE
プル
TREMBLE
プル
YOU DID?!
LOOK!! YOU DO THIS PART LIKE THIS!!
AND THEN LIKE THIS!!
OH... YEAH... I GET IT NOW...
...
IT'S INCREDIBLE... YOU'RE SUCH A BOZO, BUT YOU'RE SO GOOD AT SCHOOL...
OH...Y-Y-YOU'RE MAKING ME BLUSH!!
THERE'S THE BOOST!!

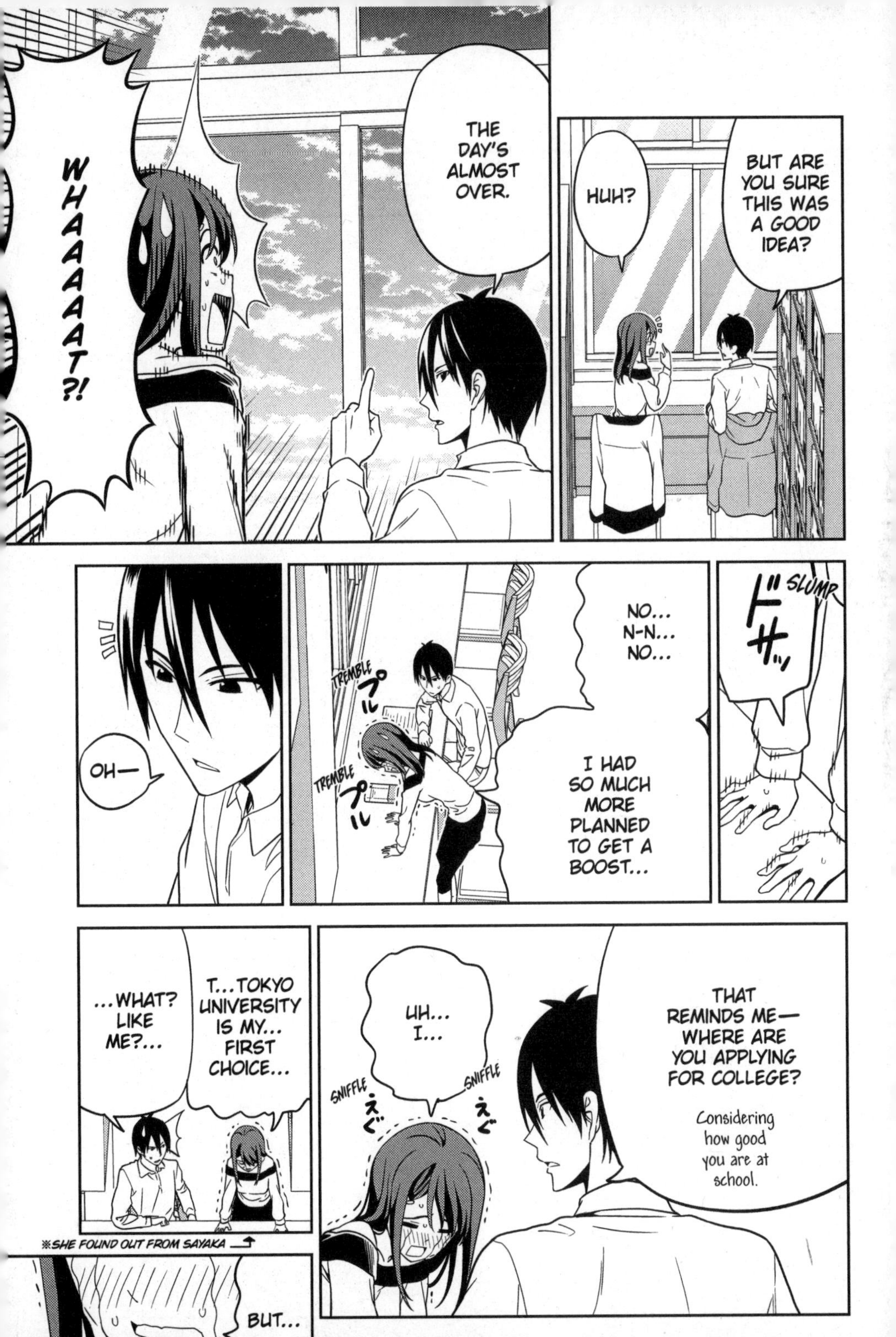
BUT ARE YOU SURE THIS WAS A GOOD IDEA?
HUH?
THE DAY'S ALMOST OVER.
WHAAAAAAAT?!
ドサッ SLUMP
NO... N-N... NO...
I HAD SO MUCH MORE PLANNED TO GET A BOOST...
プル TREMBLE
プル TREMBLE
OH—
THAT REMINDS ME— WHERE ARE YOU APPLYING FOR COLLEGE?
Considering how good you are at school.
UH... I...
えぐ SNIFFLE
えぐ SNIFFLE
T...TOKYO UNIVERSITY IS MY... FIRST CHOICE...
...WHAT? LIKE ME?...
※SHE FOUND OUT FROM SAYAKA
BUT...

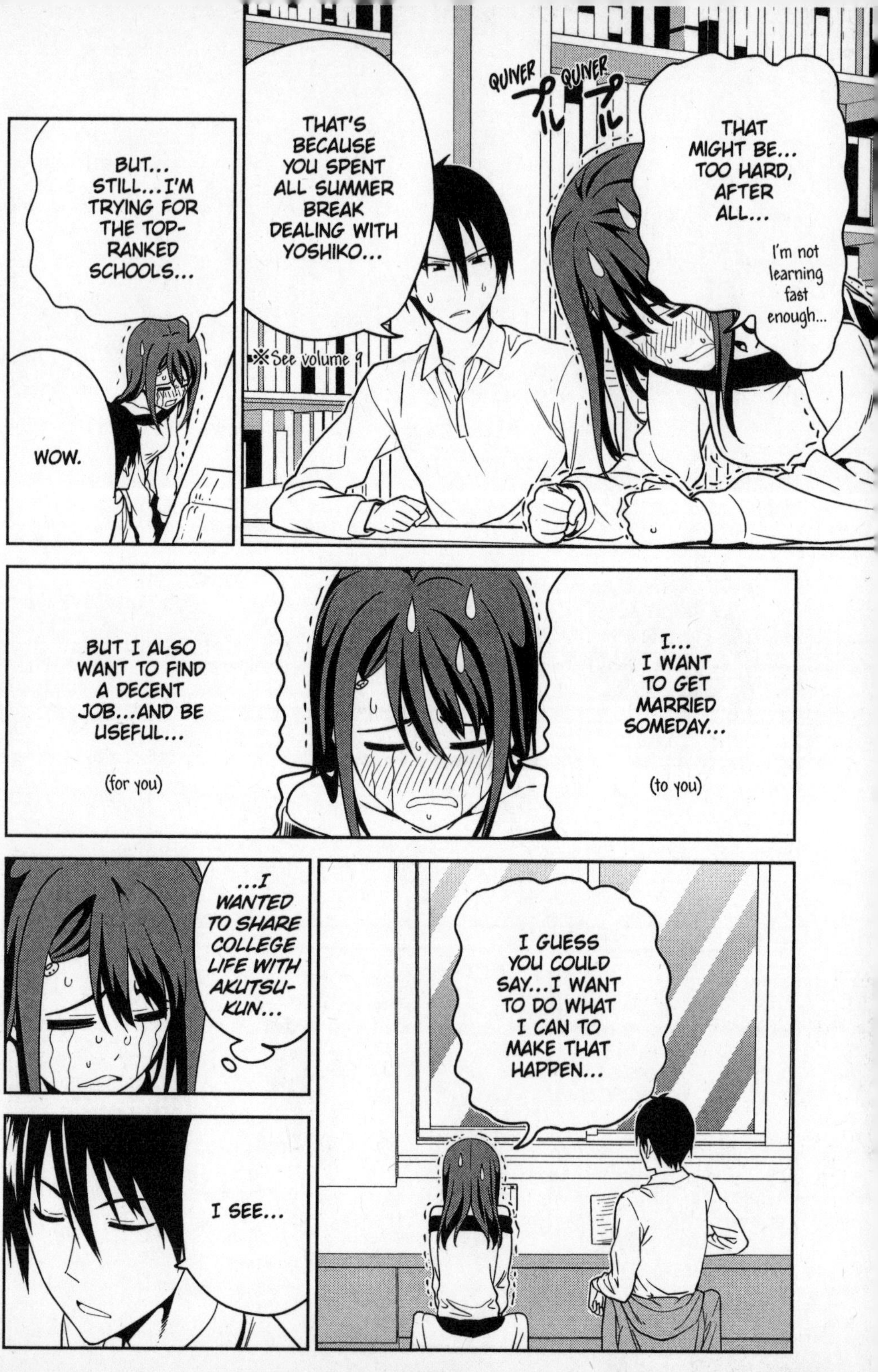
QUIVER QUIVER
プルプル
THAT MIGHT BE... TOO HARD, AFTER ALL...
I'm not learning fast enough...
THAT'S BECAUSE YOU SPENT ALL SUMMER BREAK DEALING WITH YOSHIKO...
※See volume 9
BUT... STILL... I'M TRYING FOR THE TOP-RANKED SCHOOLS...
WOW.
I... I WANT TO GET MARRIED SOMEDAY...
(to you)
BUT I ALSO WANT TO FIND A DECENT JOB...AND BE USEFUL...
(for you)
I GUESS YOU COULD SAY...I WANT TO DO WHAT I CAN TO MAKE THAT HAPPEN...
...I WANTED TO SHARE COLLEGE LIFE WITH AKUTSU-KUN...
I SEE...

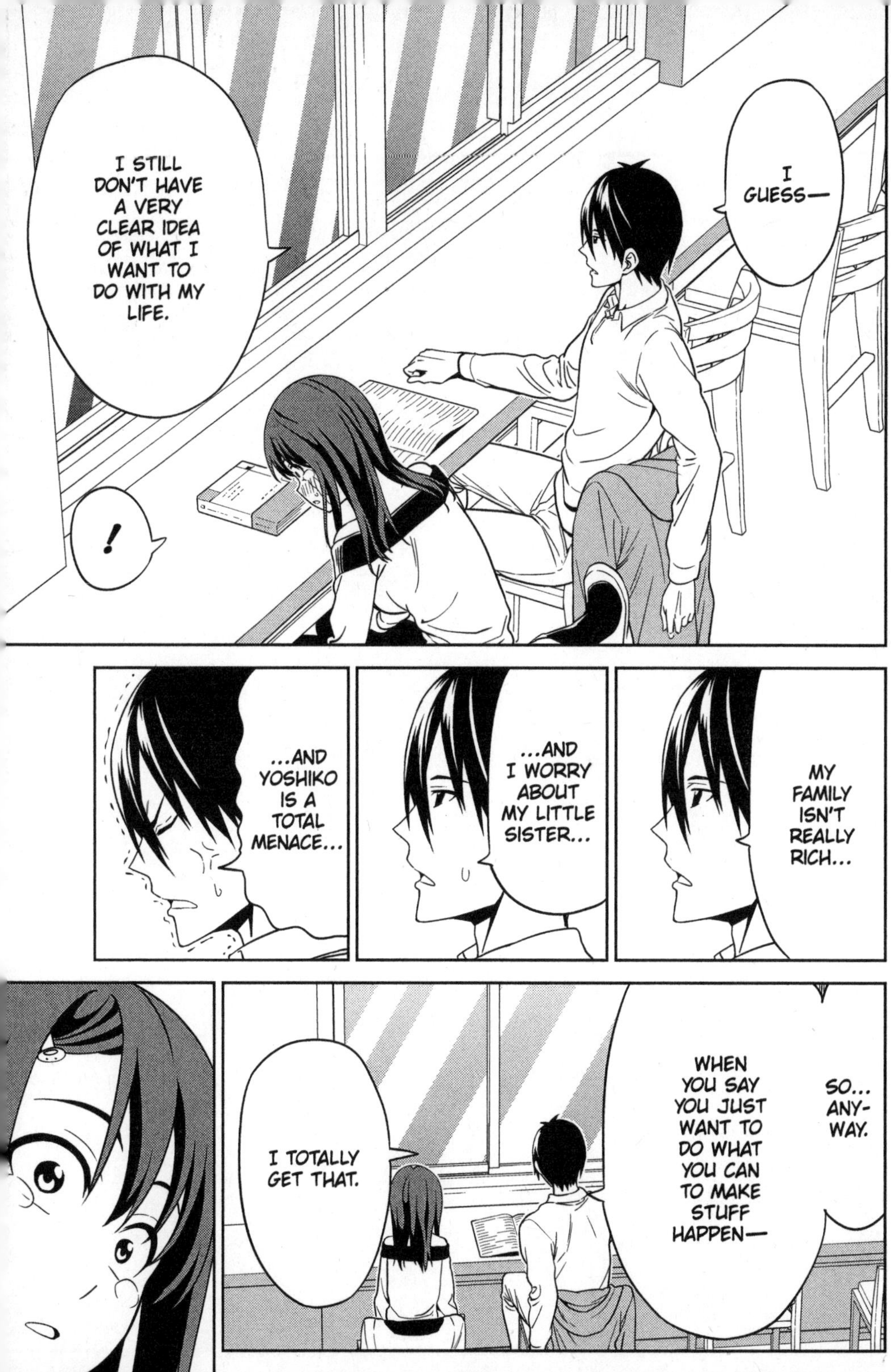
I GUESS—
I STILL DON'T HAVE A VERY CLEAR IDEA OF WHAT I WANT TO DO WITH MY LIFE.
!
MY FAMILY ISN'T REALLY RICH...
...AND I WORRY ABOUT MY LITTLE SISTER...
...AND YOSHIKO IS A TOTAL MENACE...
SO... ANY-WAY.
WHEN YOU SAY YOU JUST WANT TO DO WHAT YOU CAN TO MAKE STUFF HAPPEN—
I TOTALLY GET THAT.

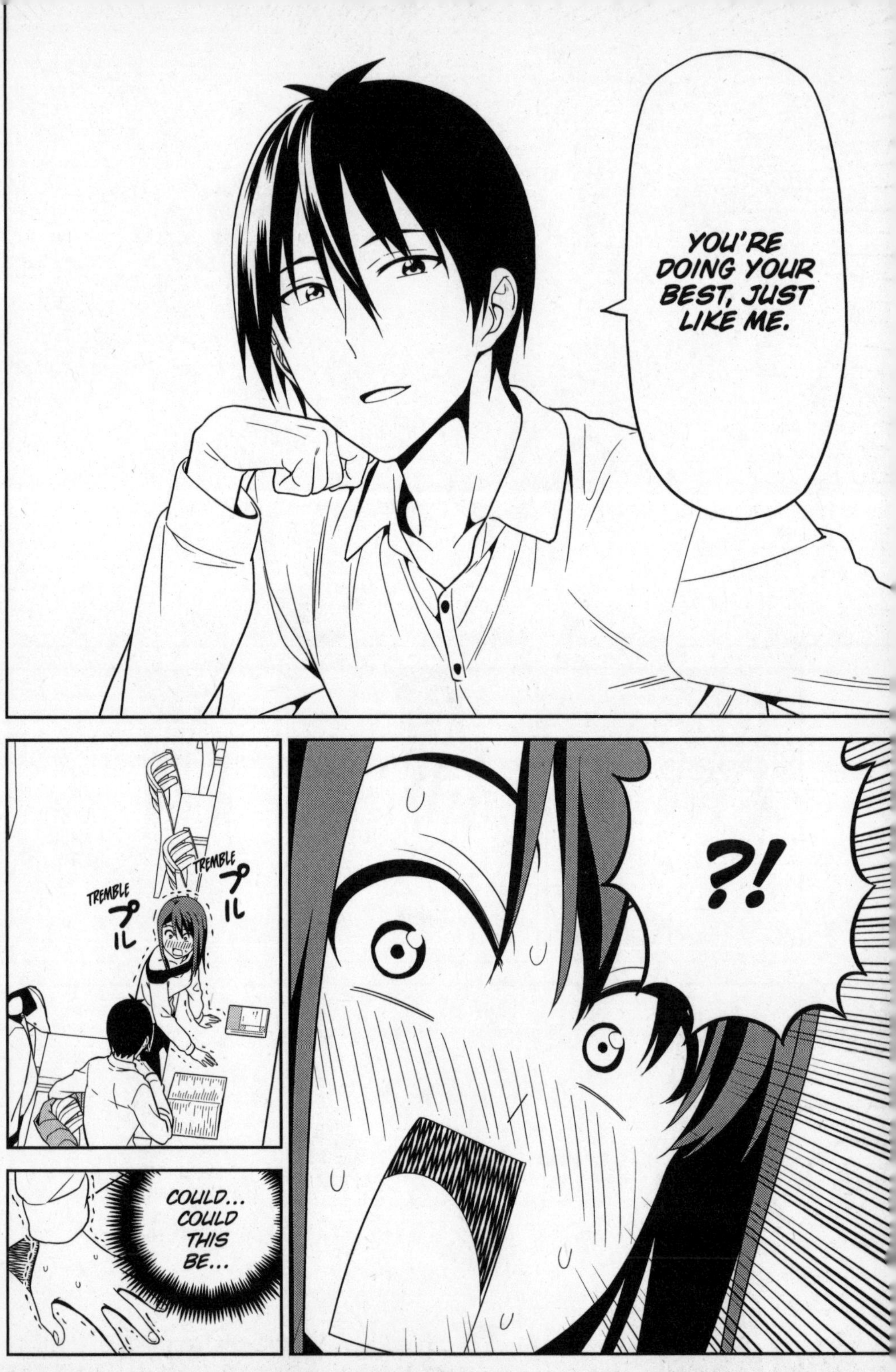
YOU'RE DOING YOUR BEST, JUST LIKE ME.
?!
TREMBLE プル
TREMBLE プル
COULD... COULD THIS BE...

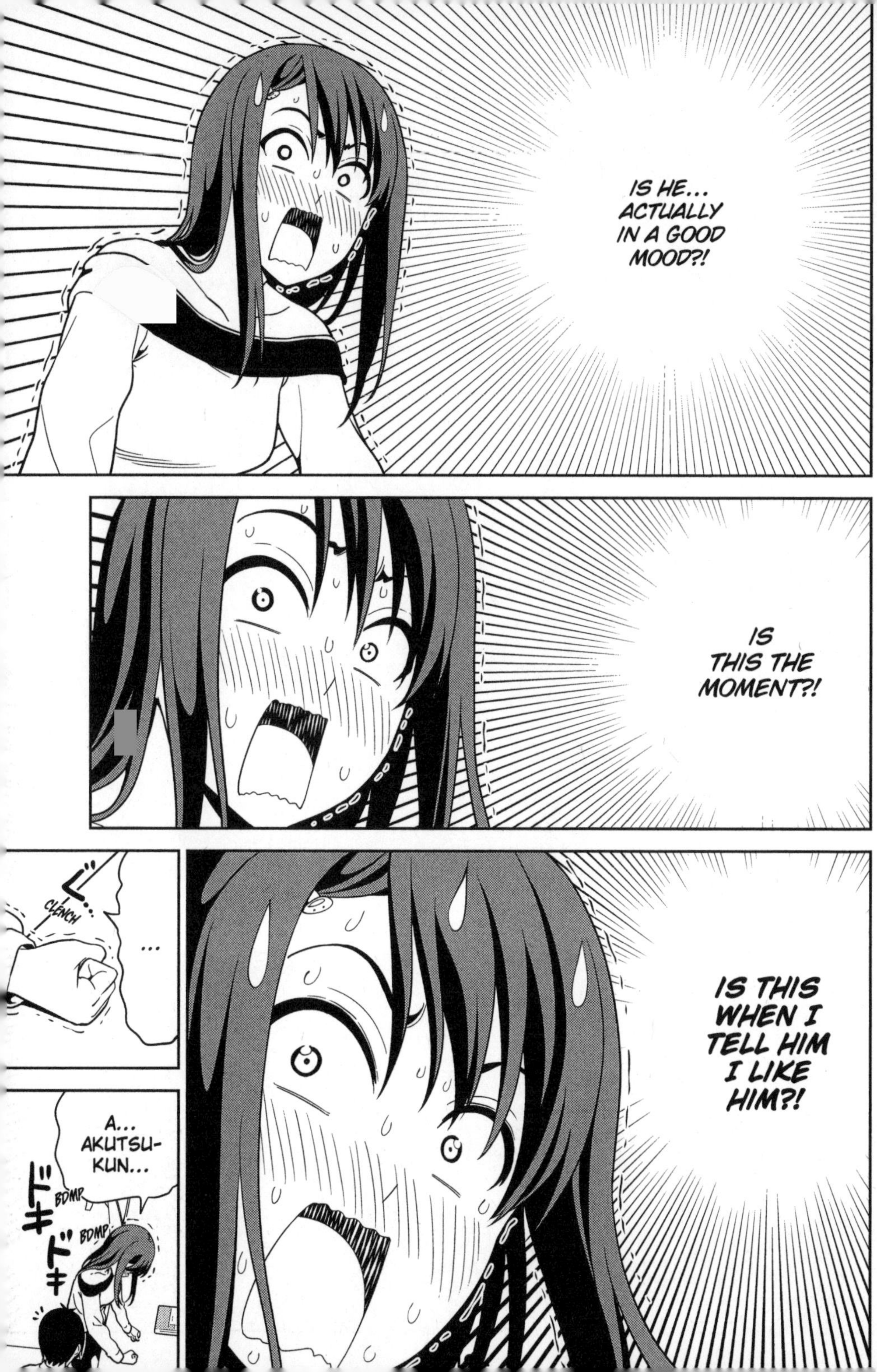
IS HE... ACTUALLY IN A GOOD MOOD?!
IS THIS THE MOMENT?!
IS THIS WHEN I TELL HIM I LIKE HIM?!
CLENCH
...
A... AKUTSU-KUN...
ドキ BDMP
ドキ BDMP

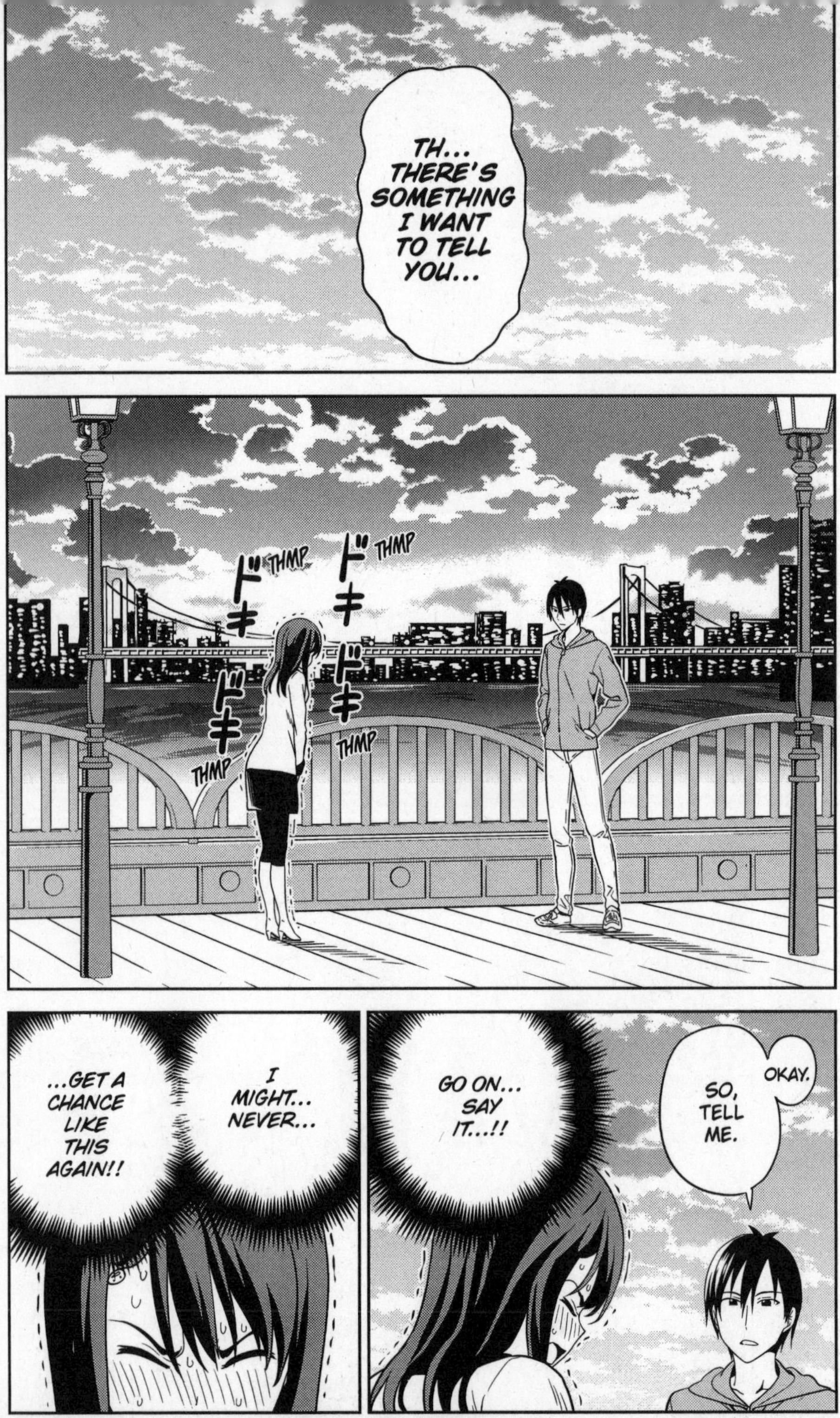
TH... THERE'S SOMETHING I WANT TO TELL YOU...
ドキ THMP
ドキ THMP
ドキ THMP
ドキ THMP
OKAY.
SO, TELL ME.
GO ON... SAY IT...!!
I MIGHT... NEVER...
...GET A CHANCE LIKE THIS AGAIN!!

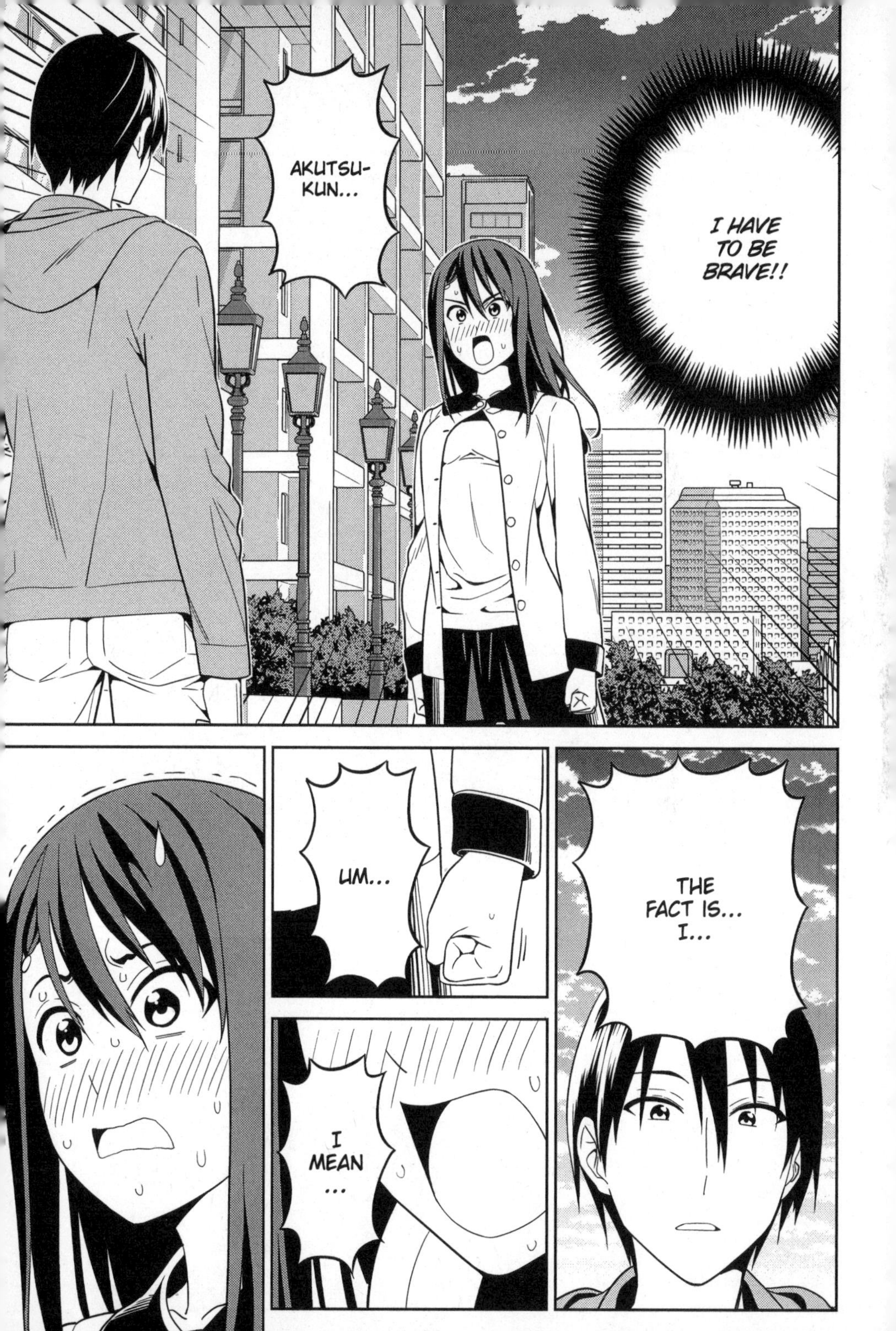
I HAVE TO BE BRAVE!!
AKUTSU-KUN...
THE FACT IS... I...
UM...
I MEAN ...

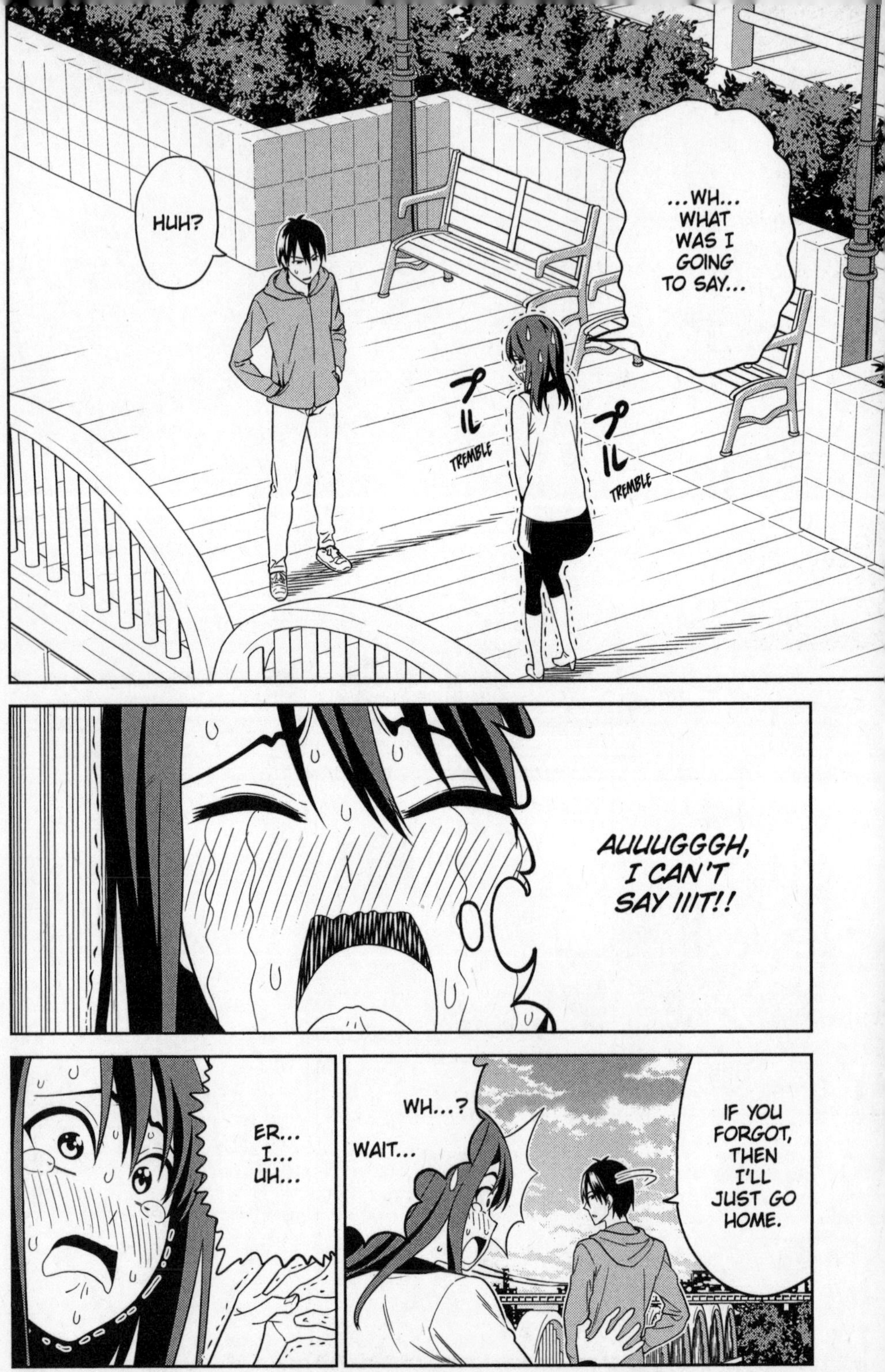
...WH... WHAT WAS I GOING TO SAY...
HUH?
プル
TREMBLE
プル
TREMBLE
AUUUGGGH, I CAN'T SAY IIIT!!
IF YOU FORGOT, THEN I'LL JUST GO HOME.
WH...?
WAIT...
ER... I... UH...

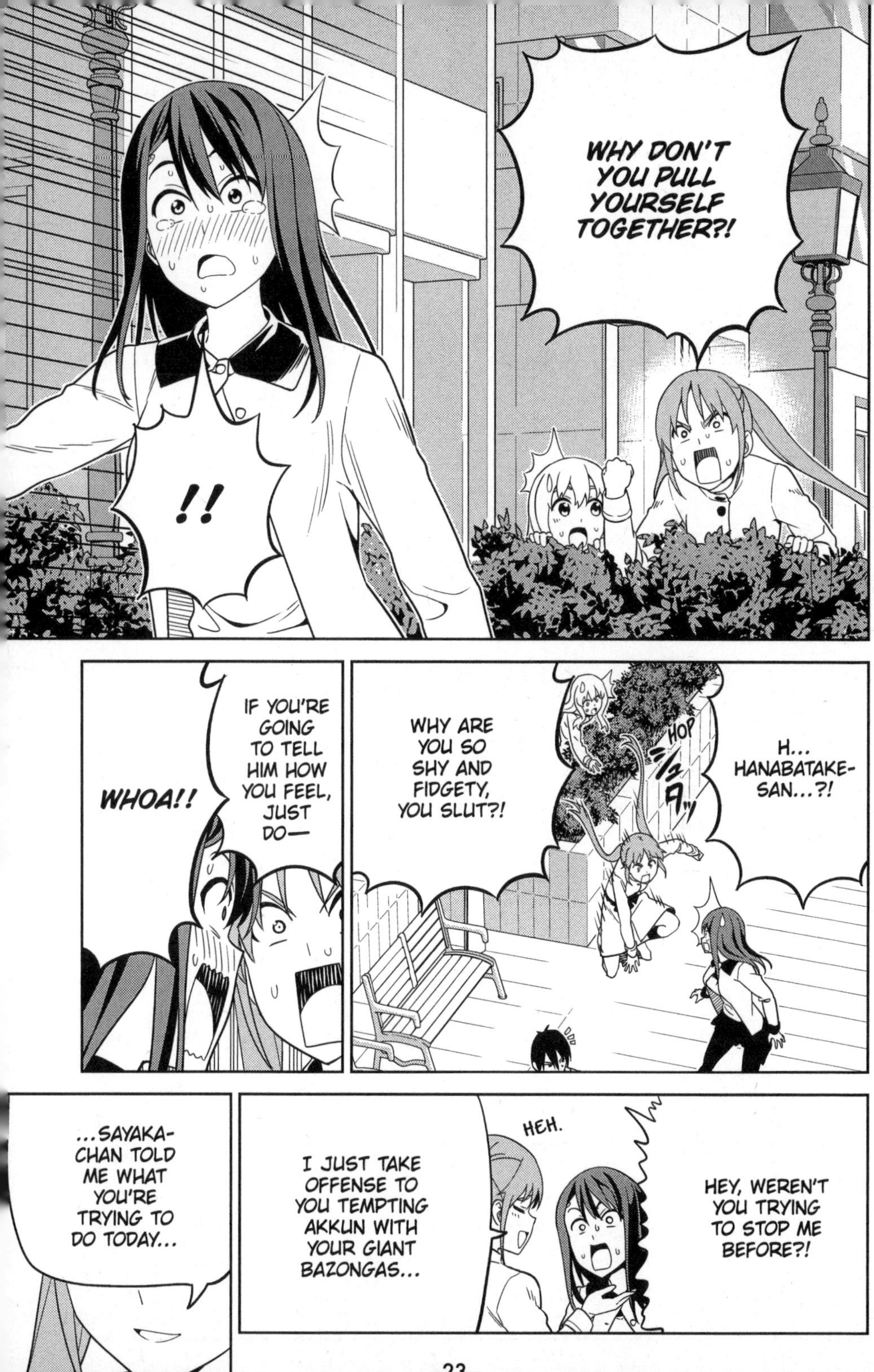
WHY DON'T YOU PULL YOURSELF TOGETHER?!
!!
H... HANABATAKE-SAN...?!
WHY ARE YOU SO SHY AND FIDGETY, YOU SLUT?!
HOP
IF YOU'RE GOING TO TELL HIM HOW YOU FEEL, JUST DO—
WHOA!!
HEY, WEREN'T YOU TRYING TO STOP ME BEFORE?!
HEH.
I JUST TAKE OFFENSE TO YOU TEMPTING AKKUN WITH YOUR GIANT BAZONGAS...
...SAYAKA-CHAN TOLD ME WHAT YOU'RE TRYING TO DO TODAY...

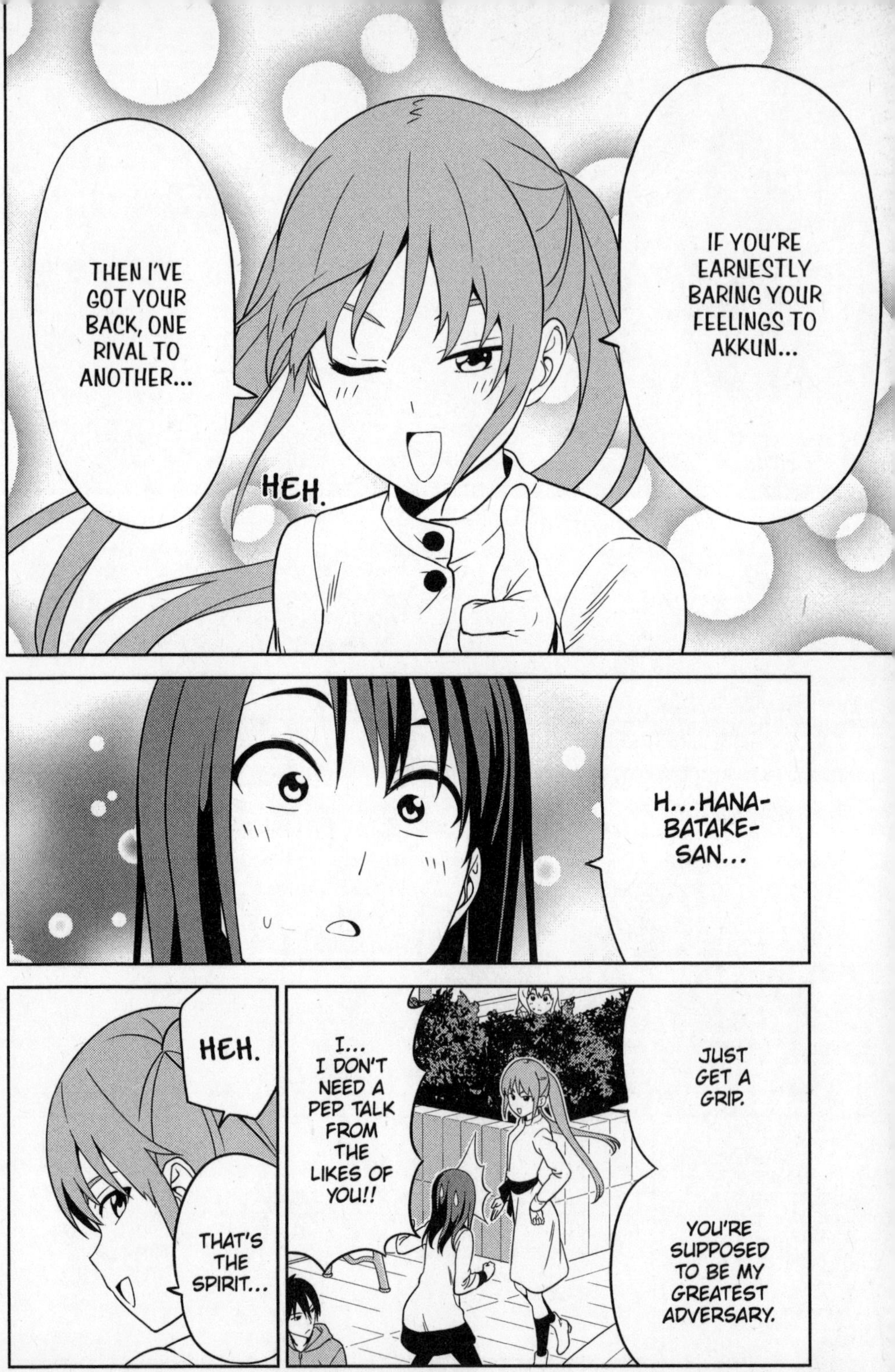
IF YOU'RE EARNESTLY BARING YOUR FEELINGS TO AKKUN...
THEN I'VE GOT YOUR BACK, ONE RIVAL TO ANOTHER...
HEH.
H...HANA-BATAKE-SAN...
JUST GET A GRIP.
YOU'RE SUPPOSED TO BE MY GREATEST ADVERSARY.
I... I DON'T NEED A PEP TALK FROM THE LIKES OF YOU!!
HEH.
THAT'S THE SPIRIT...

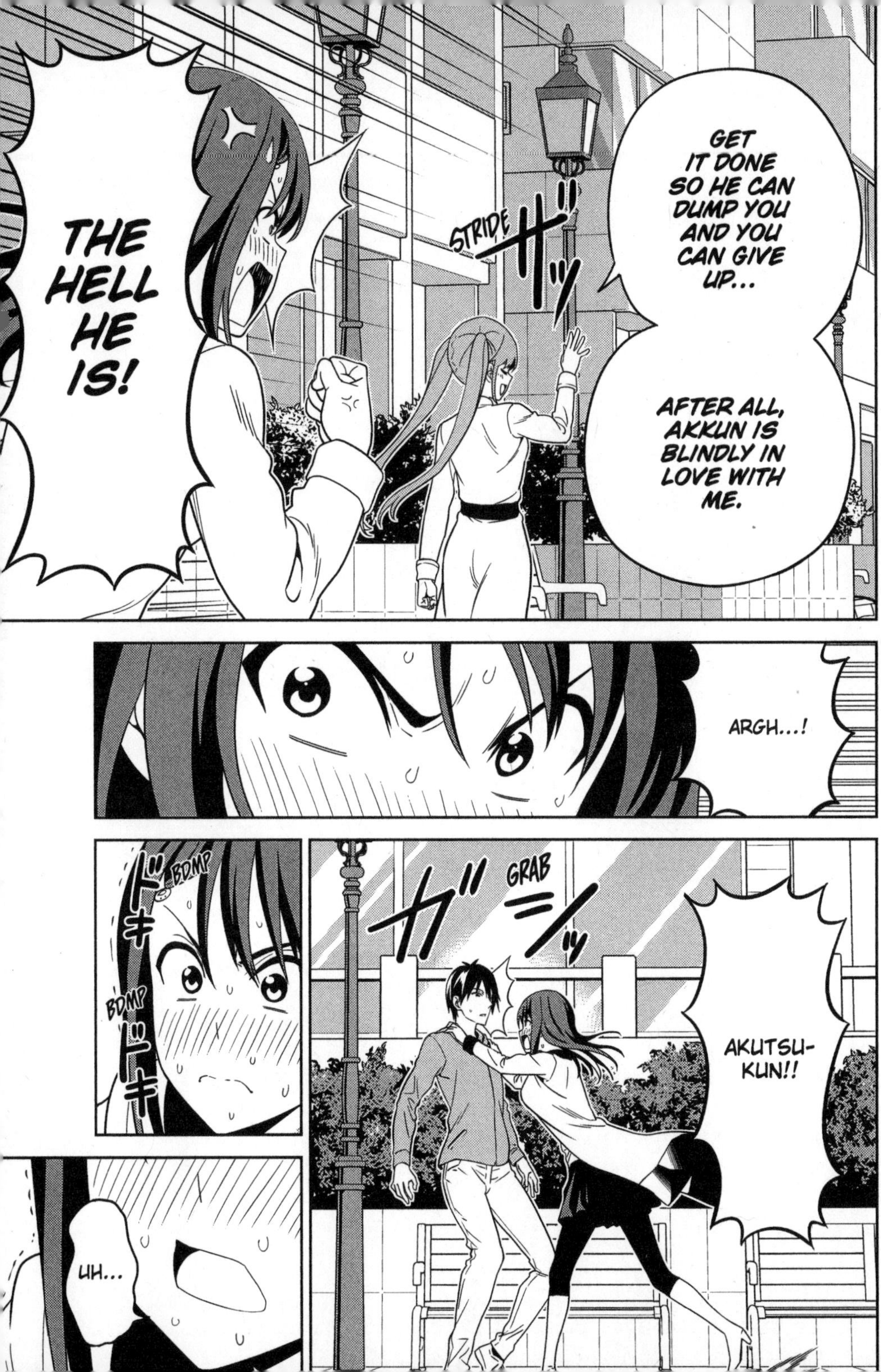
GET IT DONE SO HE CAN DUMP YOU AND YOU CAN GIVE UP...
AFTER ALL, AKKUN IS BLINDLY IN LOVE WITH ME.
STRIDE
THE HELL HE IS!
ARGH...!
GRAB
AKUTSU-KUN!!
BDMP
BDMP
UH...

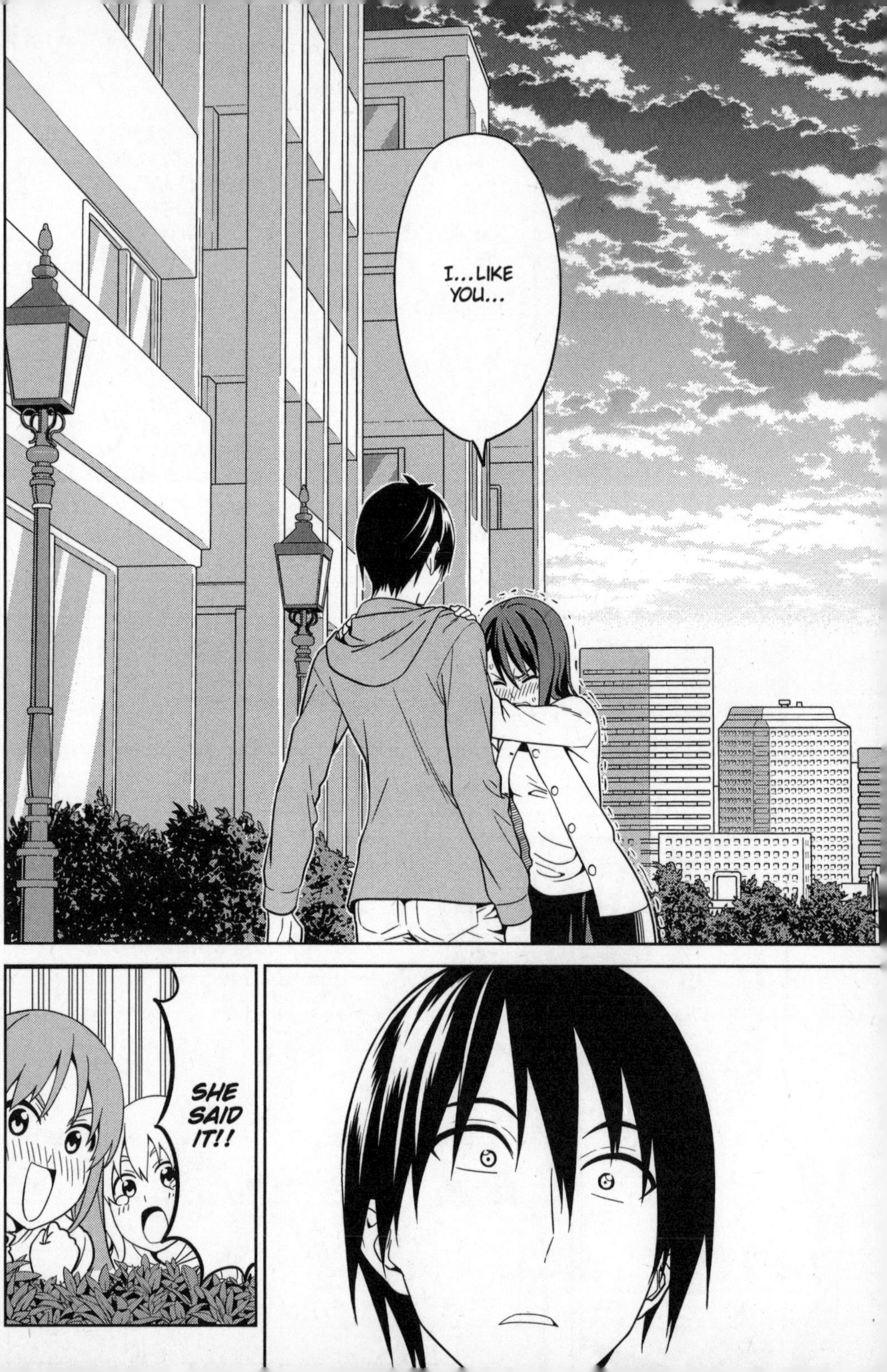
I...LIKE YOU...
SHE SAID IT!!

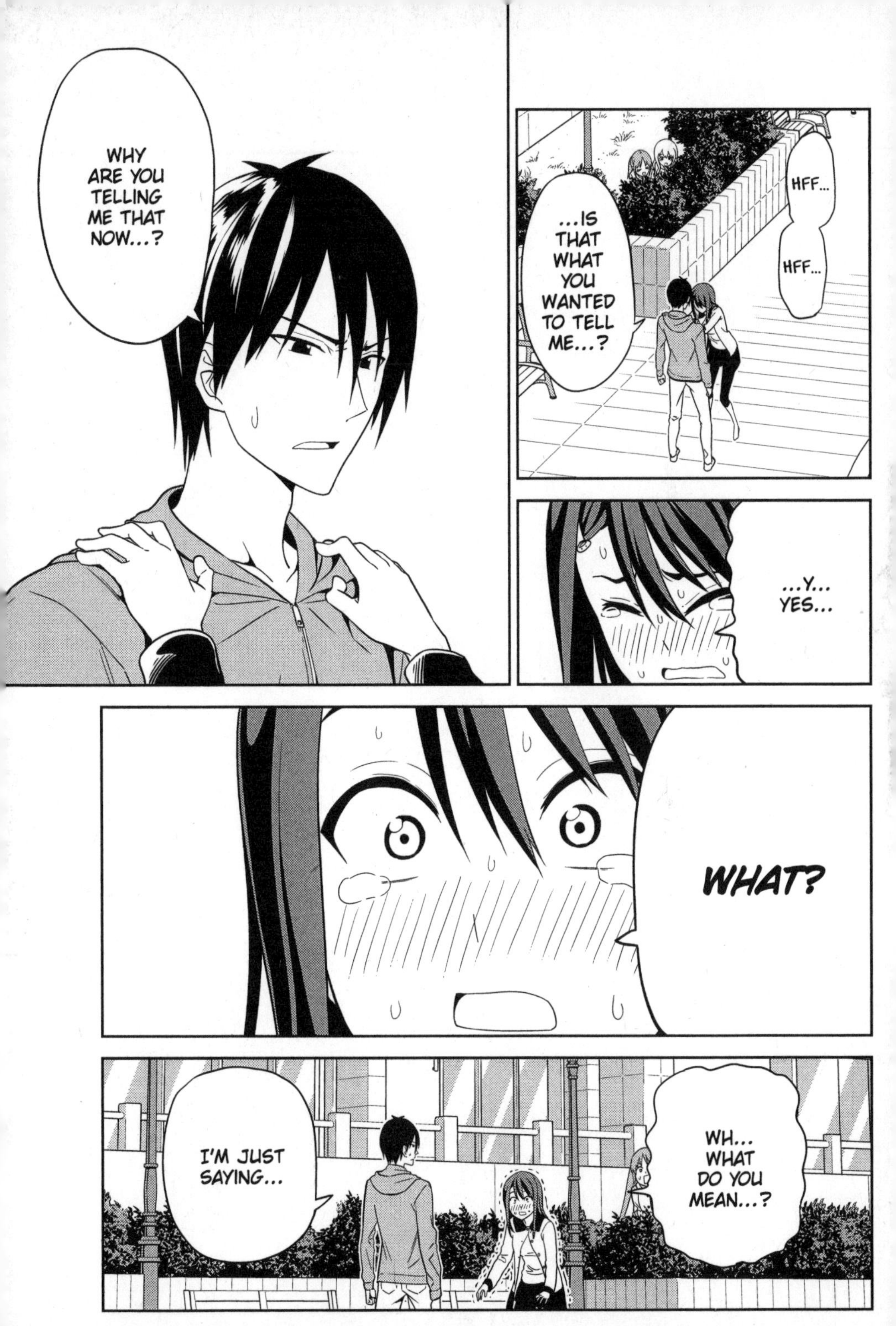
HFF...
HFF...
...IS THAT WHAT YOU WANTED TO TELL ME...?
...Y... YES...
WHY ARE YOU TELLING ME THAT NOW...?
WHAT?
WH... WHAT DO YOU MEAN...?
I'M JUST SAYING...

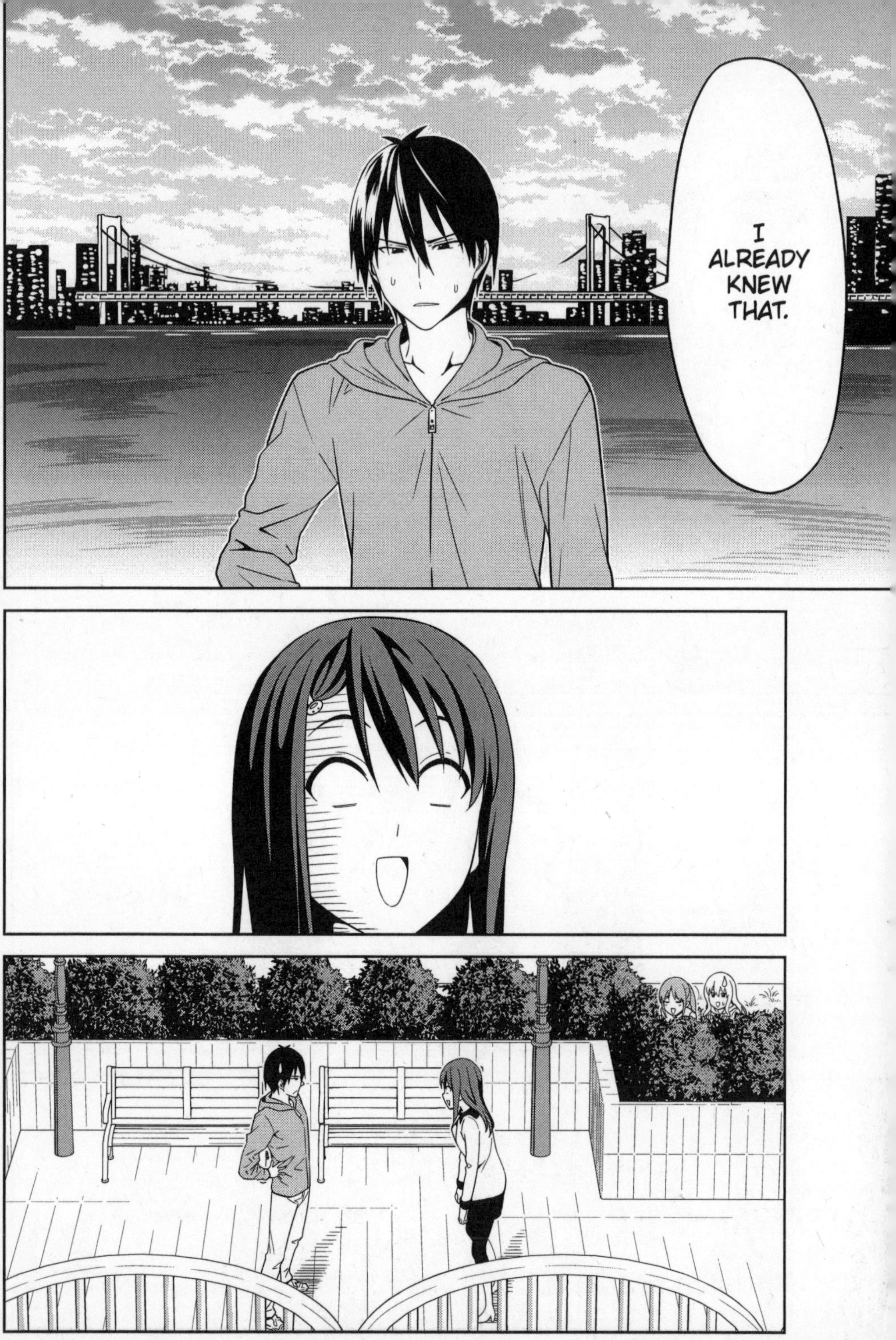
I ALREADY KNEW THAT.

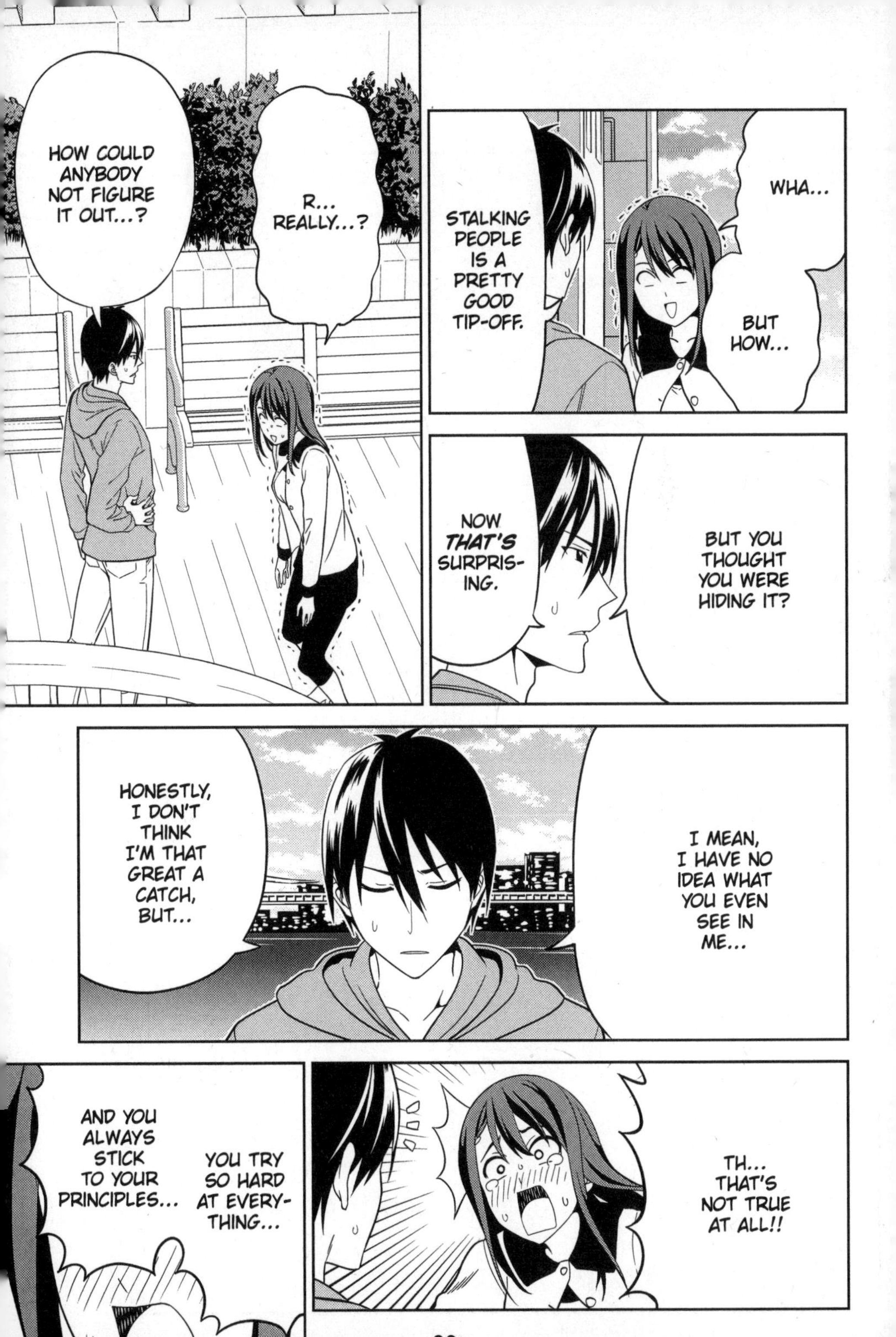
WHA...
BUT HOW...
STALKING PEOPLE IS A PRETTY GOOD TIP-OFF.
BUT YOU THOUGHT YOU WERE HIDING IT?
NOW *THAT'S* SURPRIS-ING.
R... REALLY...?
HOW COULD ANYBODY NOT FIGURE IT OUT...?
I MEAN, I HAVE NO IDEA WHAT YOU EVEN SEE IN ME...
HONESTLY, I DON'T THINK I'M THAT GREAT A CATCH, BUT...
TH... THAT'S NOT TRUE AT ALL!!
YOU TRY SO HARD AT EVERY-THING...
AND YOU ALWAYS STICK TO YOUR PRINCIPLES...

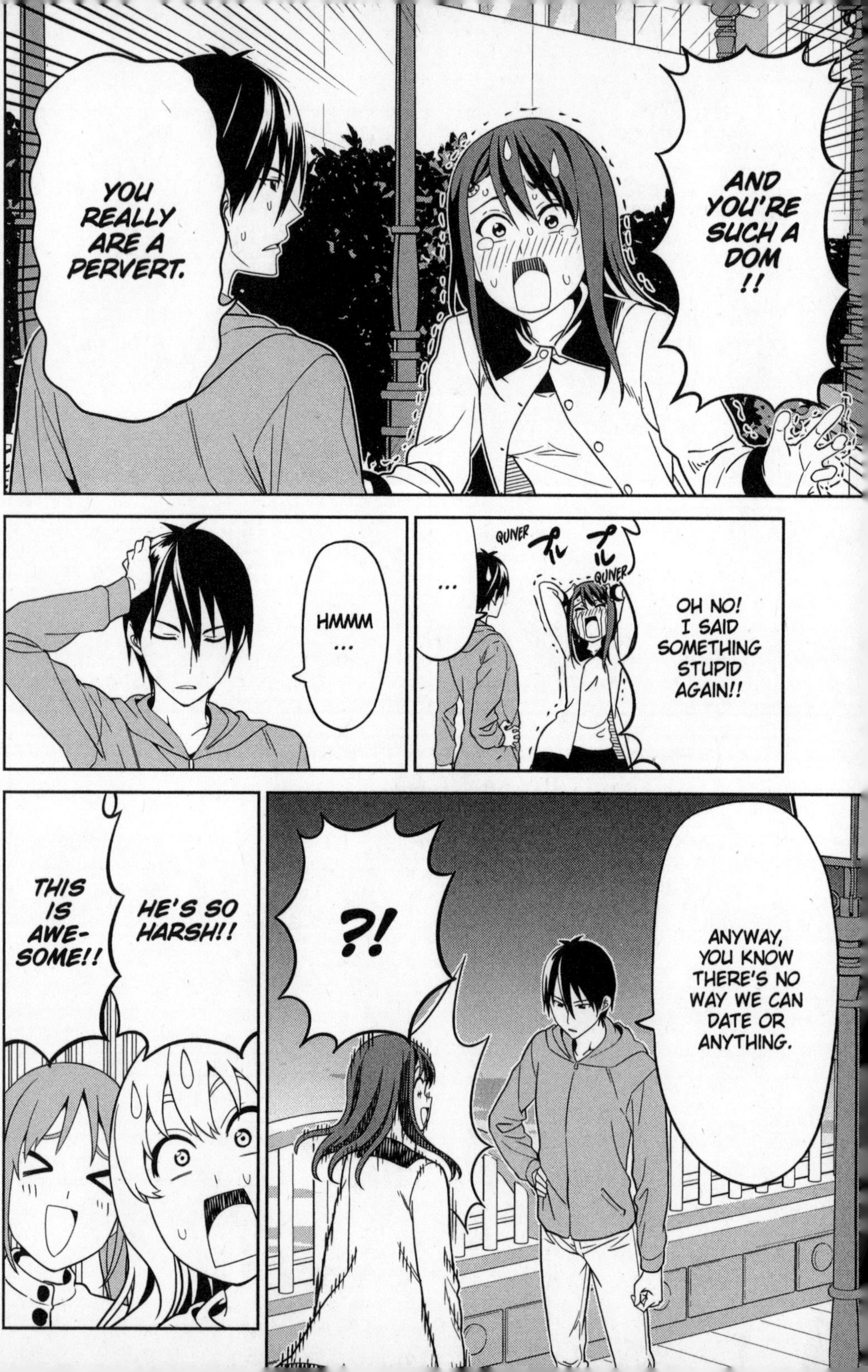
AND YOU'RE SUCH A DOM!!
YOU REALLY ARE A PERVERT.
...
QUIVER
プルプル
QUIVER
OH NO! I SAID SOMETHING STUPID AGAIN!!
HMMM ...
ANYWAY, YOU KNOW THERE'S NO WAY WE CAN DATE OR ANYTHING.
?!
HE'S SO HARSH!!
THIS IS AWE-SOME!!

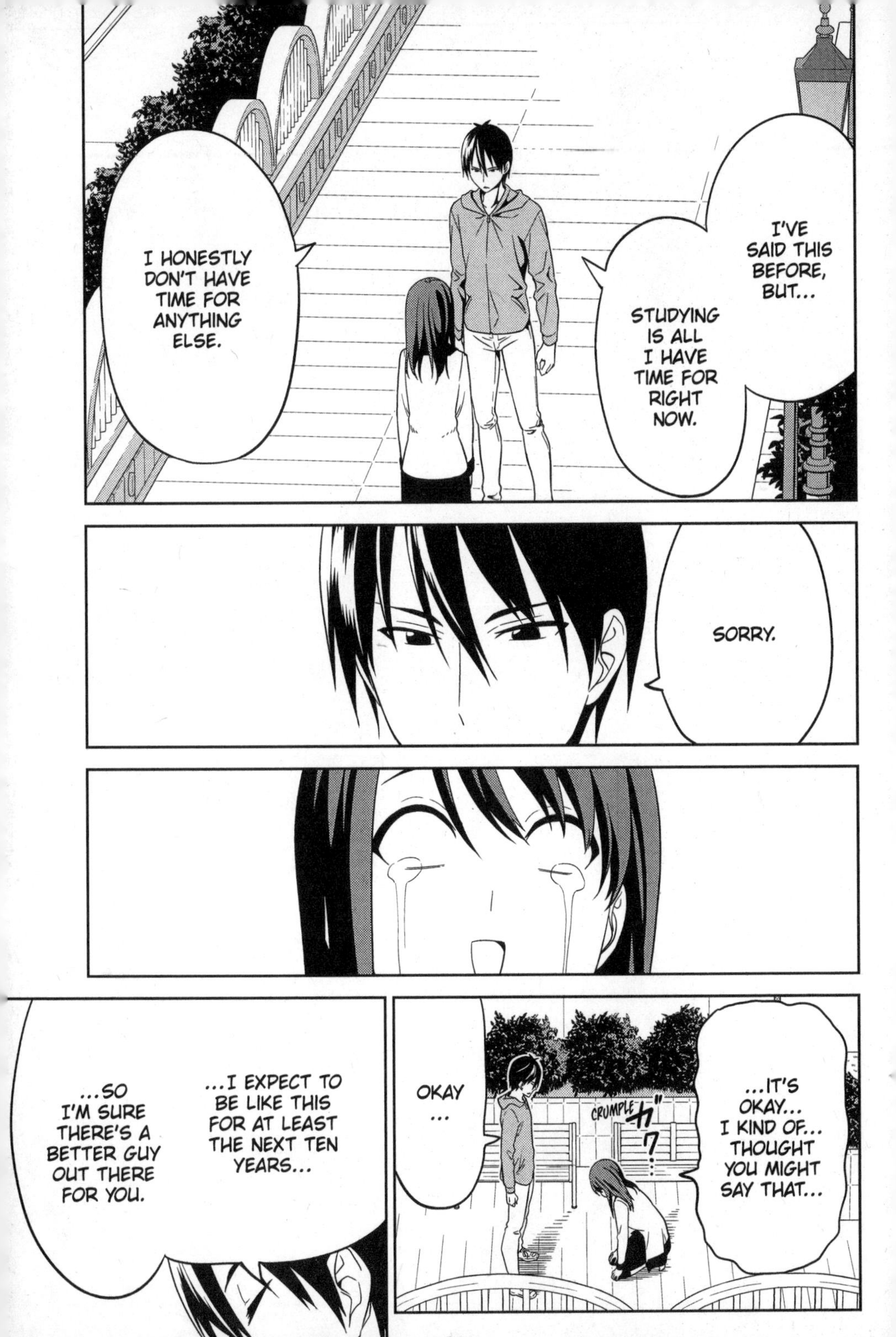
I'VE SAID THIS BEFORE, BUT...
STUDYING IS ALL I HAVE TIME FOR RIGHT NOW.
I HONESTLY DON'T HAVE TIME FOR ANYTHING ELSE.
SORRY.
...IT'S OKAY... I KIND OF... THOUGHT YOU MIGHT SAY THAT...
CRUMPLE
OKAY ...
...I EXPECT TO BE LIKE THIS FOR AT LEAST THE NEXT TEN YEARS...
...SO I'M SURE THERE'S A BETTER GUY OUT THERE FOR YOU.

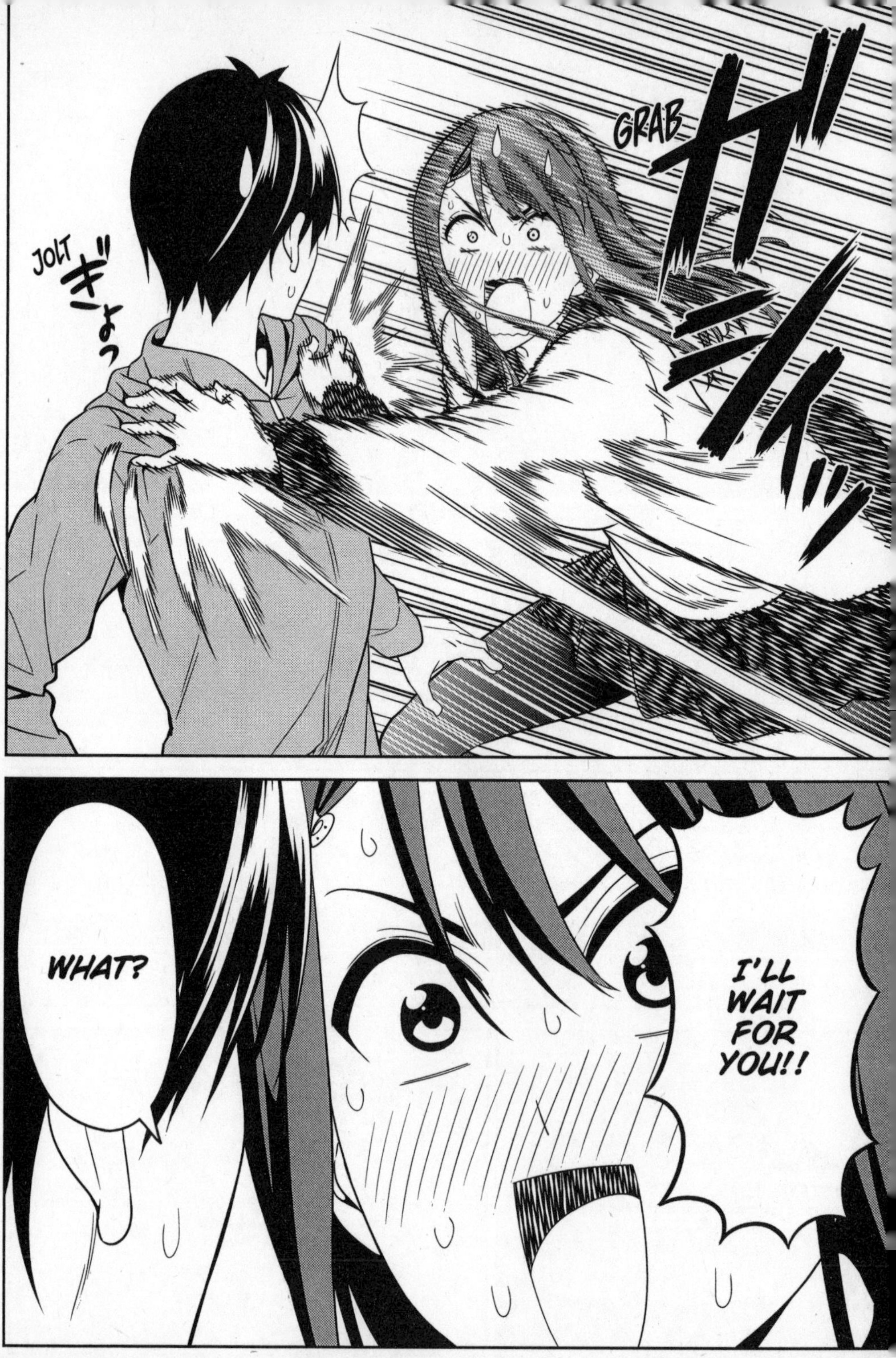
GRAB
JOLT
ぎょっ
I'LL WAIT FOR YOU!!
WHAT?

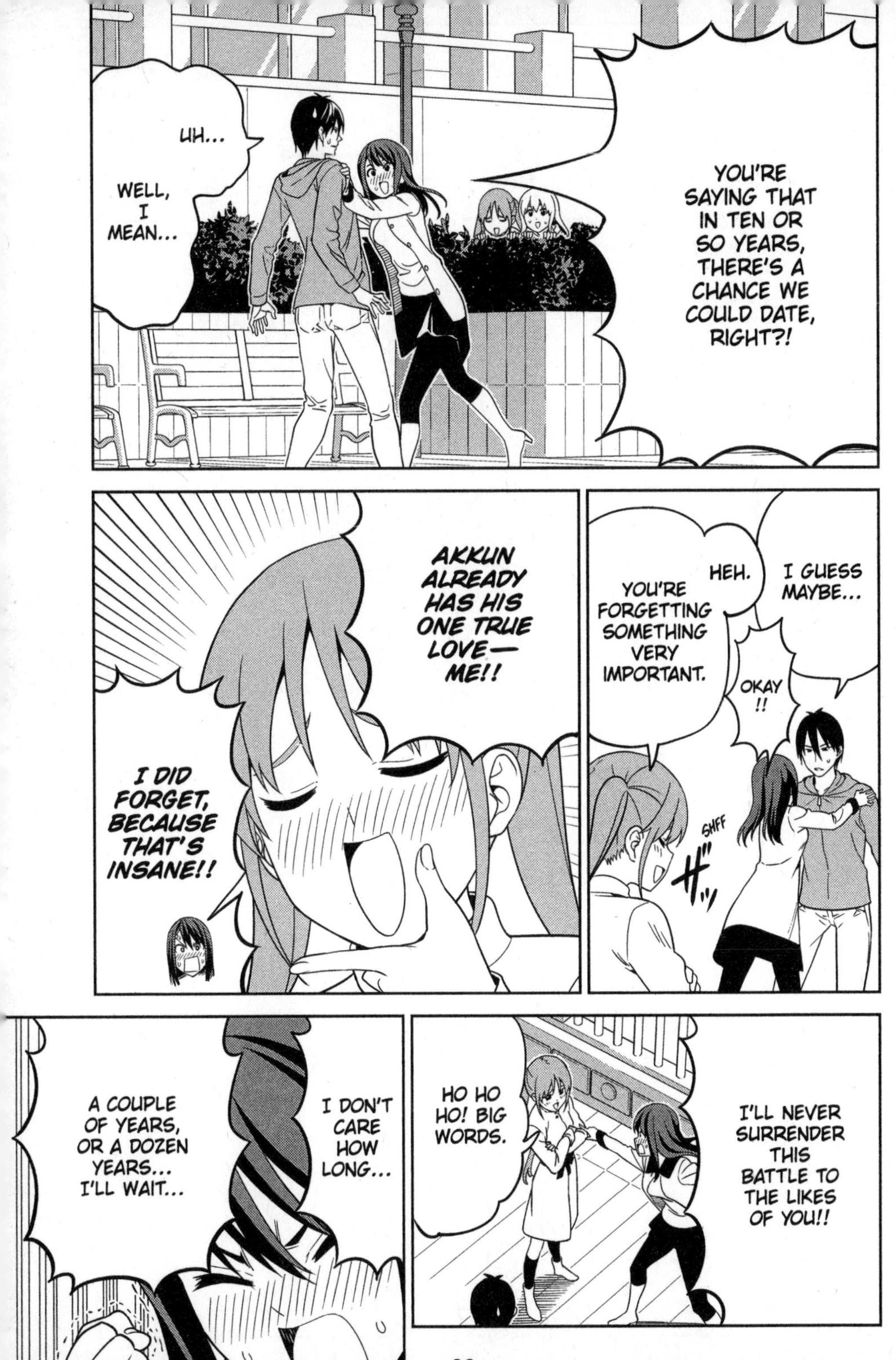
YOU'RE SAYING THAT IN TEN OR SO YEARS, THERE'S A CHANCE WE COULD DATE, RIGHT?!
UH...
WELL, I MEAN...
I GUESS MAYBE...
HEH.
YOU'RE FORGETTING SOMETHING VERY IMPORTANT.
OKAY!!
SHFF
AKKUN ALREADY HAS HIS ONE TRUE LOVE— ME!!
I DID FORGET, BECAUSE THAT'S INSANE!!
I'LL NEVER SURRENDER THIS BATTLE TO THE LIKES OF YOU!!
HO HO HO! BIG WORDS.
I DON'T CARE HOW LONG...
A COUPLE OF YEARS, OR A DOZEN YEARS... I'LL WAIT...

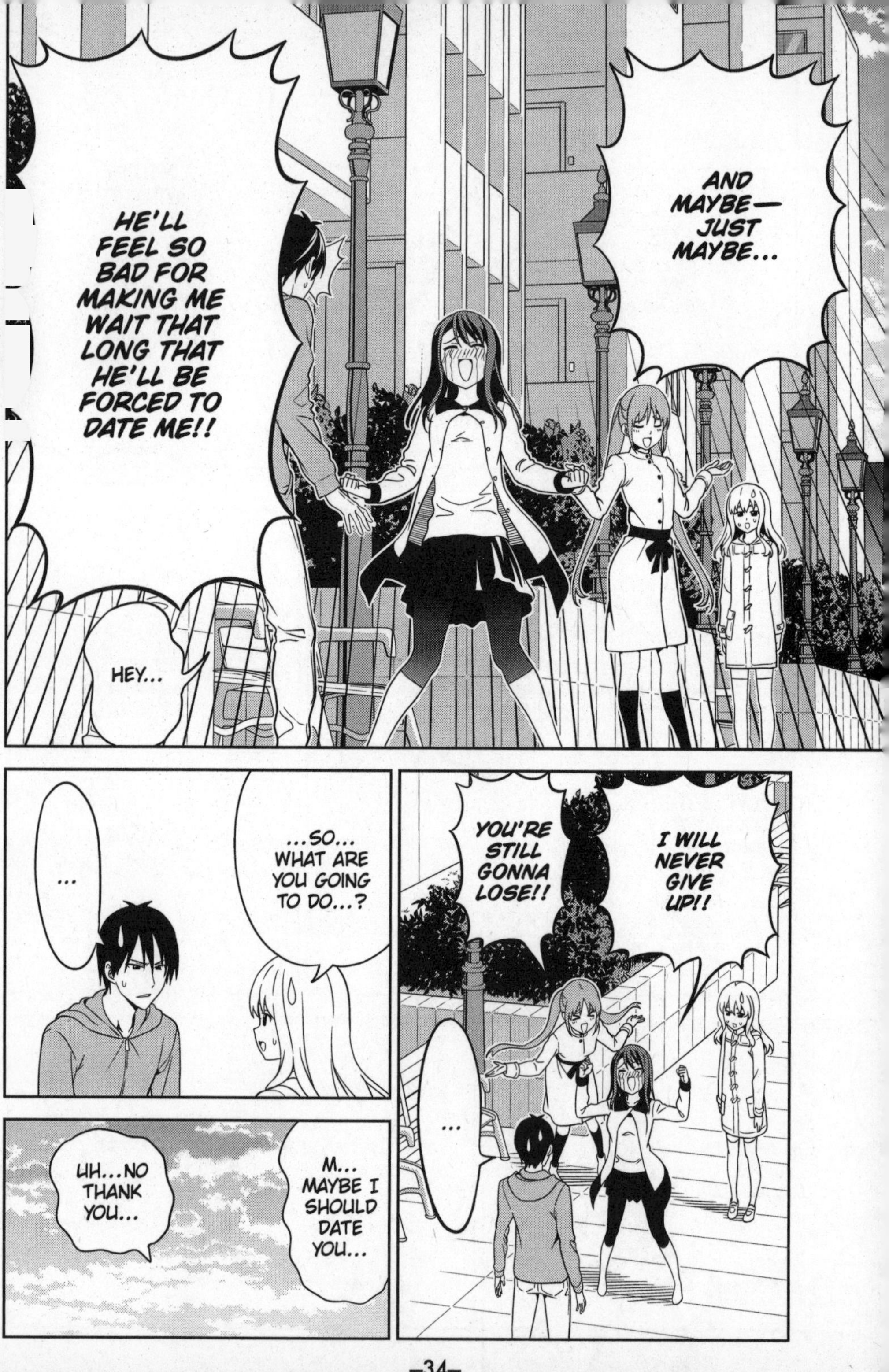
AND MAYBE— JUST MAYBE...
HE'LL FEEL SO BAD FOR MAKING ME WAIT THAT LONG THAT HE'LL BE FORCED TO DATE ME!!
HEY...
I WILL NEVER GIVE UP!!
YOU'RE STILL GONNA LOSE!!
...
...SO... WHAT ARE YOU GOING TO DO...?
...
M... MAYBE I SHOULD DATE YOU...
UH...NO THANK YOU...

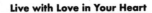

Live with Love in Your Heart

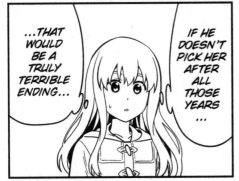

IF HE DOESN'T PICK HER AFTER ALL THOSE YEARS...
...THAT WOULD BE A TRULY TERRIBLE ENDING...
BUT THAT ALMOST SEEMS LIKE THE PERFECT LIFE FOR HEAD MONITOR-SAN...
A REALI-ZATION.

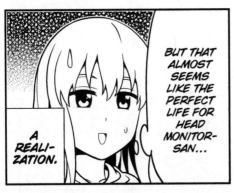

Aho-Girl

\ˈahô͵gərl \ *Japanese, noun.*
A clueless girl.

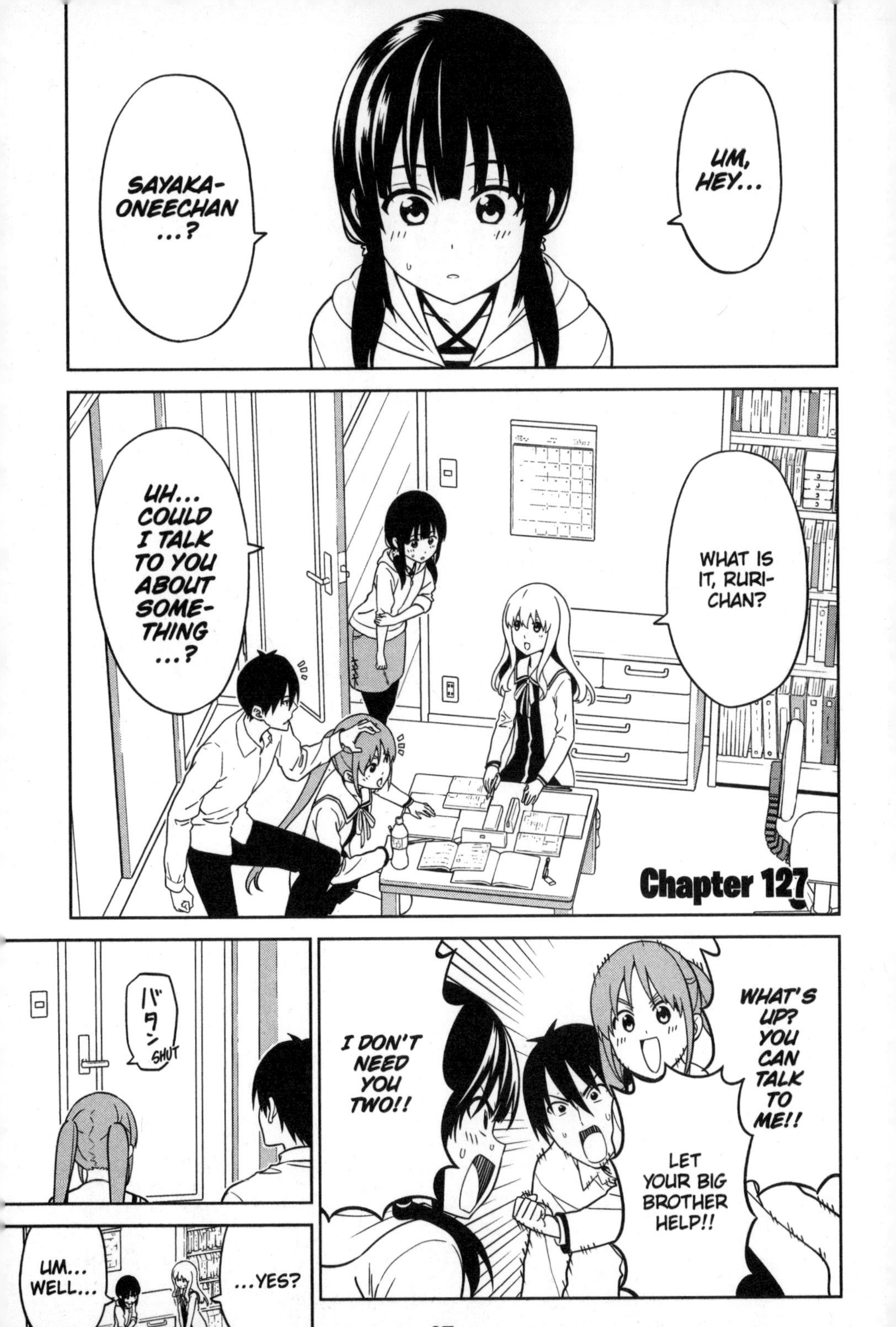
UM, HEY...
SAYAKA-ONEECHAN ...?
WHAT IS IT, RURI-CHAN?
UH... COULD I TALK TO YOU ABOUT SOME-THING ...?
Chapter 127
WHAT'S UP? YOU CAN TALK TO ME!!
LET YOUR BIG BROTHER HELP!!
I DON'T NEED YOU TWO!!
バタン
SHUT
UM... WELL...
...YES?

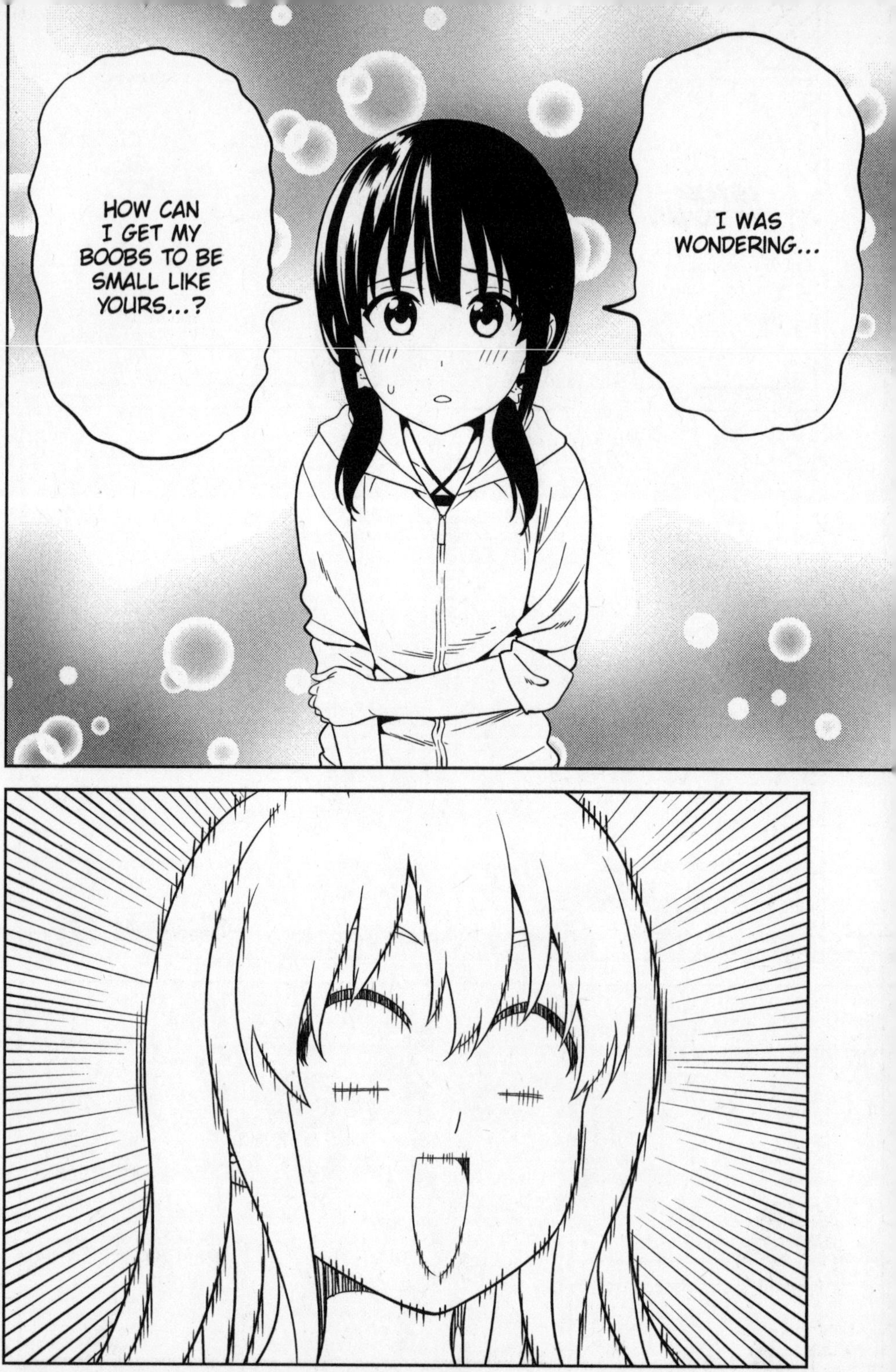
I WAS WONDERING...
HOW CAN I GET MY BOOBS TO BE SMALL LIKE YOURS...?

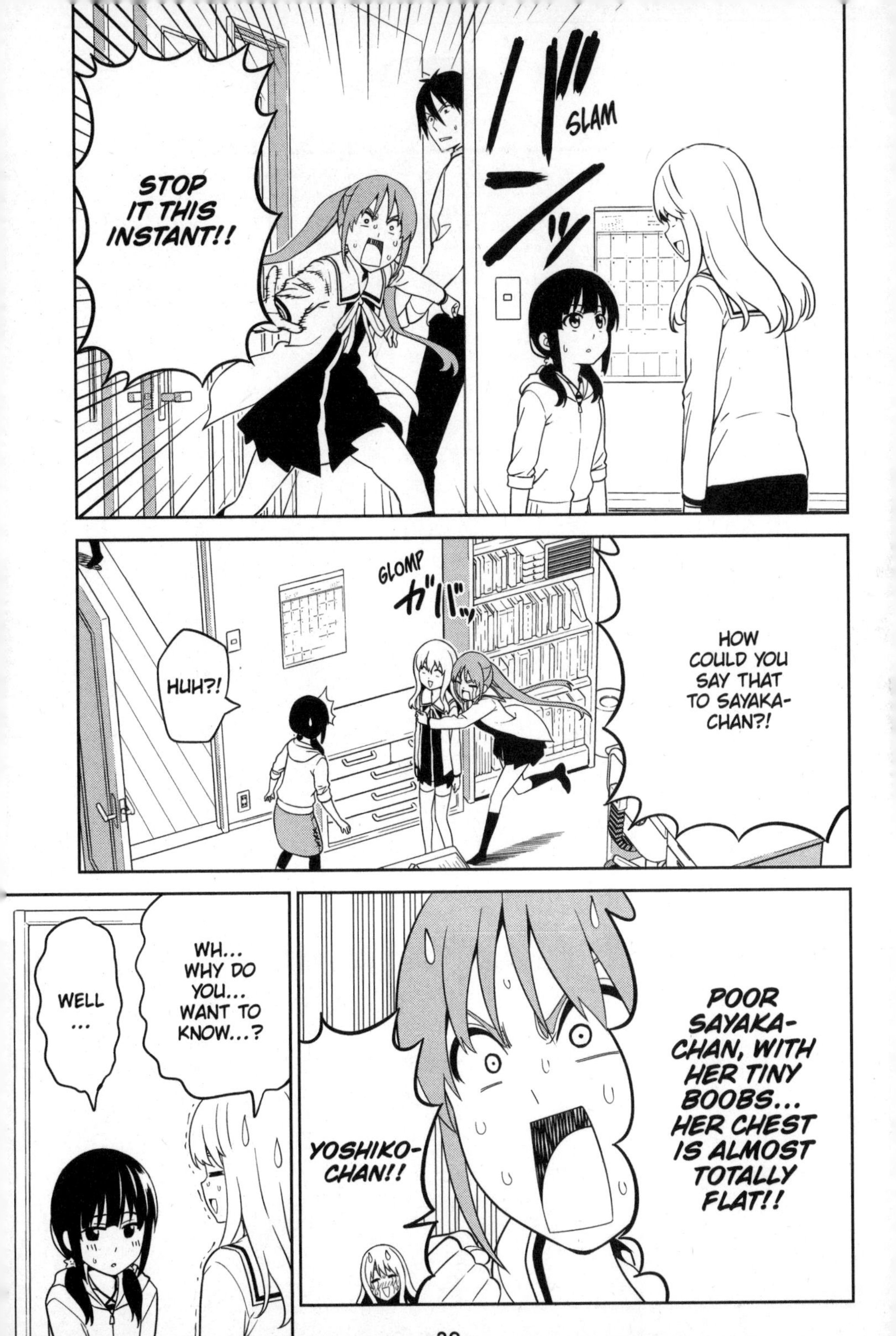
SLAM
STOP IT THIS INSTANT!!
GLOMP
ガバッ
HOW COULD YOU SAY THAT TO SAYAKA-CHAN?!
HUH?!
POOR SAYAKA-CHAN, WITH HER TINY BOOBS... HER CHEST IS ALMOST TOTALLY FLAT!!
YOSHIKO-CHAN!!
WH... WHY DO YOU... WANT TO KNOW...?
WELL ...

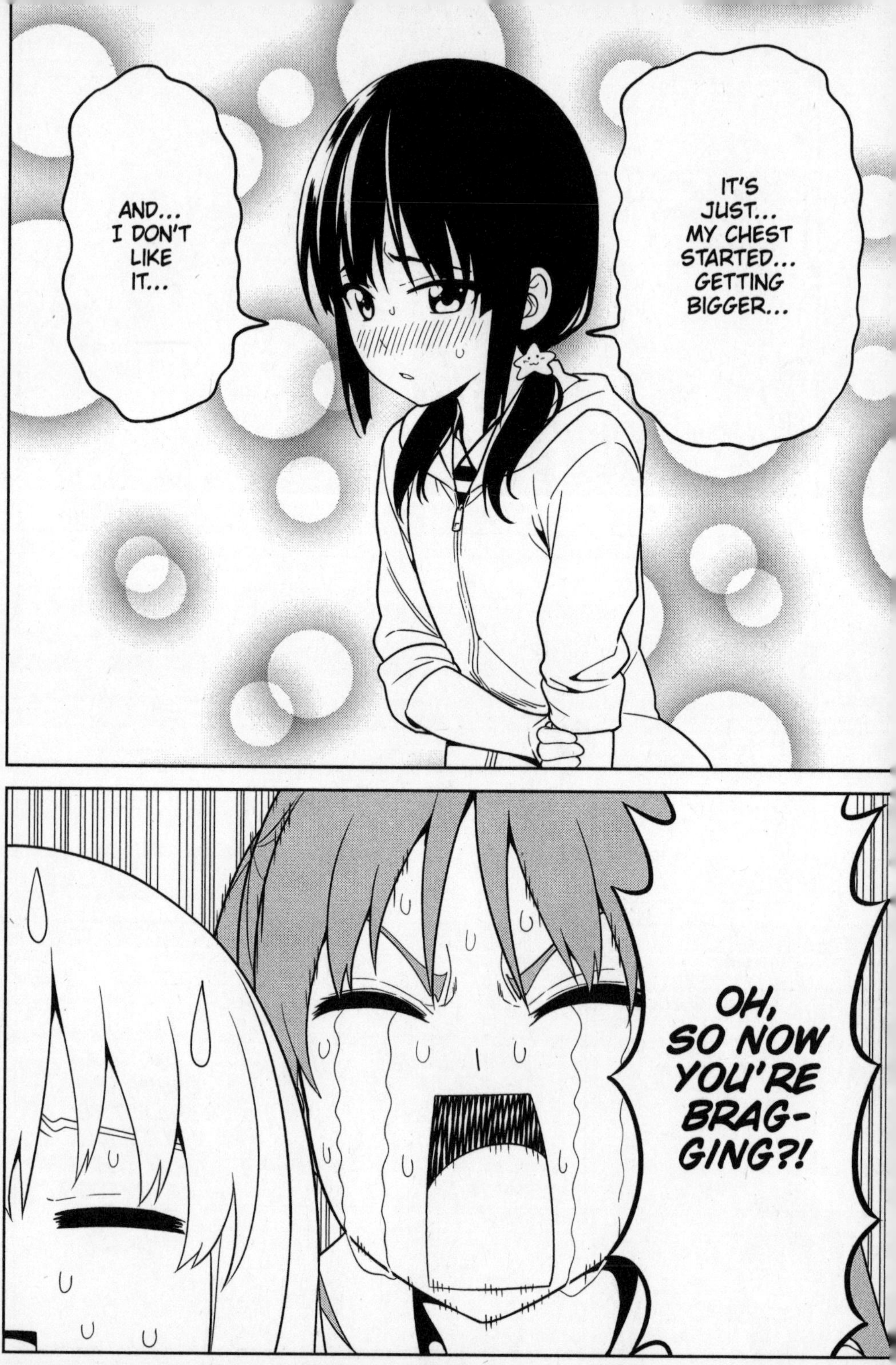
IT'S JUST... MY CHEST STARTED... GETTING BIGGER...
AND... I DON'T LIKE IT...
OH, SO NOW YOU'RE BRAG-GING?!

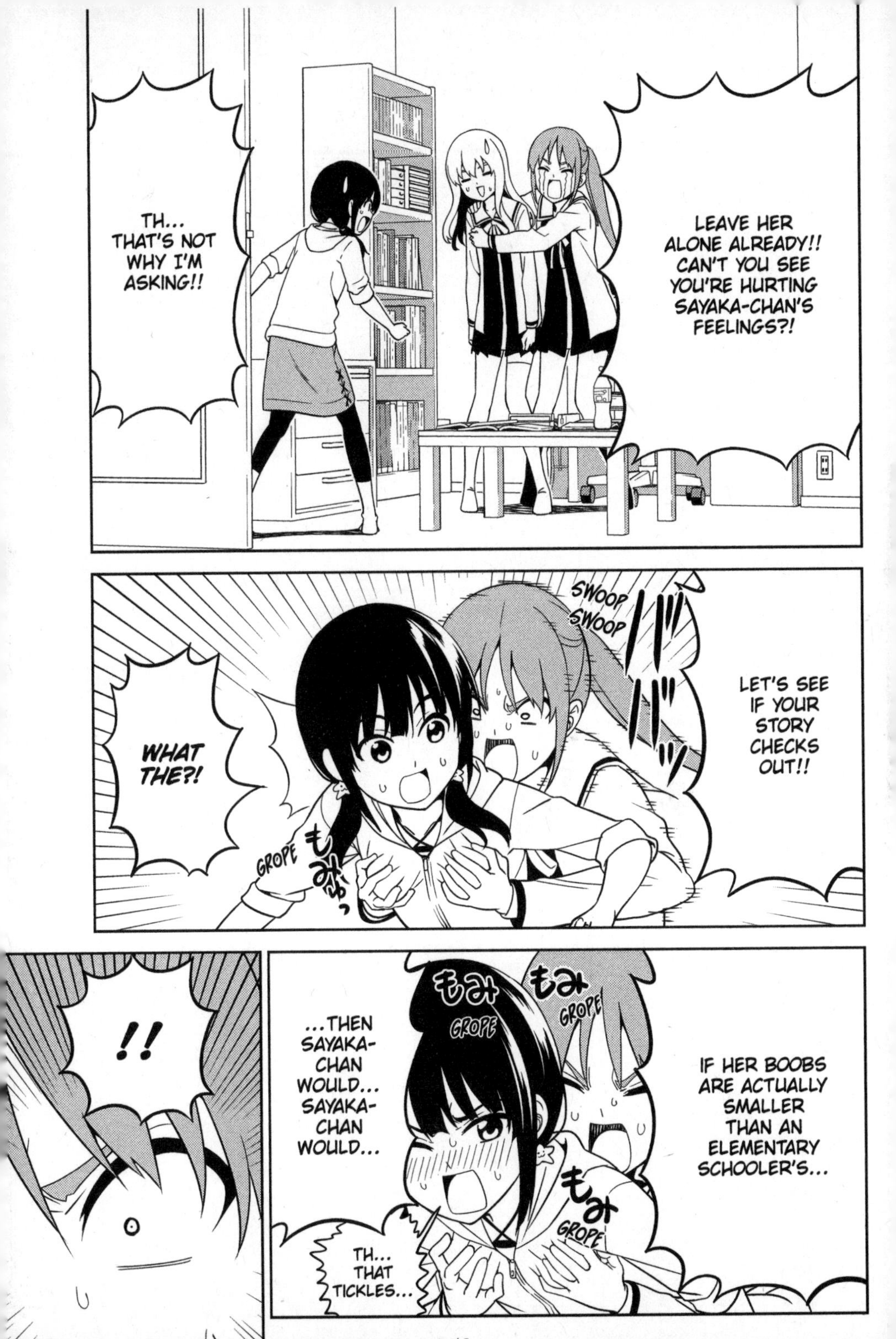
LEAVE HER ALONE ALREADY!! CAN'T YOU SEE YOU'RE HURTING SAYAKA-CHAN'S FEELINGS?!
TH... THAT'S NOT WHY I'M ASKING!!
LET'S SEE IF YOUR STORY CHECKS OUT!!
SWOOP SWOOP
WHAT THE?!
GROPE
もみゅっ
IF HER BOOBS ARE ACTUALLY SMALLER THAN AN ELEMENTARY SCHOOLER'S...
もみ
GROPE
もみ
GROPE
...THEN SAYAKA-CHAN WOULD... SAYAKA-CHAN WOULD...
もみ
GROPE
TH... THAT TICKLES...
!!

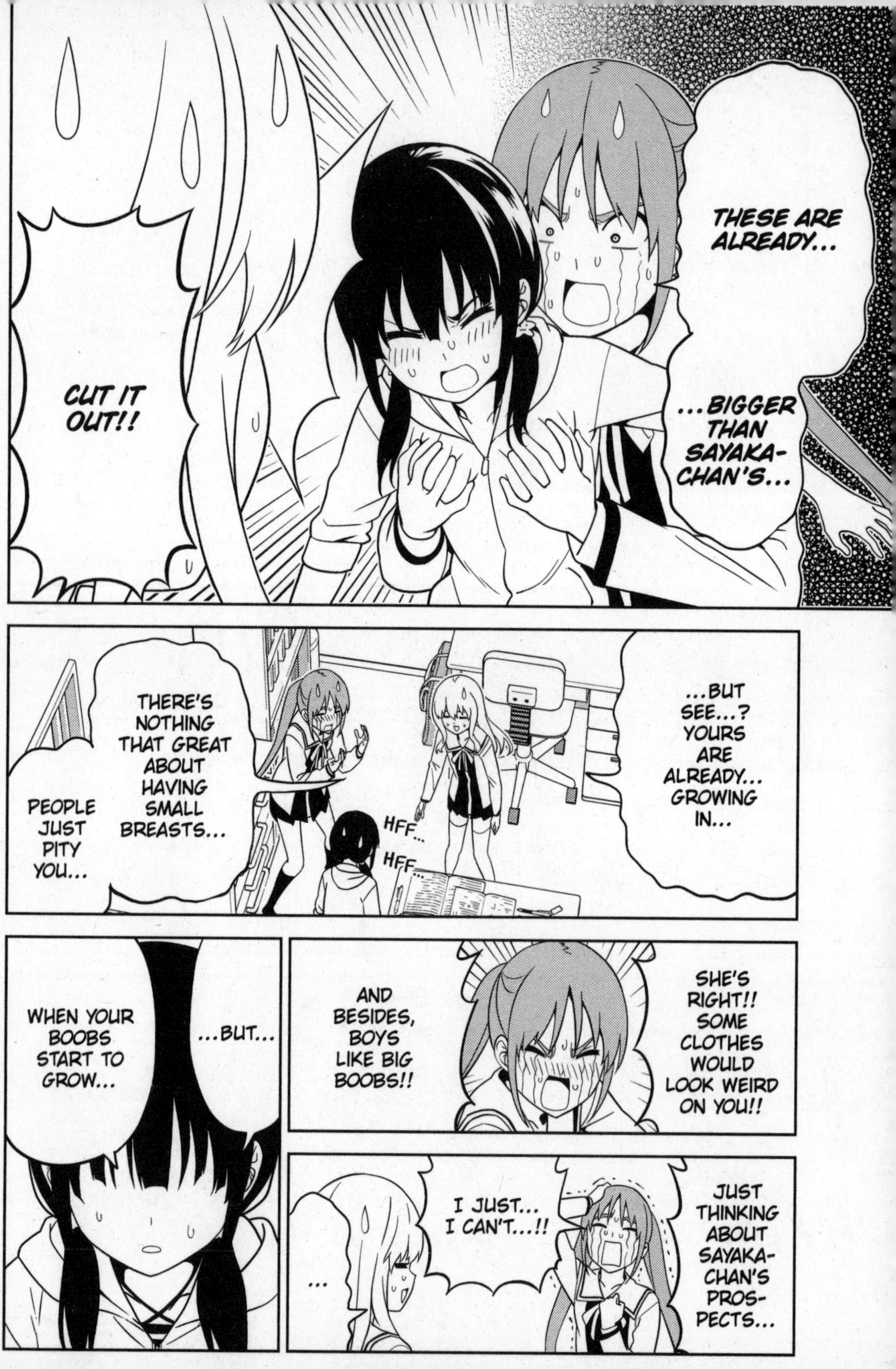
THESE ARE ALREADY...
...BIGGER THAN SAYAKA-CHAN'S...
CUT IT OUT!!
...BUT SEE...? YOURS ARE ALREADY... GROWING IN...
HFF... HFF...
THERE'S NOTHING THAT GREAT ABOUT HAVING SMALL BREASTS...
PEOPLE JUST PITY YOU...
SHE'S RIGHT!! SOME CLOTHES WOULD LOOK WEIRD ON YOU!!
AND BESIDES, BOYS LIKE BIG BOOBS!!
JUST THINKING ABOUT SAYAKA-CHAN'S PROSPECTS...
I JUST... I CAN'T...!!
...
...BUT...
WHEN YOUR BOOBS START TO GROW...

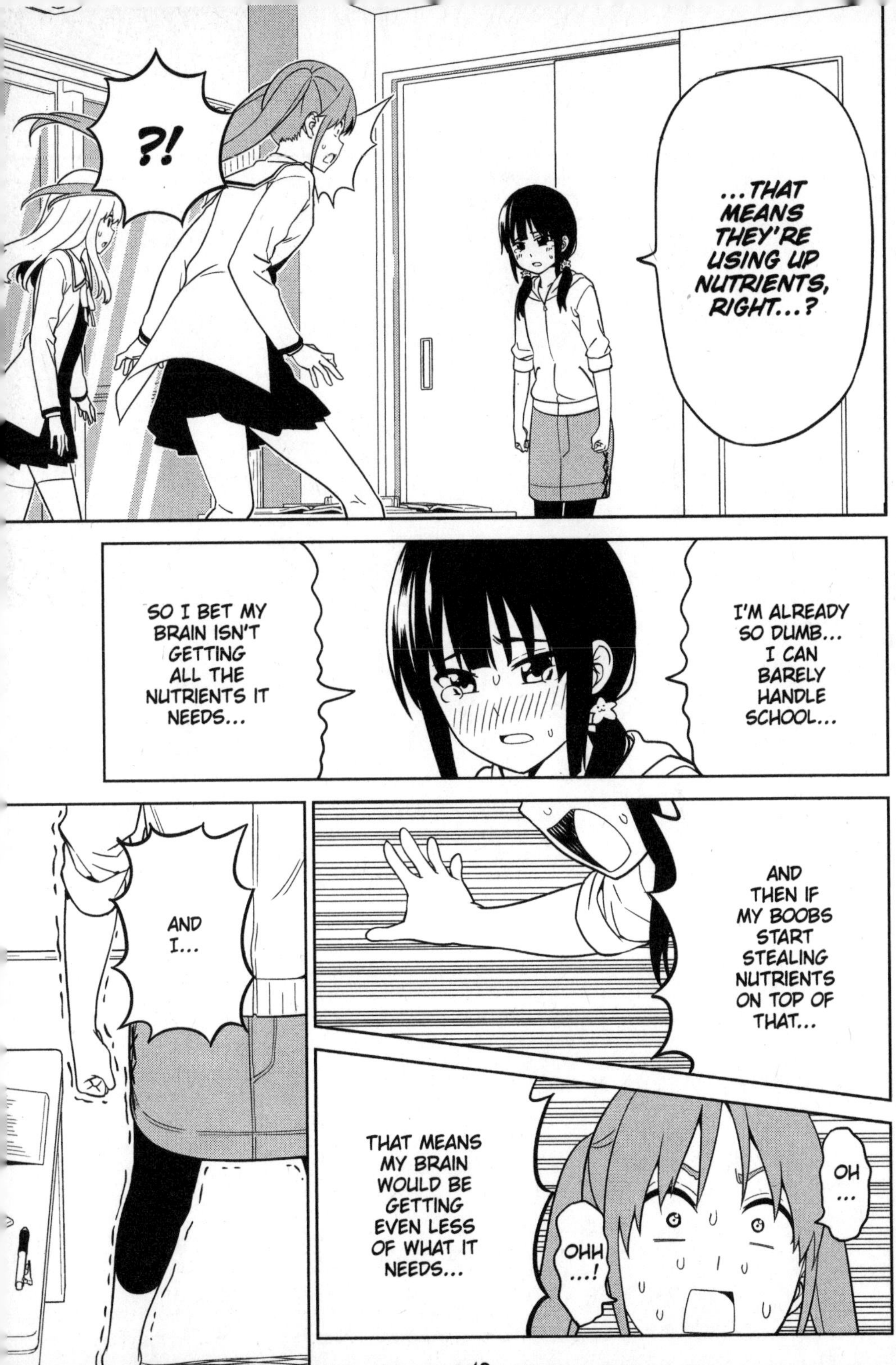
...THAT MEANS THEY'RE USING UP NUTRIENTS, RIGHT...?
?!
I'M ALREADY SO DUMB... I CAN BARELY HANDLE SCHOOL...
SO I BET MY BRAIN ISN'T GETTING ALL THE NUTRIENTS IT NEEDS...
AND THEN IF MY BOOBS START STEALING NUTRIENTS ON TOP OF THAT...
OH ...
THAT MEANS MY BRAIN WOULD BE GETTING EVEN LESS OF WHAT IT NEEDS...
OHH ...!
AND I...

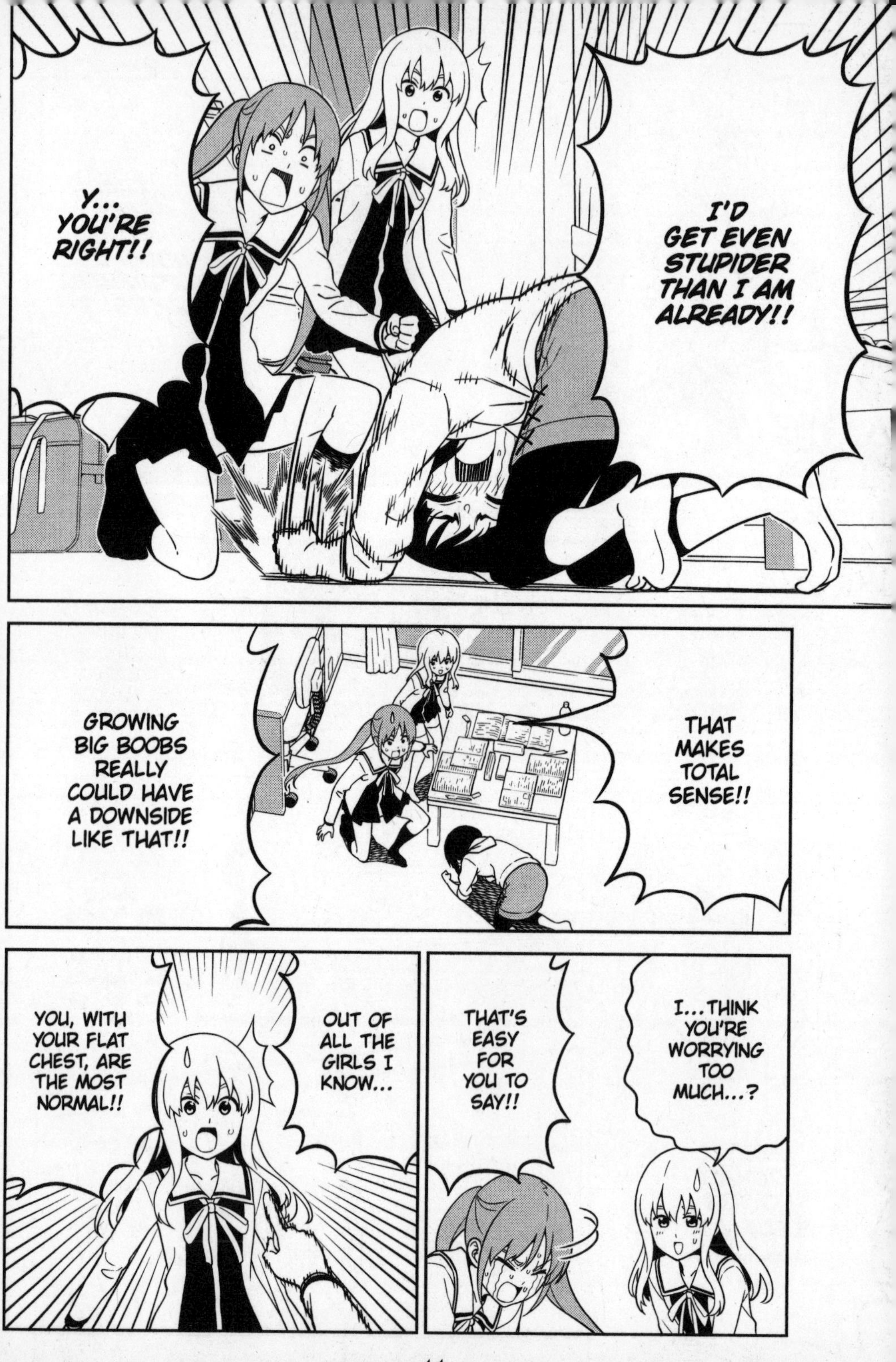
I'D GET EVEN STUPIDER THAN I AM ALREADY!!
Y... YOU'RE RIGHT!!
THAT MAKES TOTAL SENSE!!
GROWING BIG BOOBS REALLY COULD HAVE A DOWNSIDE LIKE THAT!!
I...THINK YOU'RE WORRYING TOO MUCH...?
THAT'S EASY FOR YOU TO SAY!!
OUT OF ALL THE GIRLS I KNOW...
YOU, WITH YOUR FLAT CHEST, ARE THE MOST NORMAL!!

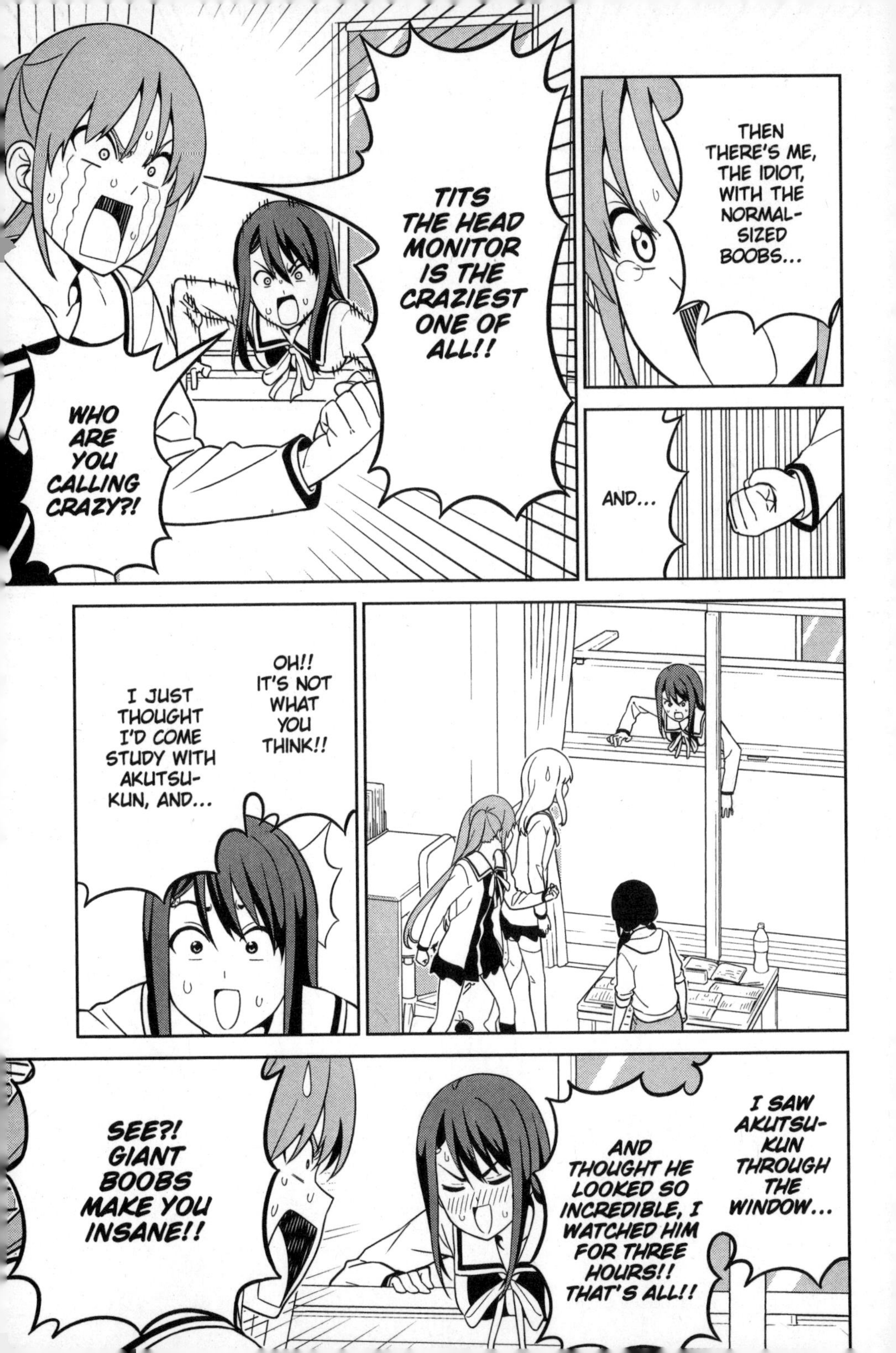
THEN THERE'S ME, THE IDIOT, WITH THE NORMAL-SIZED BOOBS...
AND...
TITS THE HEAD MONITOR IS THE CRAZIEST ONE OF ALL!!
WHO ARE YOU CALLING CRAZY?!
OH!! IT'S NOT WHAT YOU THINK!!
I JUST THOUGHT I'D COME STUDY WITH AKUTSU-KUN, AND...
I SAW AKUTSU-KUN THROUGH THE WINDOW...
AND THOUGHT HE LOOKED SO INCREDIBLE, I WATCHED HIM FOR THREE HOURS!! THAT'S ALL!!
SEE?! GIANT BOOBS MAKE YOU INSANE!!

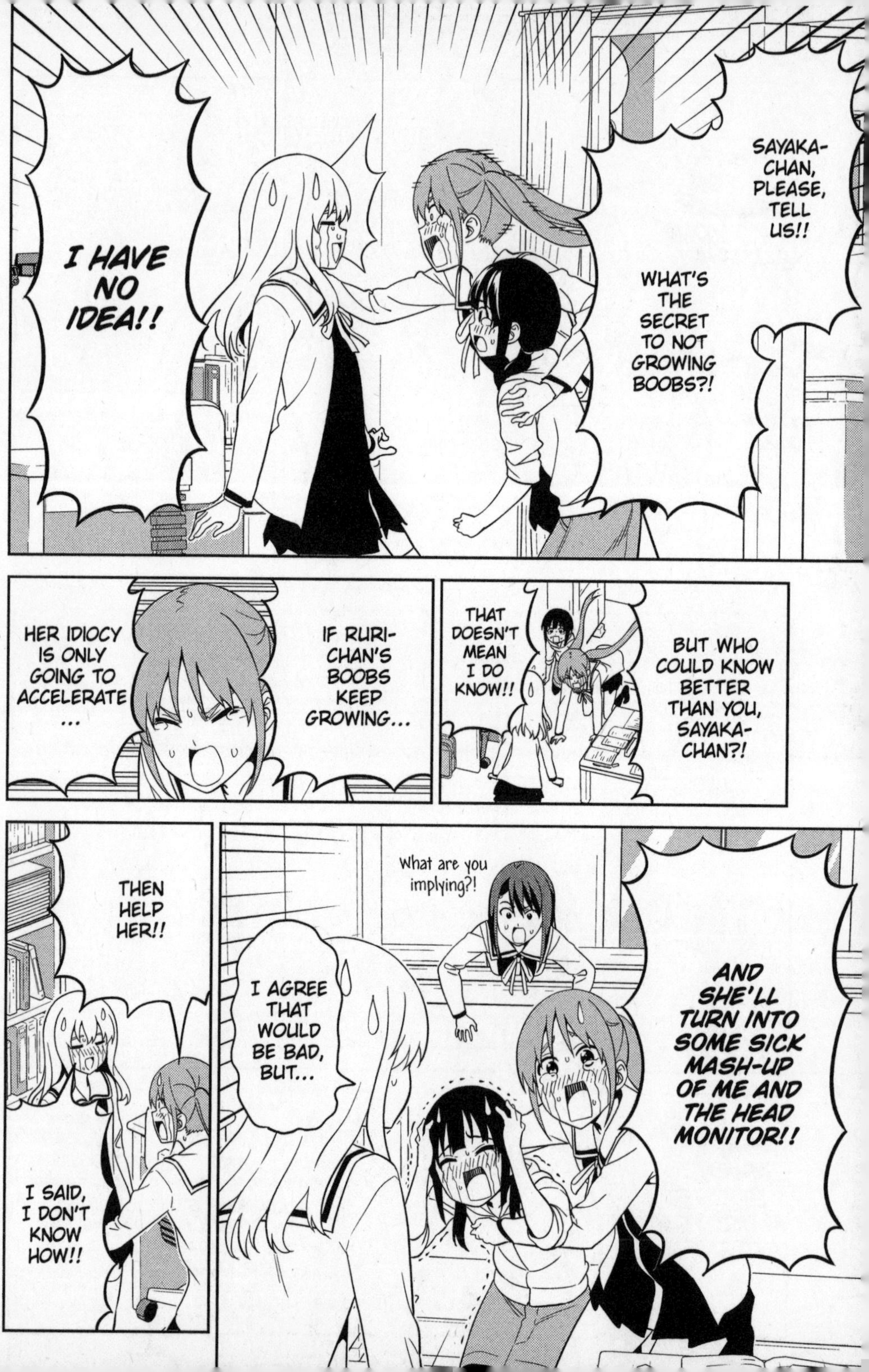
SAYAKA-CHAN, PLEASE, TELL US!!
WHAT'S THE SECRET TO NOT GROWING BOOBS?!
I HAVE NO IDEA!!
BUT WHO COULD KNOW BETTER THAN YOU, SAYAKA-CHAN?!
THAT DOESN'T MEAN I DO KNOW!!
IF RURI-CHAN'S BOOBS KEEP GROWING...
HER IDIOCY IS ONLY GOING TO ACCELERATE...
AND SHE'LL TURN INTO SOME SICK MASH-UP OF ME AND THE HEAD MONITOR!!
What are you implying?!
I AGREE THAT WOULD BE BAD, BUT...
THEN HELP HER!!
I SAID, I DON'T KNOW HOW!!

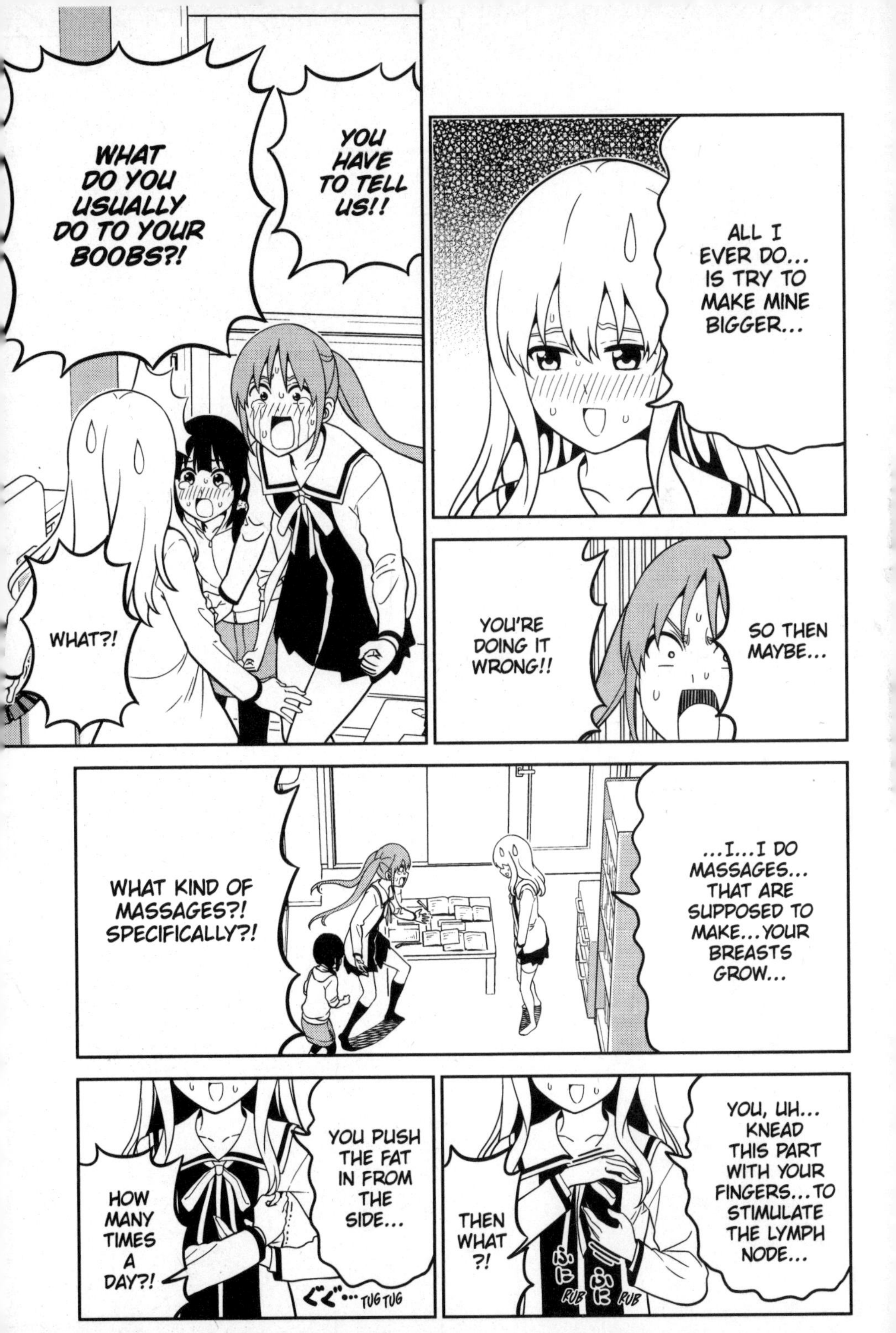
YOU HAVE TO TELL US!!
WHAT DO YOU USUALLY DO TO YOUR BOOBS?!
WHAT?!
ALL I EVER DO... IS TRY TO MAKE MINE BIGGER...
SO THEN MAYBE...
YOU'RE DOING IT WRONG!!
...I...I DO MASSAGES... THAT ARE SUPPOSED TO MAKE...YOUR BREASTS GROW...
WHAT KIND OF MASSAGES?! SPECIFICALLY?!
YOU, UH... KNEAD THIS PART WITH YOUR FINGERS...TO STIMULATE THE LYMPH NODE...
THEN WHAT?!
ふに RUB ふに RUB
YOU PUSH THE FAT IN FROM THE SIDE...
HOW MANY TIMES A DAY?!
ぐぐ… TUG TUG

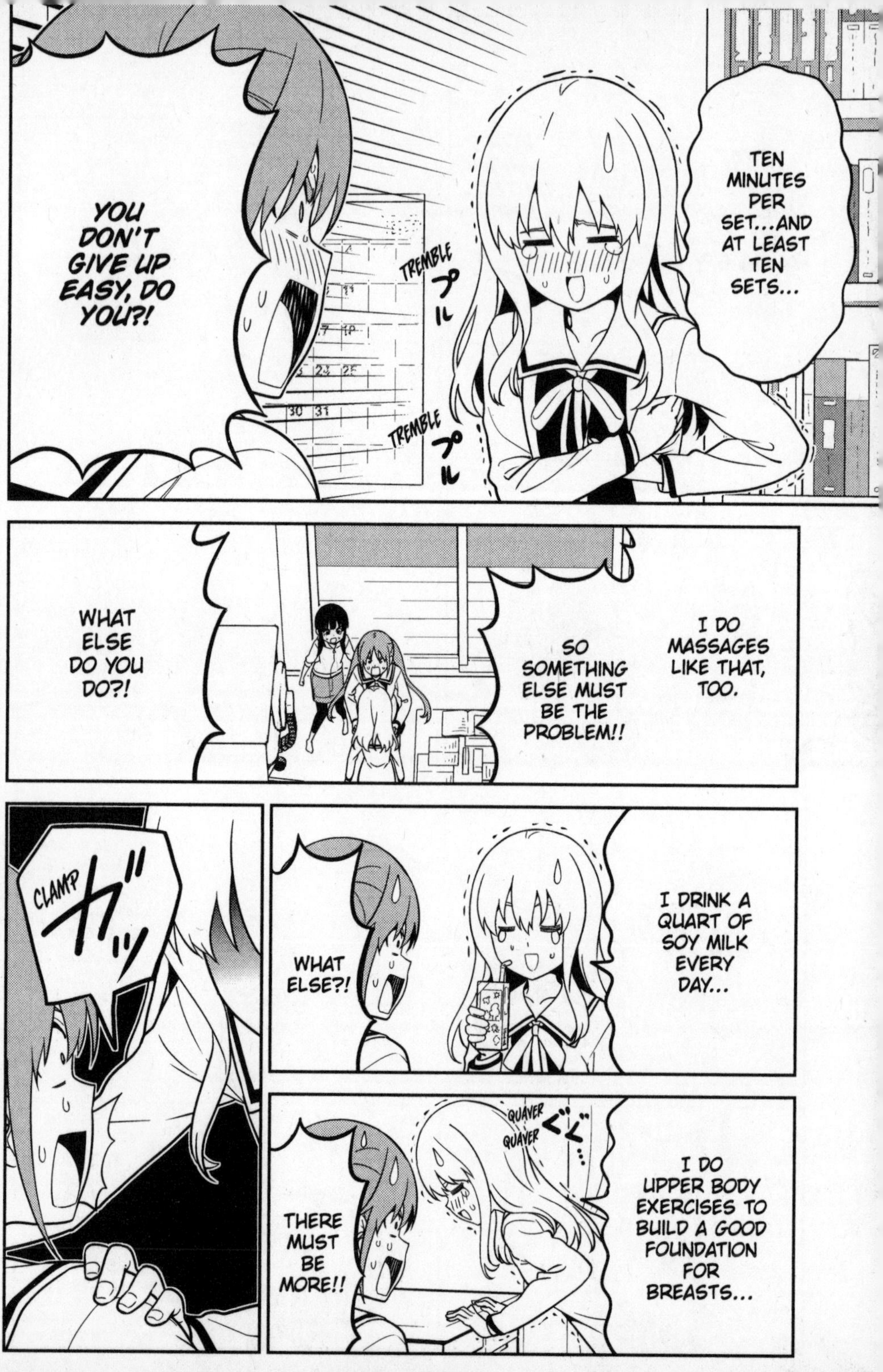
TEN MINUTES PER SET...AND AT LEAST TEN SETS...
TREMBLE プル
TREMBLE プル
YOU DON'T GIVE UP EASY, DO YOU?!
I DO MASSAGES LIKE THAT, TOO.
SO SOMETHING ELSE MUST BE THE PROBLEM!!
WHAT ELSE DO YOU DO?!
I DRINK A QUART OF SOY MILK EVERY DAY...
WHAT ELSE?!
QUAVER QUAVER ぐぐ...
I DO UPPER BODY EXERCISES TO BUILD A GOOD FOUNDATION FOR BREASTS...
THERE MUST BE MORE!!
CLAMP ガッ

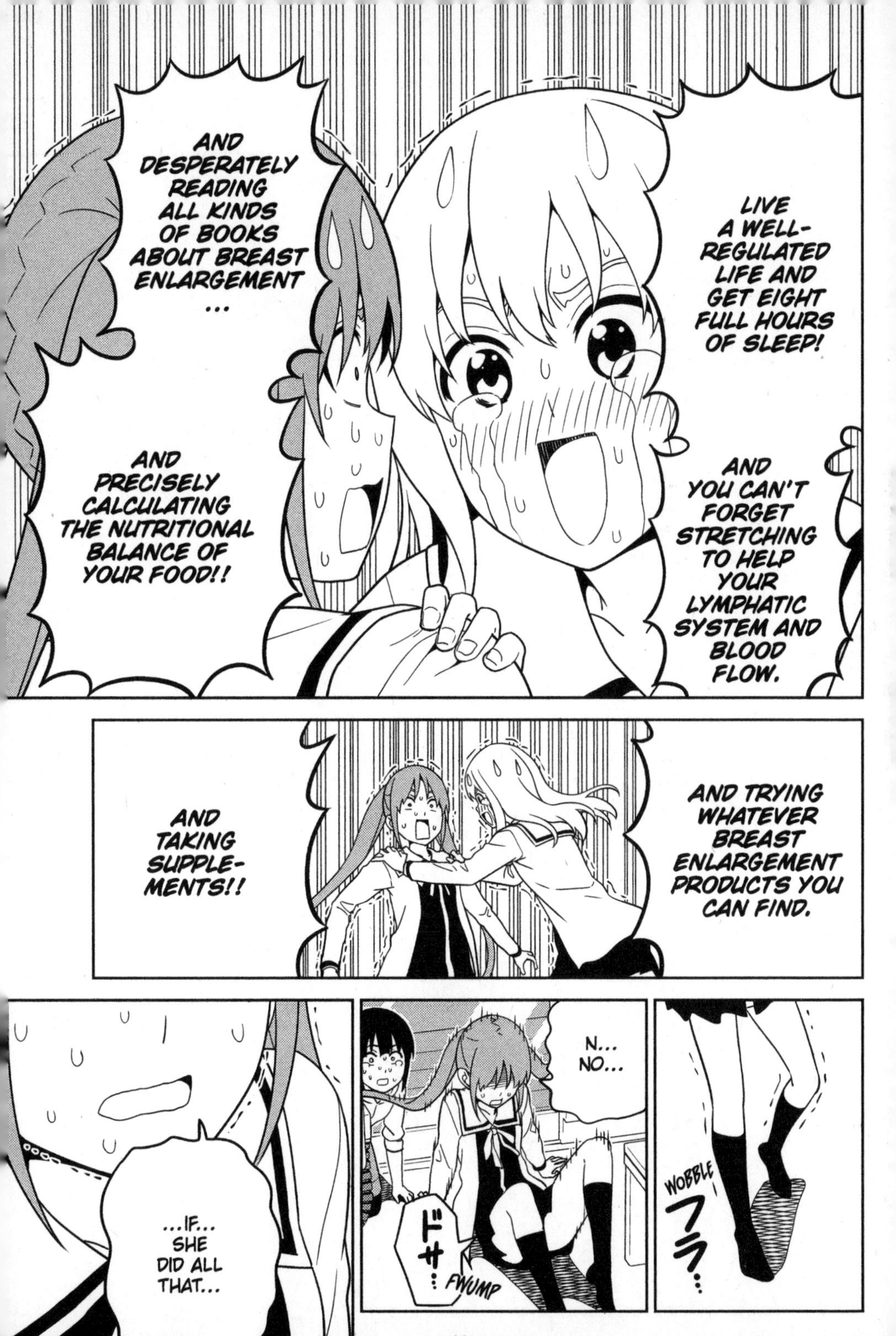
LIVE A WELL-REGULATED LIFE AND GET EIGHT FULL HOURS OF SLEEP!
AND DESPERATELY READING ALL KINDS OF BOOKS ABOUT BREAST ENLARGEMENT ...
AND YOU CAN'T FORGET STRETCHING TO HELP YOUR LYMPHATIC SYSTEM AND BLOOD FLOW.
AND PRECISELY CALCULATING THE NUTRITIONAL BALANCE OF YOUR FOOD!!
AND TRYING WHATEVER BREAST ENLARGEMENT PRODUCTS YOU CAN FIND.
AND TAKING SUPPLE-MENTS!!
WOBBLE
フラ…
N... NO...
ドサ…
FWUMP
...IF... SHE DID ALL THAT...

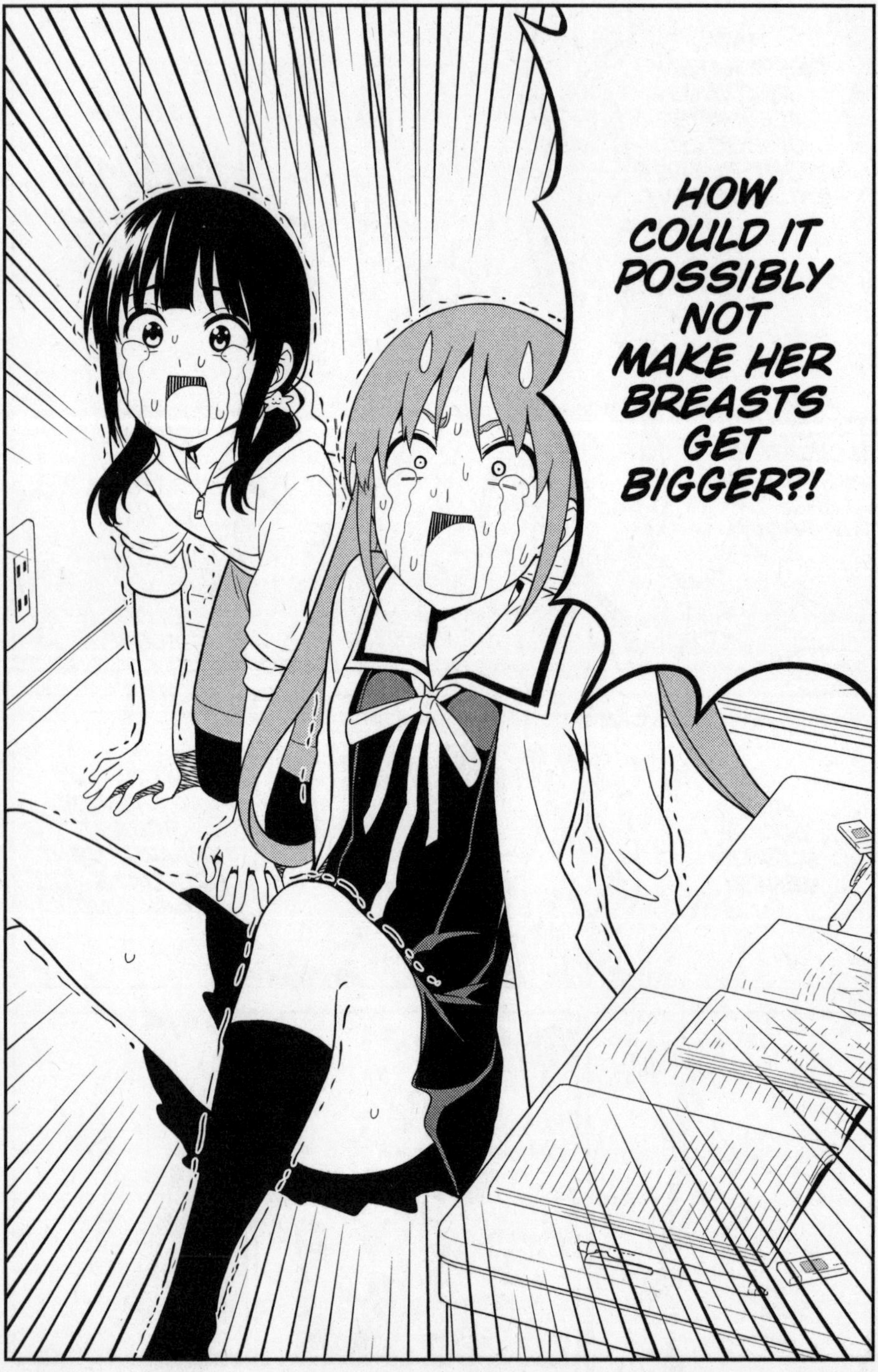
HOW COULD IT POSSIBLY NOT MAKE HER BREASTS GET BIGGER?!

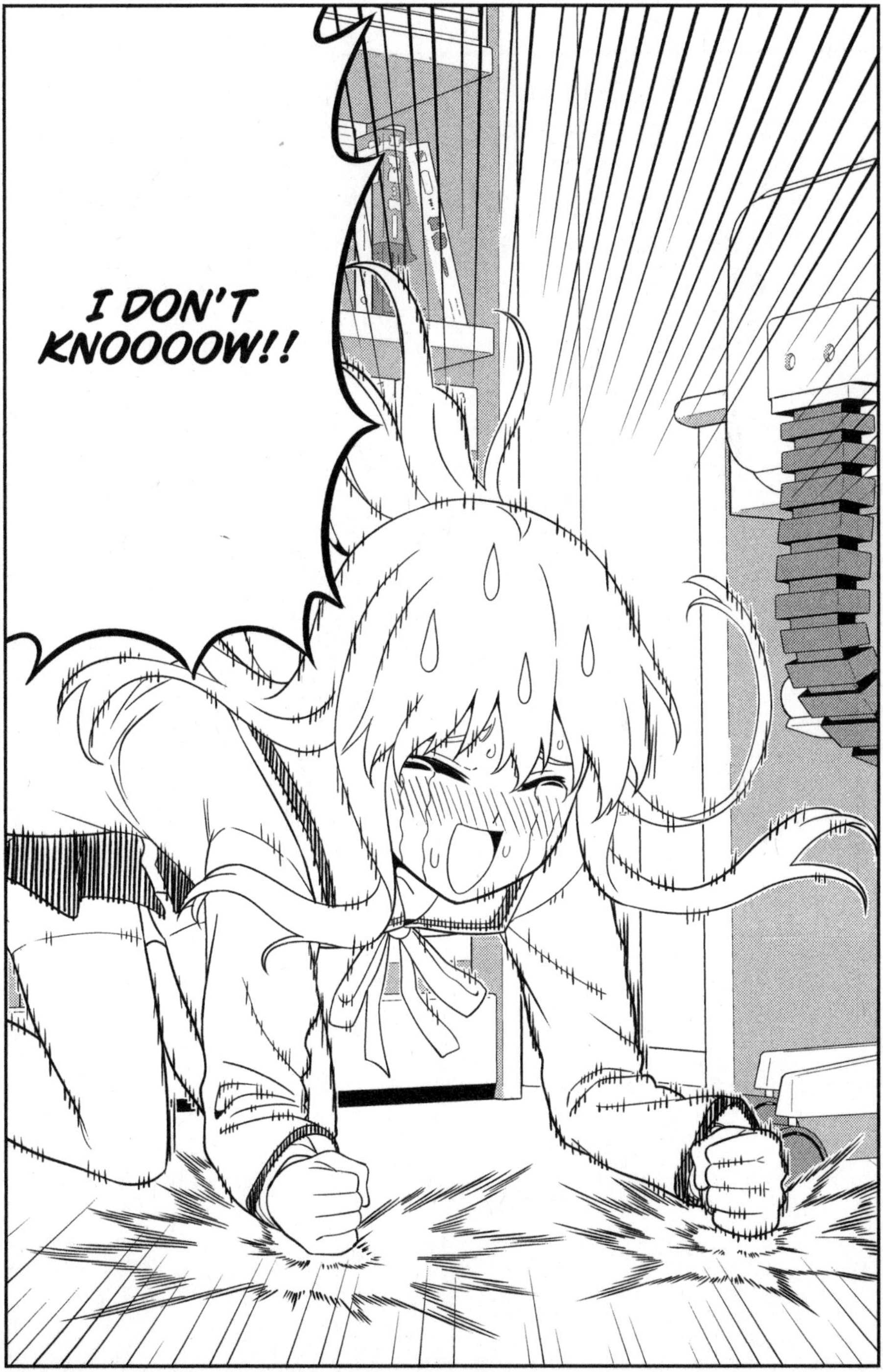
I DON'T KNOOOOW!!

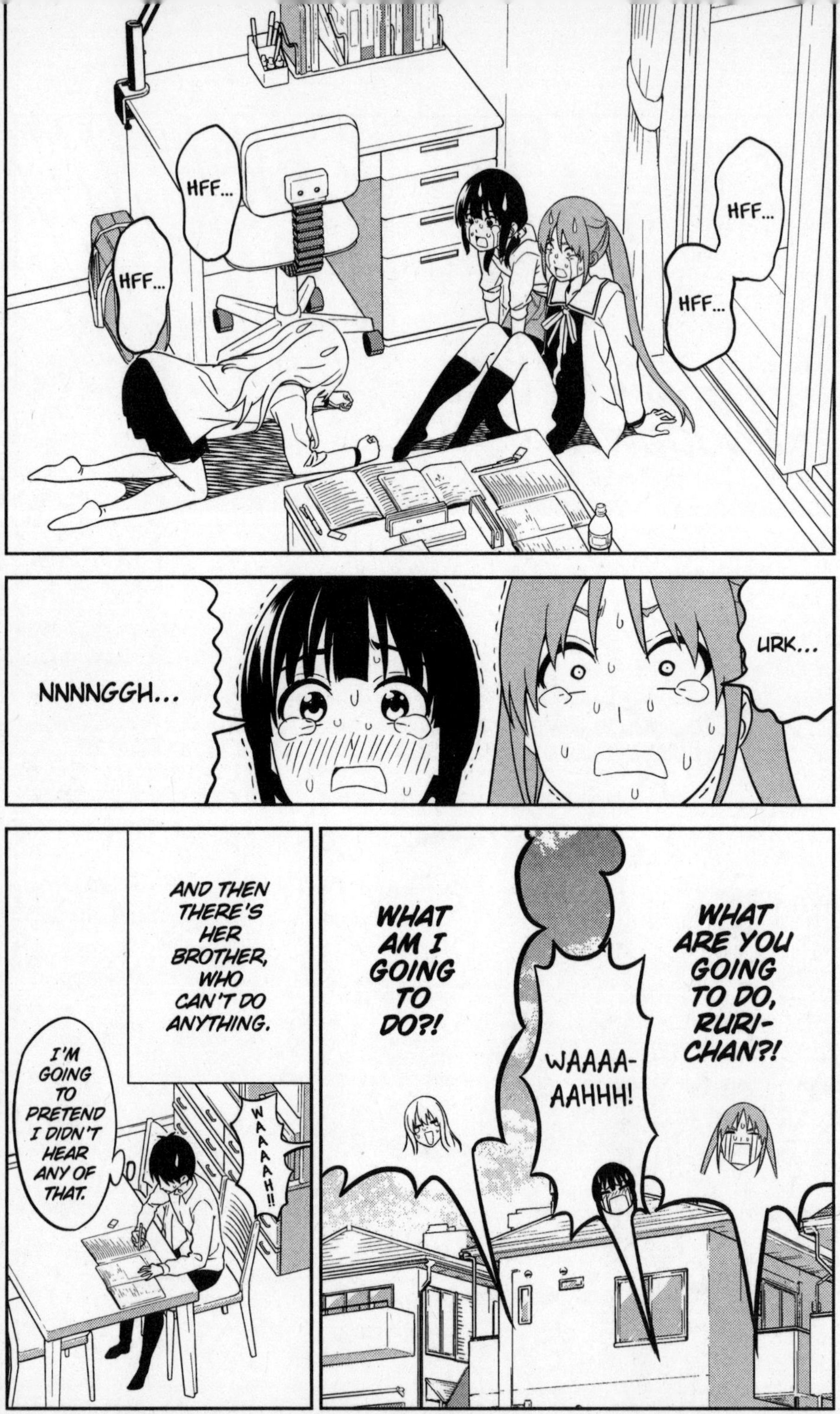
HFF...
HFF...
HFF...
HFF...
URK...
NNNNGGH...
WHAT ARE YOU GOING TO DO, RURI-CHAN?!
WAAAA-AAHHH!
WHAT AM I GOING TO DO?!
AND THEN THERE'S HER BROTHER, WHO CAN'T DO ANYTHING.
WAAAAAH!!
I'M GOING TO PRETEND I DIDN'T HEAR ANY OF THAT.

An Honest Man

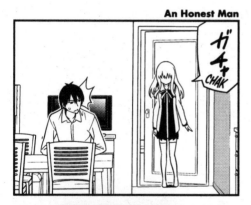

ガチャ
CHAK
...I DIDN'T HEAR ANYTHING YOU GUYS SAID...
HE'S SUCH A BAD LIAR!!

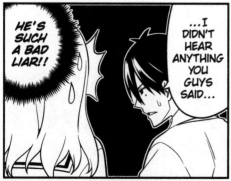

(Everyone is different, everyone is)

Aho-Girl

\'ahô,gərl\ *Japanese, noun*.

A clueless girl.

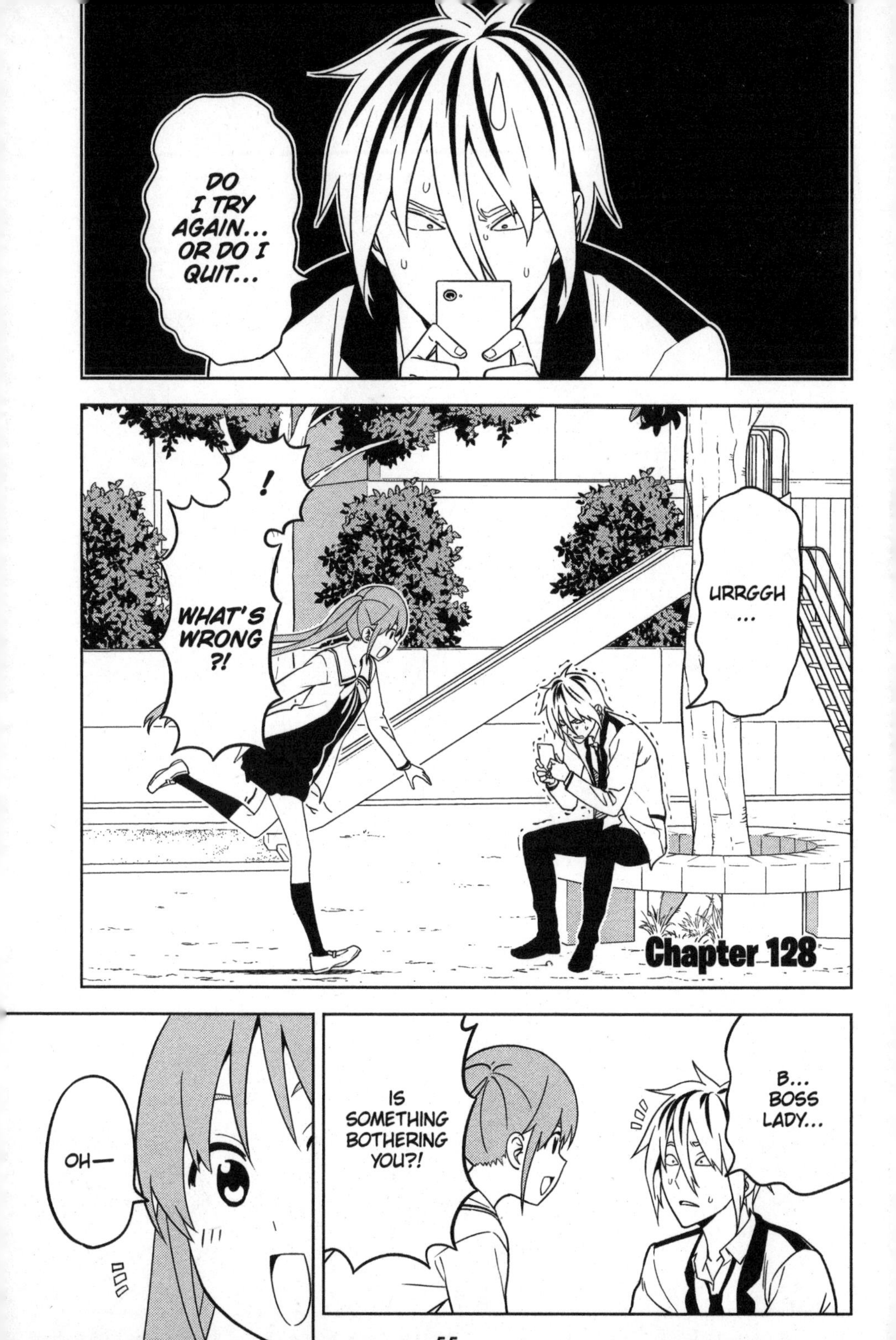
DO I TRY AGAIN... OR DO I QUIT...
URRGGH ...
!
WHAT'S WRONG ?!
Chapter 128
B... BOSS LADY...
IS SOMETHING BOTHERING YOU?!
OH—

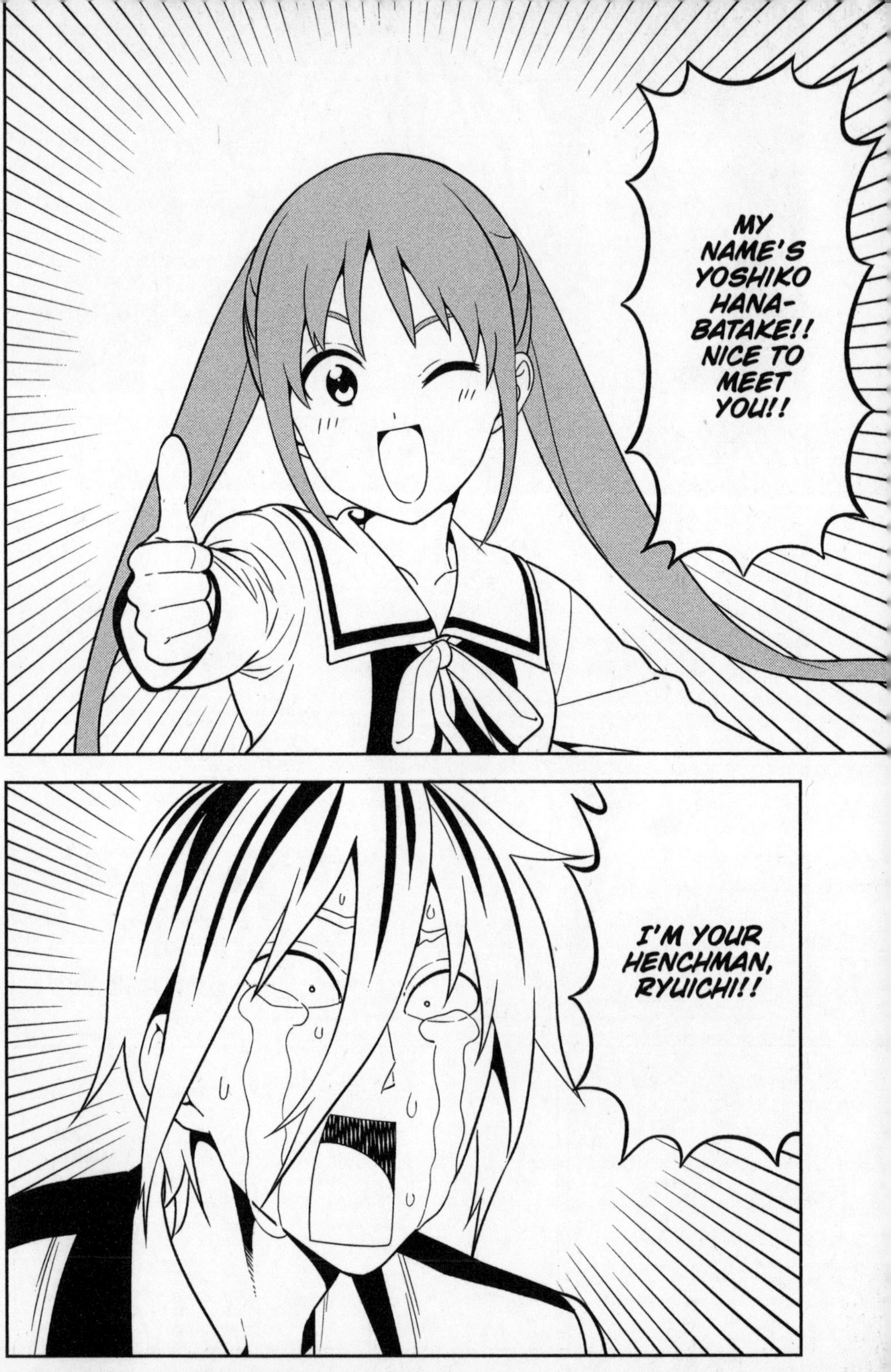
MY NAME'S YOSHIKO HANA-BATAKE!! NICE TO MEET YOU!!
I'M YOUR HENCHMAN, RYUICHI!!

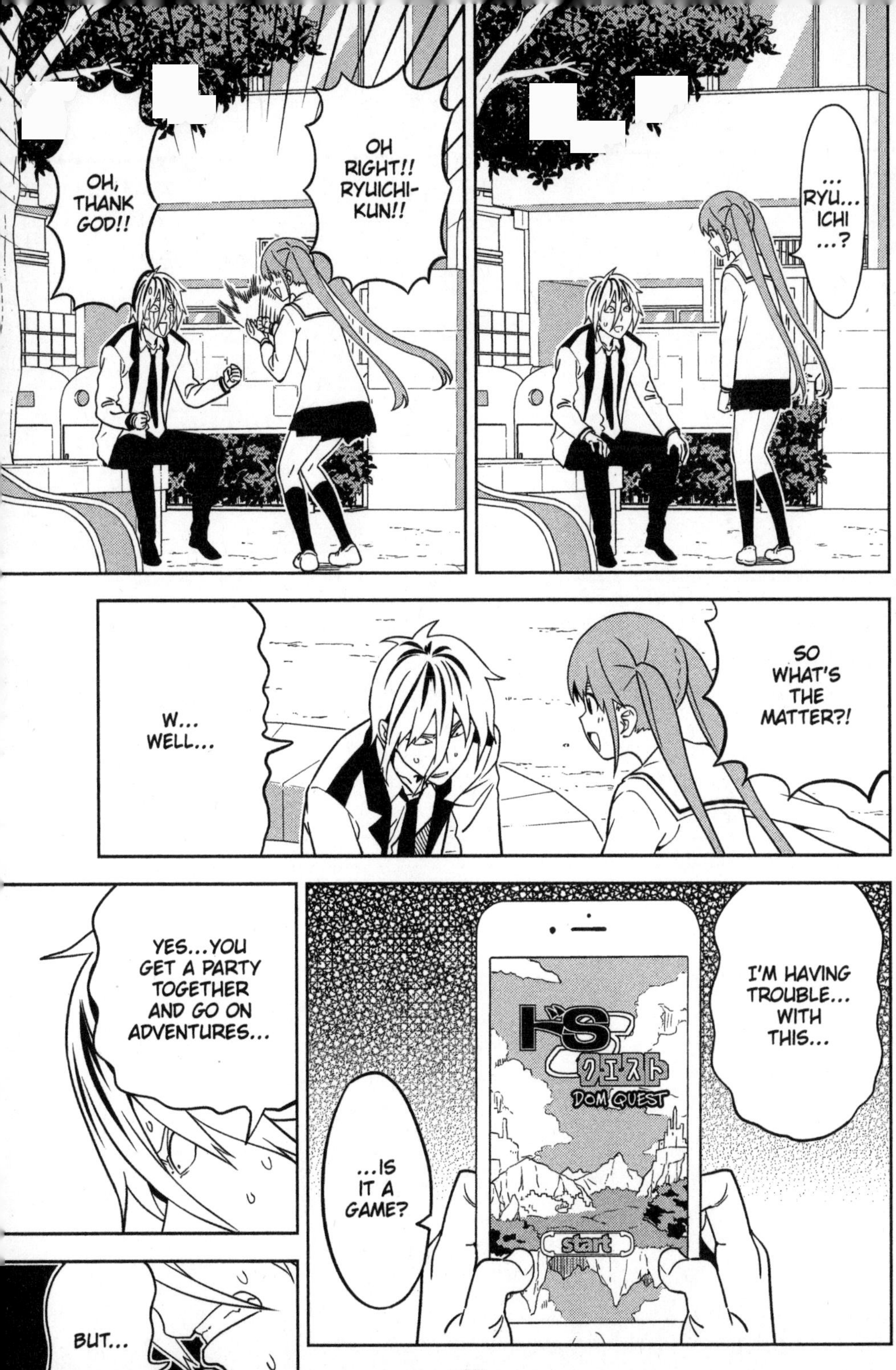
...RYU...ICHI...?
OH RIGHT!! RYUICHI-KUN!!
OH, THANK GOD!!
SO WHAT'S THE MATTER?!
W... WELL...
I'M HAVING TROUBLE... WITH THIS...
ドS クエスト
DOM QUEST
start
...IS IT A GAME?
YES...YOU GET A PARTY TOGETHER AND GO ON ADVENTURES...
BUT...

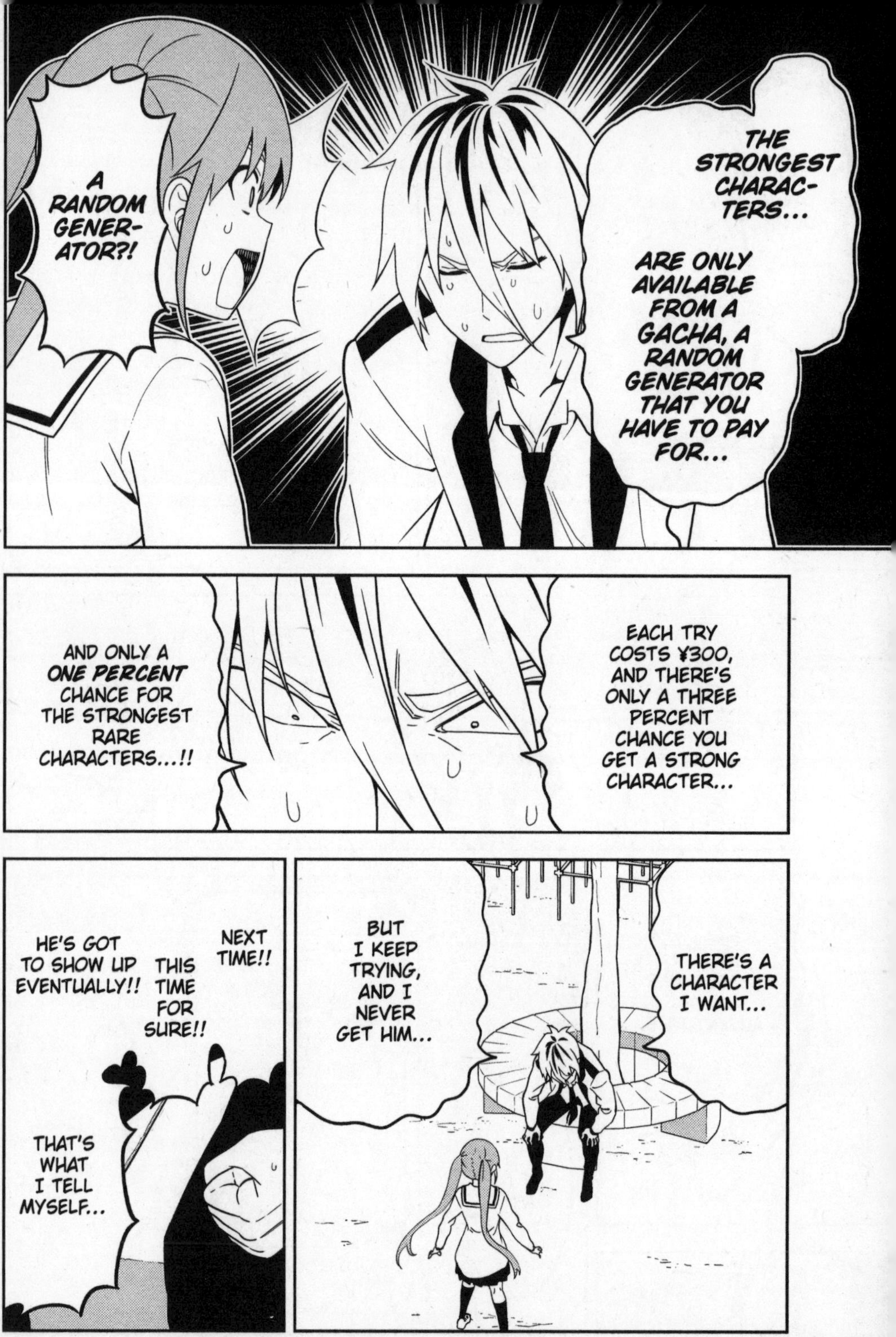
THE STRONGEST CHARACTERS...
ARE ONLY AVAILABLE FROM A GACHA, A RANDOM GENERATOR THAT YOU HAVE TO PAY FOR...
A RANDOM GENERATOR?!
EACH TRY COSTS ¥300, AND THERE'S ONLY A THREE PERCENT CHANCE YOU GET A STRONG CHARACTER...
AND ONLY A *ONE PERCENT* CHANCE FOR THE STRONGEST RARE CHARACTERS...!!
THERE'S A CHARACTER I WANT...
BUT I KEEP TRYING, AND I NEVER GET HIM...
NEXT TIME!!
THIS TIME FOR SURE!!
HE'S GOT TO SHOW UP EVENTUALLY!!
THAT'S WHAT I TELL MYSELF...

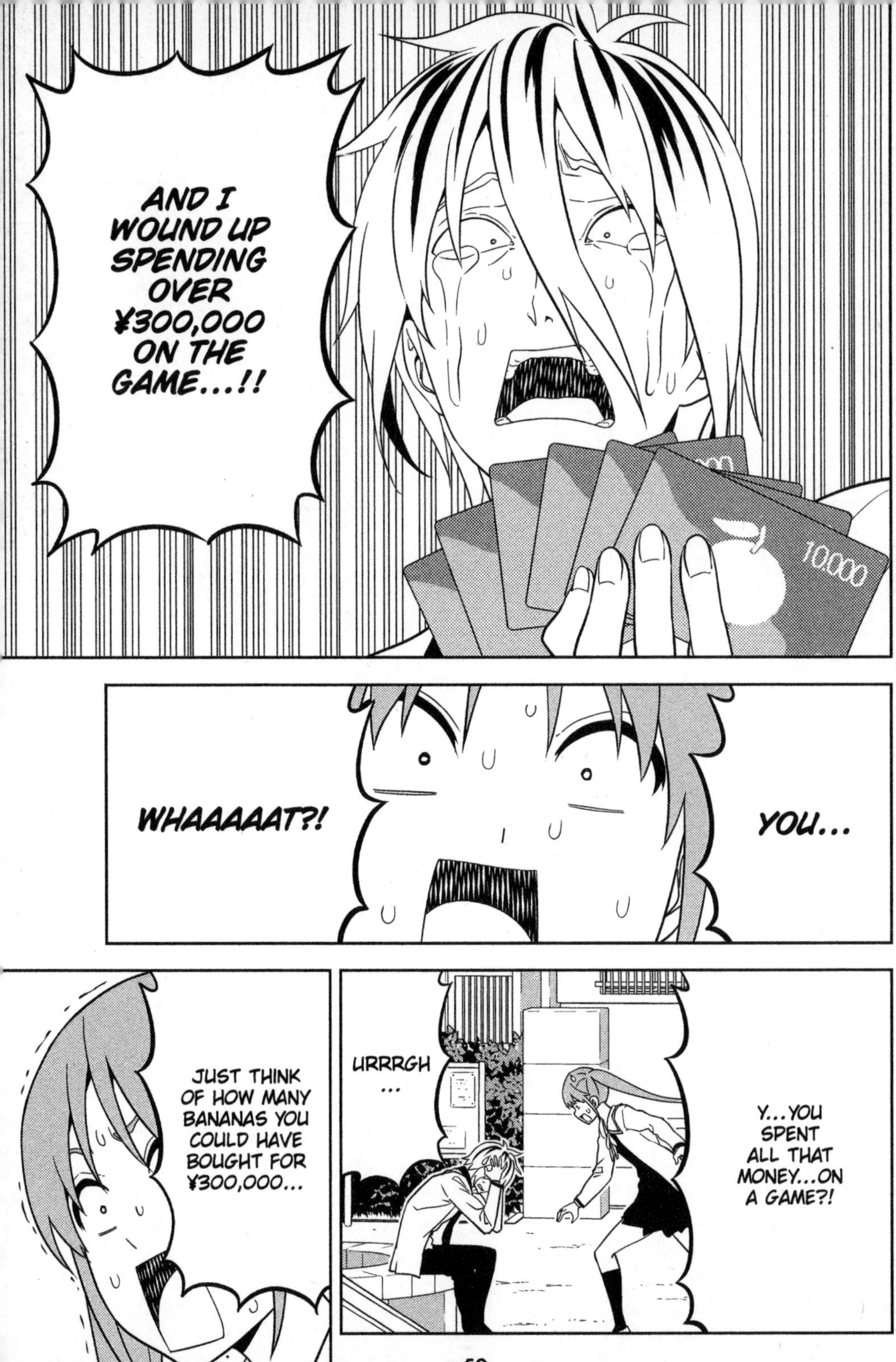
AND I WOUND UP SPENDING OVER ¥300,000 ON THE GAME...!!
10,000
YOU...
WHAAAAAT?!
Y...YOU SPENT ALL THAT MONEY...ON A GAME?!
URRRGH ...
JUST THINK OF HOW MANY BANANAS YOU COULD HAVE BOUGHT FOR ¥300,000...

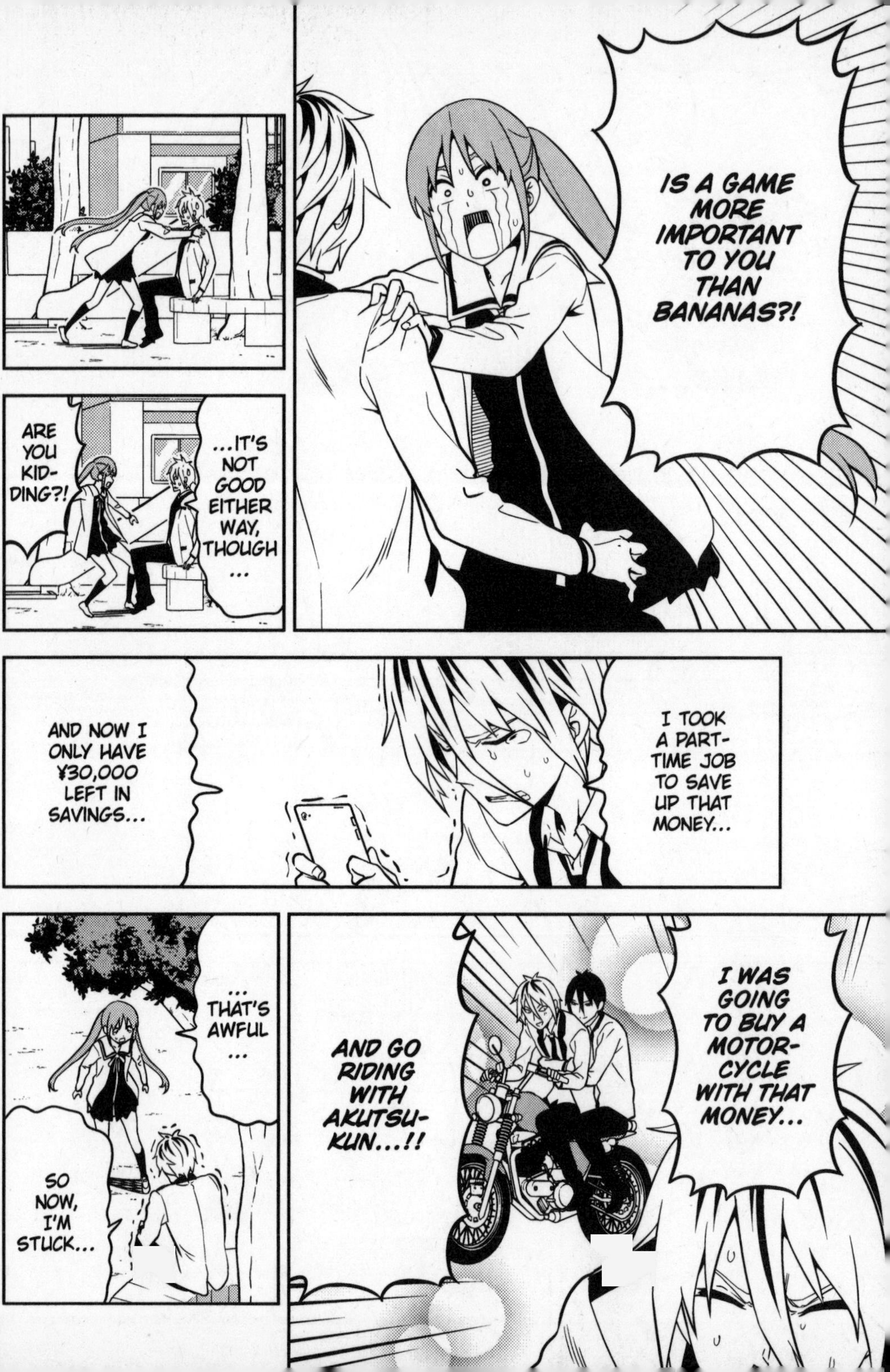
IS A GAME MORE IMPORTANT TO YOU THAN BANANAS?!
...IT'S NOT GOOD EITHER WAY, THOUGH...
ARE YOU KID-DING?!
I TOOK A PART-TIME JOB TO SAVE UP THAT MONEY...
AND NOW I ONLY HAVE ¥30,000 LEFT IN SAVINGS...
I WAS GOING TO BUY A MOTOR-CYCLE WITH THAT MONEY...
AND GO RIDING WITH AKUTSU-KUN...!!
...THAT'S AWFUL...
SO NOW, I'M STUCK...

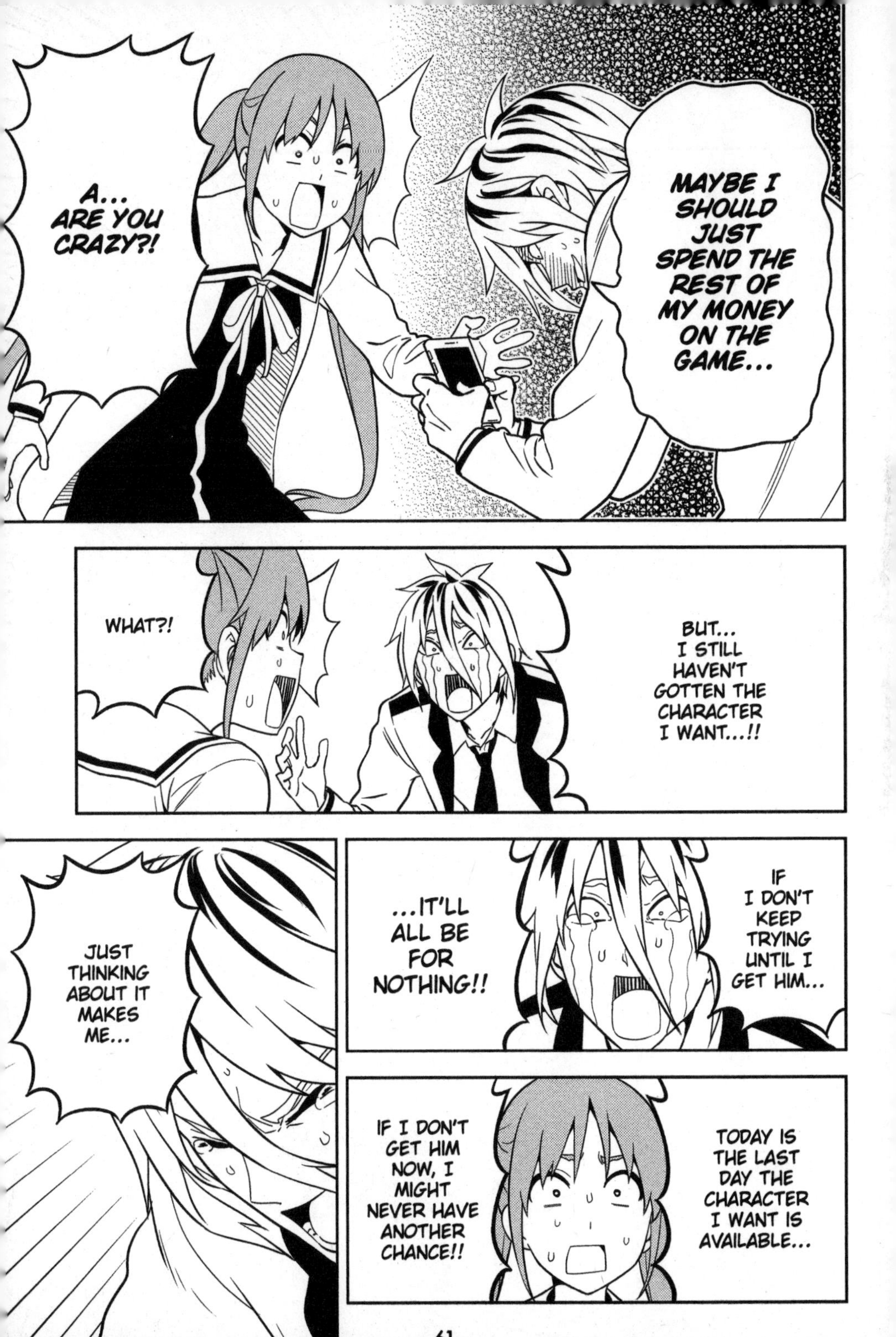
MAYBE I SHOULD JUST SPEND THE REST OF MY MONEY ON THE GAME...
A... ARE YOU CRAZY?!
BUT... I STILL HAVEN'T GOTTEN THE CHARACTER I WANT...!!
WHAT?!
IF I DON'T KEEP TRYING UNTIL I GET HIM...
...IT'LL ALL BE FOR NOTHING!!
TODAY IS THE LAST DAY THE CHARACTER I WANT IS AVAILABLE...
IF I DON'T GET HIM NOW, I MIGHT NEVER HAVE ANOTHER CHANCE!!
JUST THINKING ABOUT IT MAKES ME...

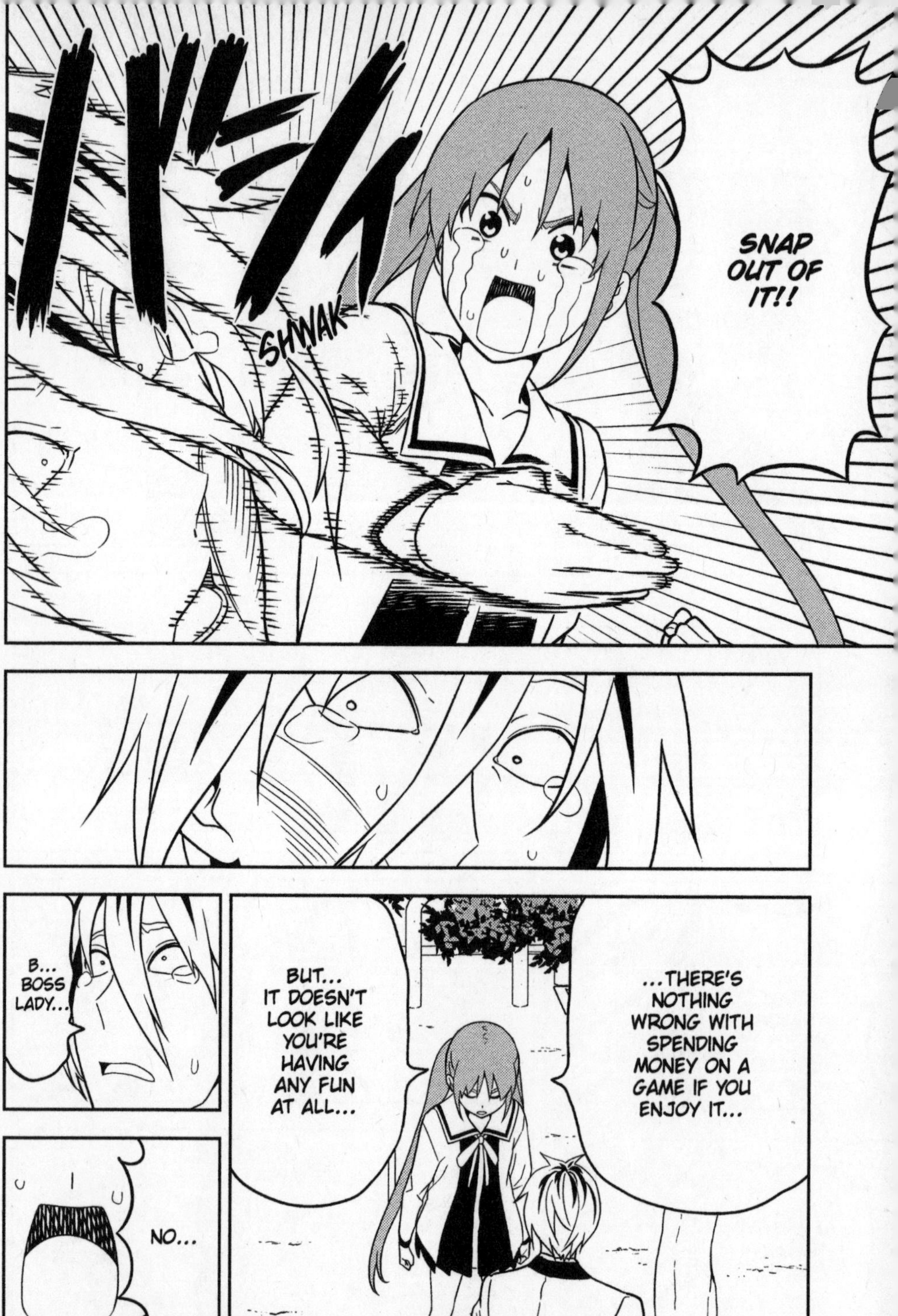
SNAP OUT OF IT!!
SHWAK
...THERE'S NOTHING WRONG WITH SPENDING MONEY ON A GAME IF YOU ENJOY IT...
BUT... IT DOESN'T LOOK LIKE YOU'RE HAVING ANY FUN AT ALL...
B... BOSS LADY...
NO...

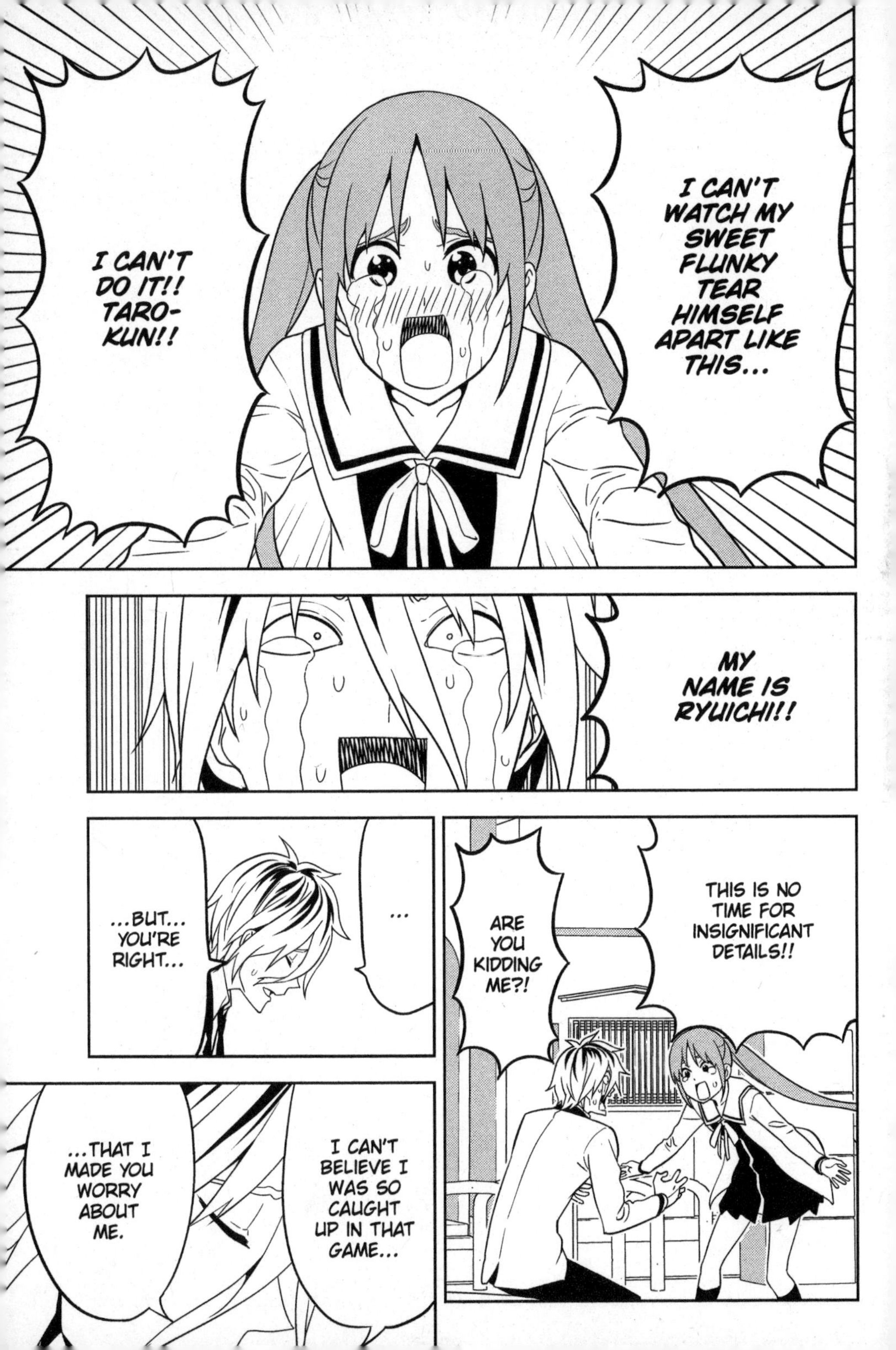
I CAN'T WATCH MY SWEET FLUNKY TEAR HIMSELF APART LIKE THIS...
I CAN'T DO IT!! TARO-KUN!!
MY NAME IS RYUICHI!!
THIS IS NO TIME FOR INSIGNIFICANT DETAILS!!
ARE YOU KIDDING ME?!
...
...BUT... YOU'RE RIGHT...
I CAN'T BELIEVE I WAS SO CAUGHT UP IN THAT GAME...
...THAT I MADE YOU WORRY ABOUT ME.

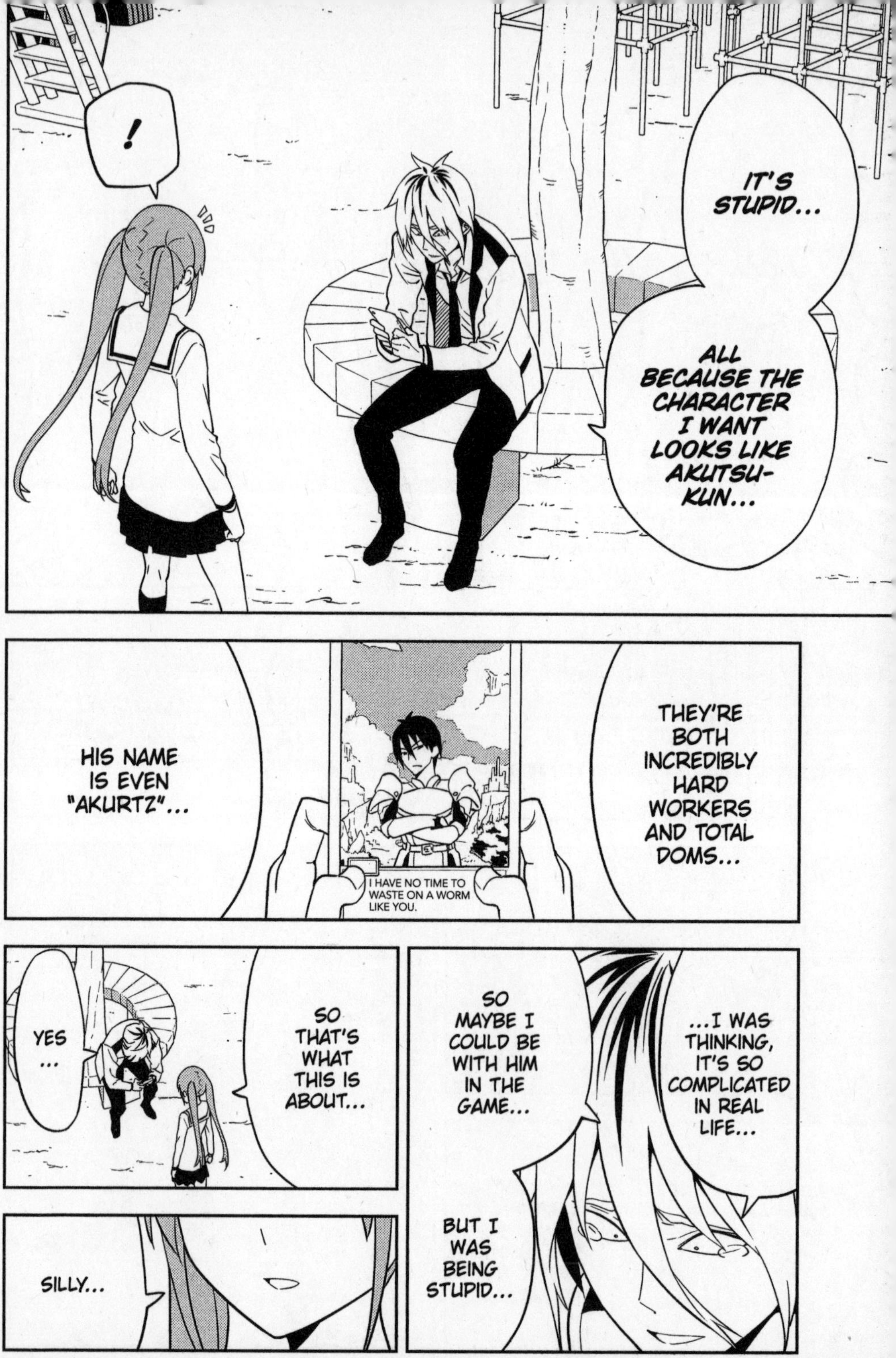
IT'S STUPID...
ALL BECAUSE THE CHARACTER I WANT LOOKS LIKE AKUTSU-KUN...
!
THEY'RE BOTH INCREDIBLY HARD WORKERS AND TOTAL DOMS...
I HAVE NO TIME TO WASTE ON A WORM LIKE YOU.
HIS NAME IS EVEN "AKURTZ"...
...I WAS THINKING, IT'S SO COMPLICATED IN REAL LIFE...
SO MAYBE I COULD BE WITH HIM IN THE GAME...
BUT I WAS BEING STUPID...
SO THAT'S WHAT THIS IS ABOUT...
YES ...
SILLY...

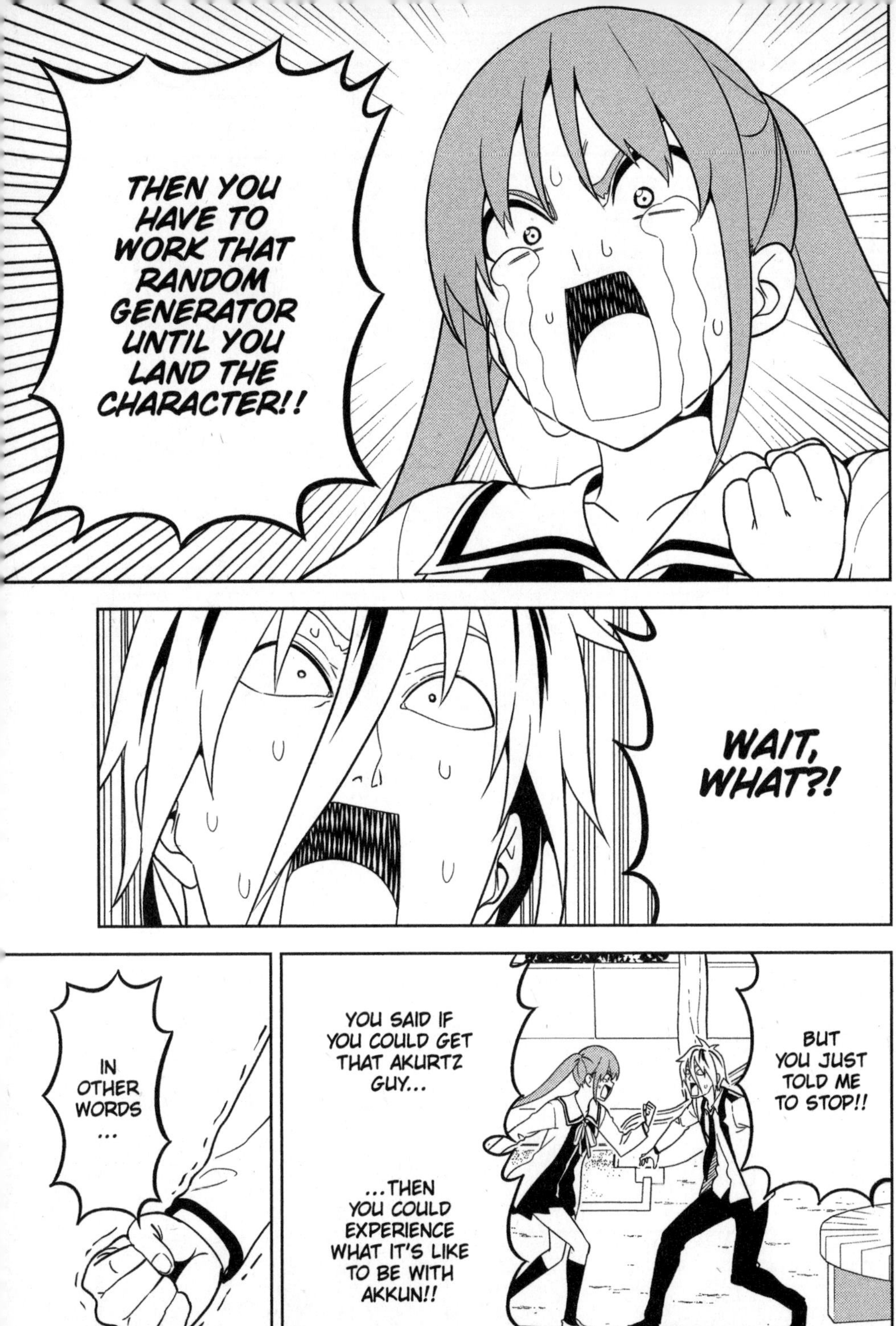
THEN YOU HAVE TO WORK THAT RANDOM GENERATOR UNTIL YOU LAND THE CHARACTER!!
WAIT, WHAT?!
BUT YOU JUST TOLD ME TO STOP!!
YOU SAID IF YOU COULD GET THAT AKURTZ GUY...
...THEN YOU COULD EXPERIENCE WHAT IT'S LIKE TO BE WITH AKKUN!!
IN OTHER WORDS ...

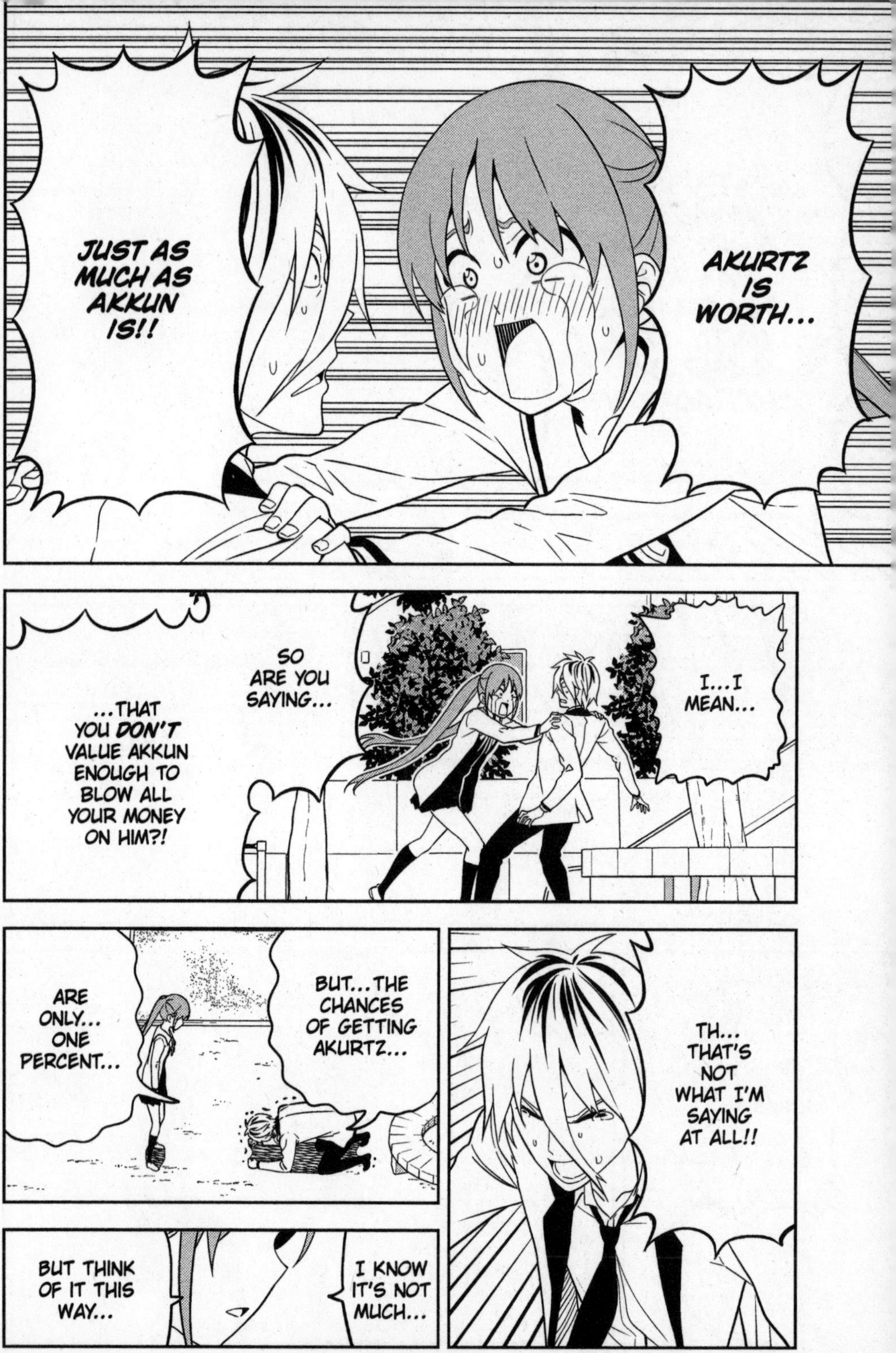
AKURTZ IS WORTH...
JUST AS MUCH AS AKKUN IS!!
I...I MEAN...
SO ARE YOU SAYING...
...THAT YOU DON'T VALUE AKKUN ENOUGH TO BLOW ALL YOUR MONEY ON HIM?!
TH... THAT'S NOT WHAT I'M SAYING AT ALL!!
BUT...THE CHANCES OF GETTING AKURTZ...
ARE ONLY... ONE PERCENT...
I KNOW IT'S NOT MUCH...
BUT THINK OF IT THIS WAY...

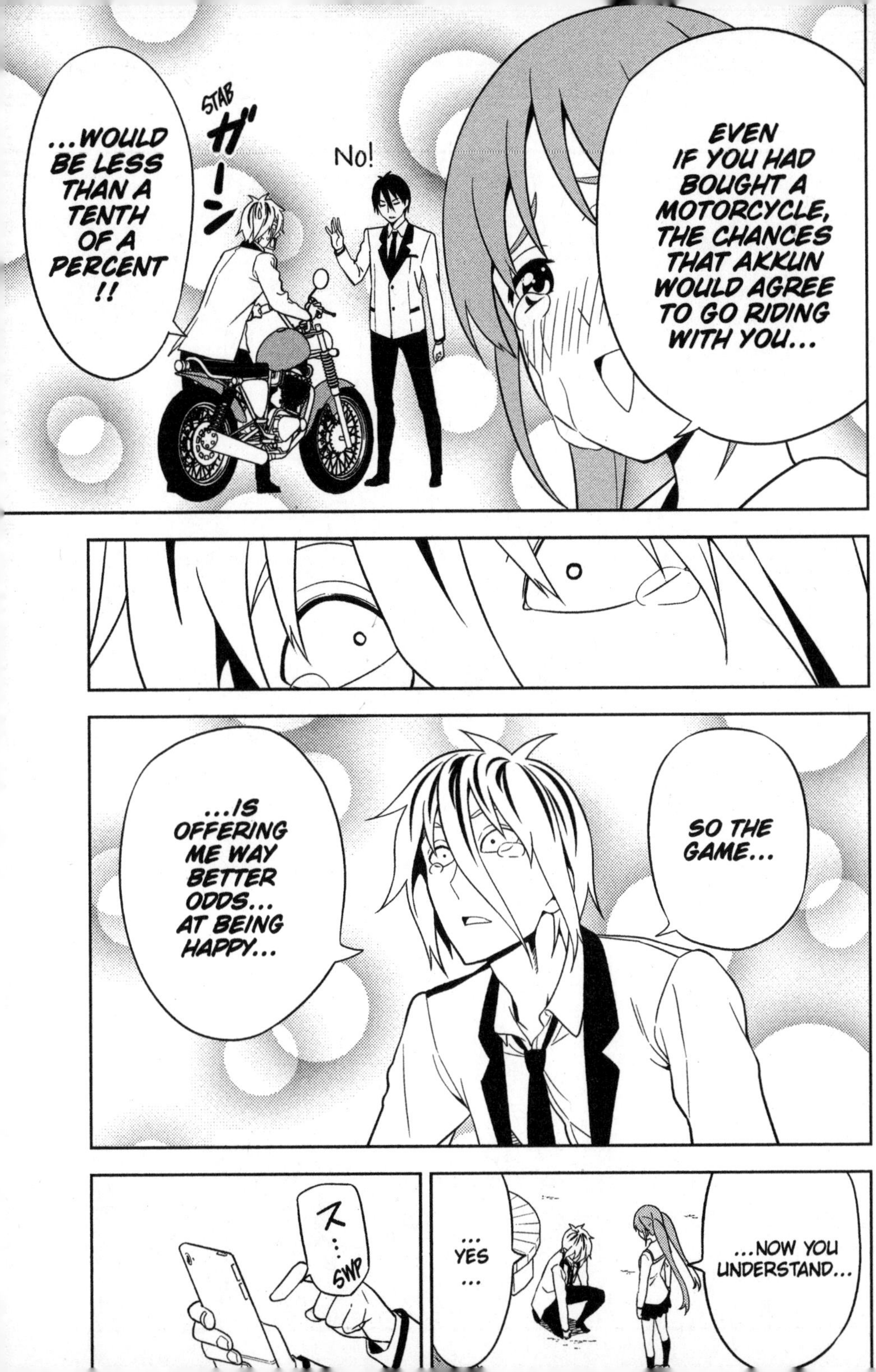
EVEN IF YOU HAD BOUGHT A MOTORCYCLE, THE CHANCES THAT AKKUN WOULD AGREE TO GO RIDING WITH YOU...
No!
STAB ガーン
...WOULD BE LESS THAN A TENTH OF A PERCENT!!
SO THE GAME...
...IS OFFERING ME WAY BETTER ODDS... AT BEING HAPPY...
...NOW YOU UNDERSTAND...
...YES...
ス... SWP

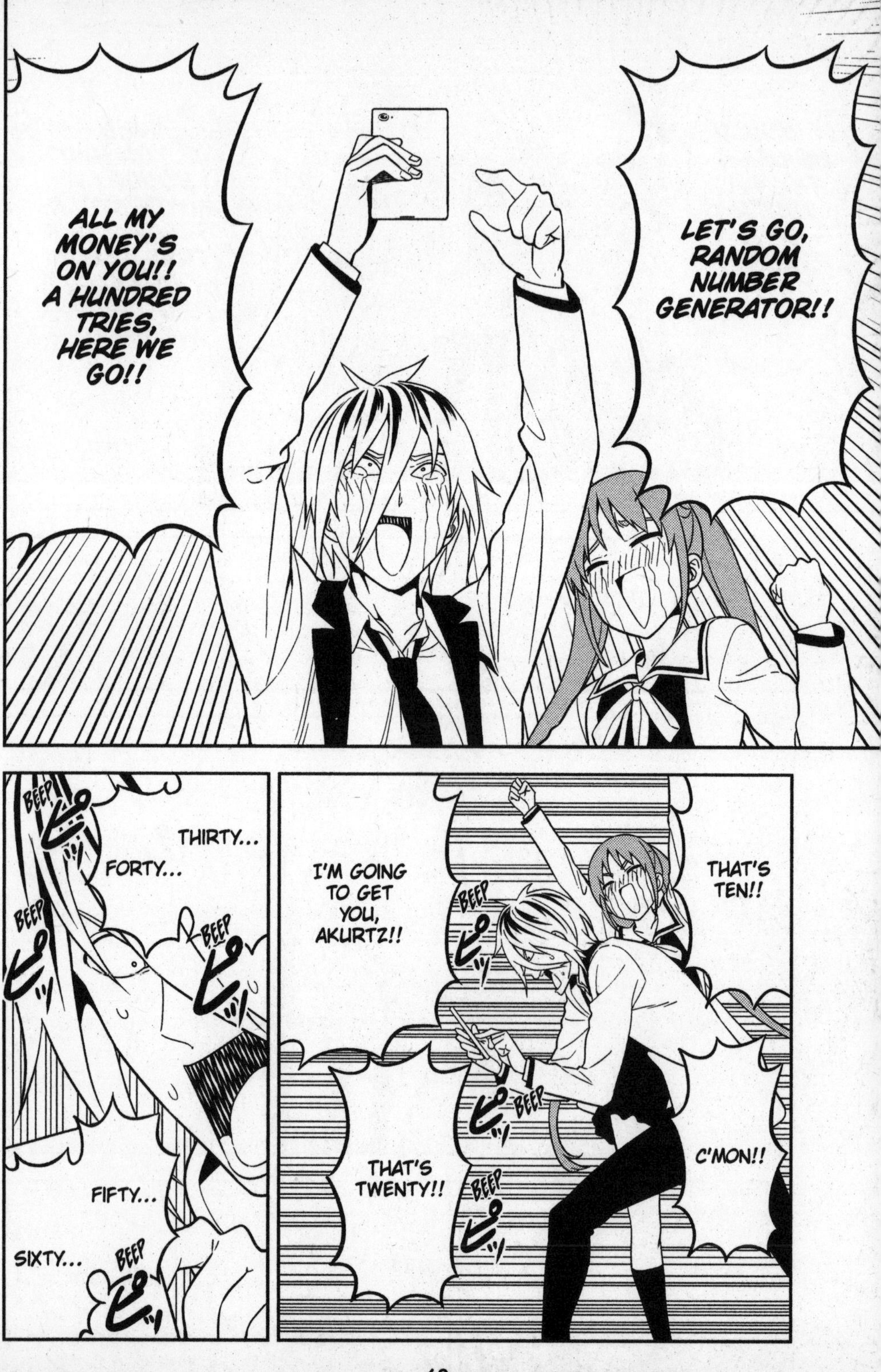
LET'S GO, RANDOM NUMBER GENERATOR!!
ALL MY MONEY'S ON YOU!! A HUNDRED TRIES, HERE WE GO!!
THAT'S TEN!!
BEEP
I'M GOING TO GET YOU, AKURTZ!!
C'MON!!
BEEP
BEEP
THAT'S TWENTY!!
THIRTY...
BEEP
FORTY...
BEEP
BEEP
FIFTY...
SIXTY...
BEEP

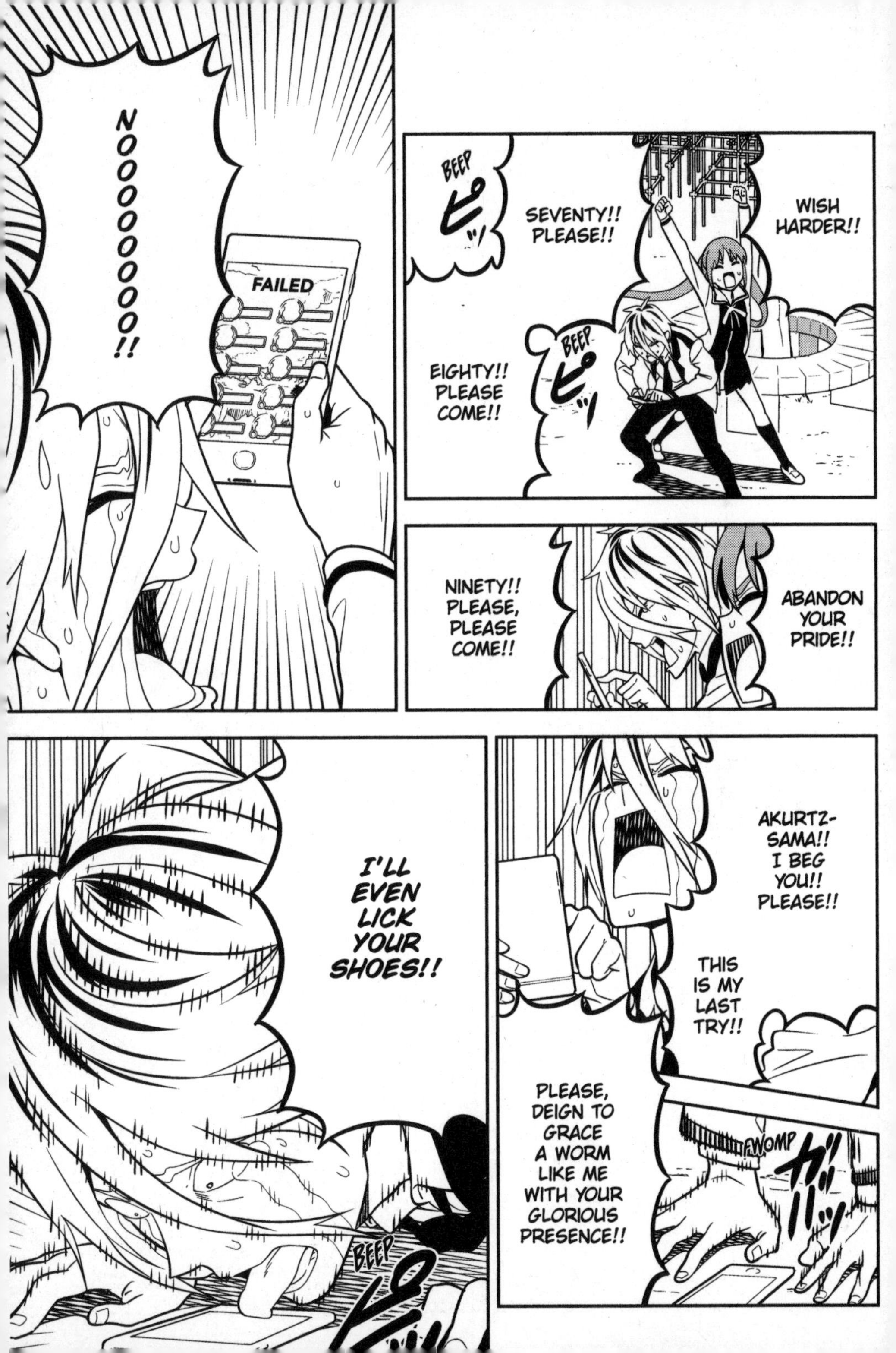
WISH HARDER!!
SEVENTY!! PLEASE!!
BEEP
ピッ
EIGHTY!! PLEASE COME!!
BEEP
ピッ
ABANDON YOUR PRIDE!!
NINETY!! PLEASE, PLEASE COME!!
FAILED
NOOOOOOOOOOO!!
AKURTZ-SAMA!! I BEG YOU!! PLEASE!!
THIS IS MY LAST TRY!!
PLEASE, DEIGN TO GRACE A WORM LIKE ME WITH YOUR GLORIOUS PRESENCE!!
WOMP
ガバッ
I'LL EVEN LICK YOUR SHOES!!
BEEP
ピッ

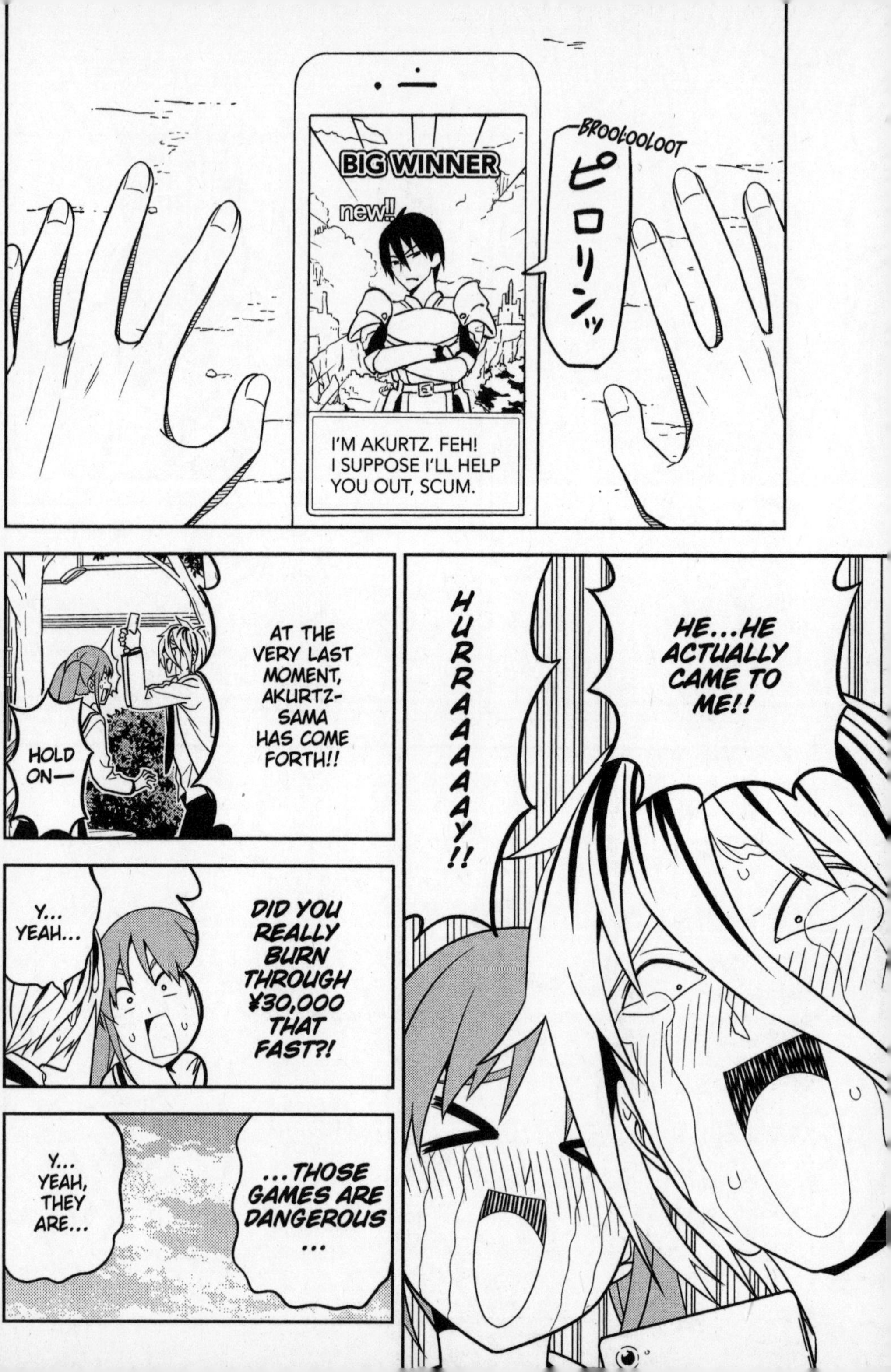
BROOLOOLOOT
ピロリンッ
BIG WINNER
new!!
I'M AKURTZ. FEH! I SUPPOSE I'LL HELP YOU OUT, SCUM.
HE...HE ACTUALLY CAME TO ME!!
HURRAAAAAAY!!
AT THE VERY LAST MOMENT, AKURTZ-SAMA HAS COME FORTH!!
HOLD ON—
DID YOU REALLY BURN THROUGH ¥30,000 THAT FAST?!
Y... YEAH...
...THOSE GAMES ARE DANGEROUS...
Y... YEAH, THEY ARE...

The Nightmare Scenario of Network Games

[IMPORTANT] DOM QUEST NOTICE OF TERMINATION OF SERVICE

We are truly grateful to the users of "DOM QUEST" who have been with us since the beginning.

Unfortunately, the "DOM QUEST" service is coming to an end.

Thank you for spending your time with us, and

WAIT...

THEIR MONETI- ZATION STRATEGY WORKED.

(If you think about it, micropayments might actually be)

Aho-Girl

\'ahô,gərl\ *Japanese, noun*.

A clueless girl.

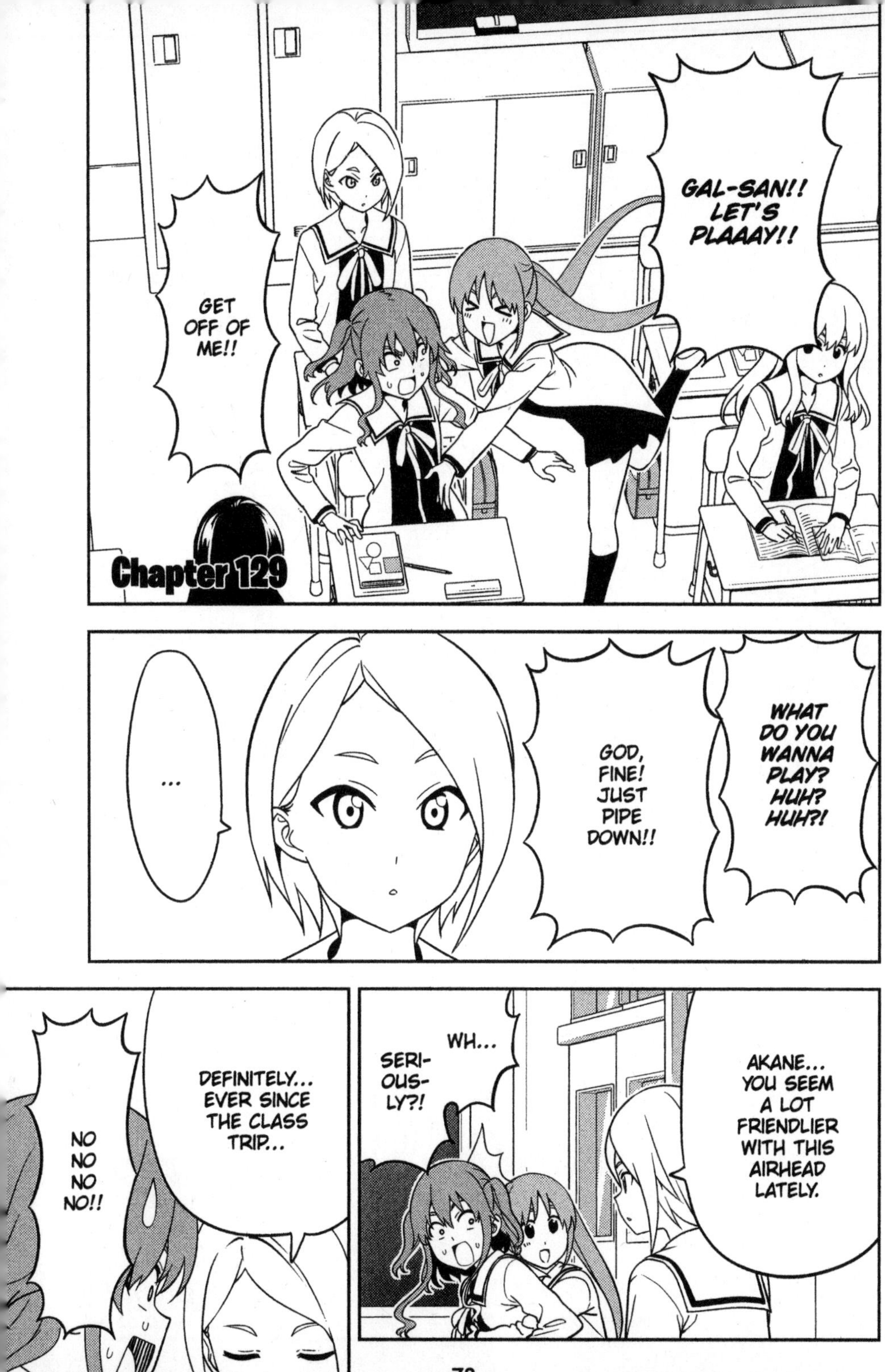
Chapter 129
GAL-SAN!! LET'S PLAAAY!!
GET OFF OF ME!!
WHAT DO YOU WANNA PLAY? HUH? HUH?!
GOD, FINE! JUST PIPE DOWN!!
...
AKANE... YOU SEEM A LOT FRIENDLIER WITH THIS AIRHEAD LATELY.
WH...
SERI-OUS-LY?!
DEFINITELY... EVER SINCE THE CLASS TRIP...
NO NO NO NO!!

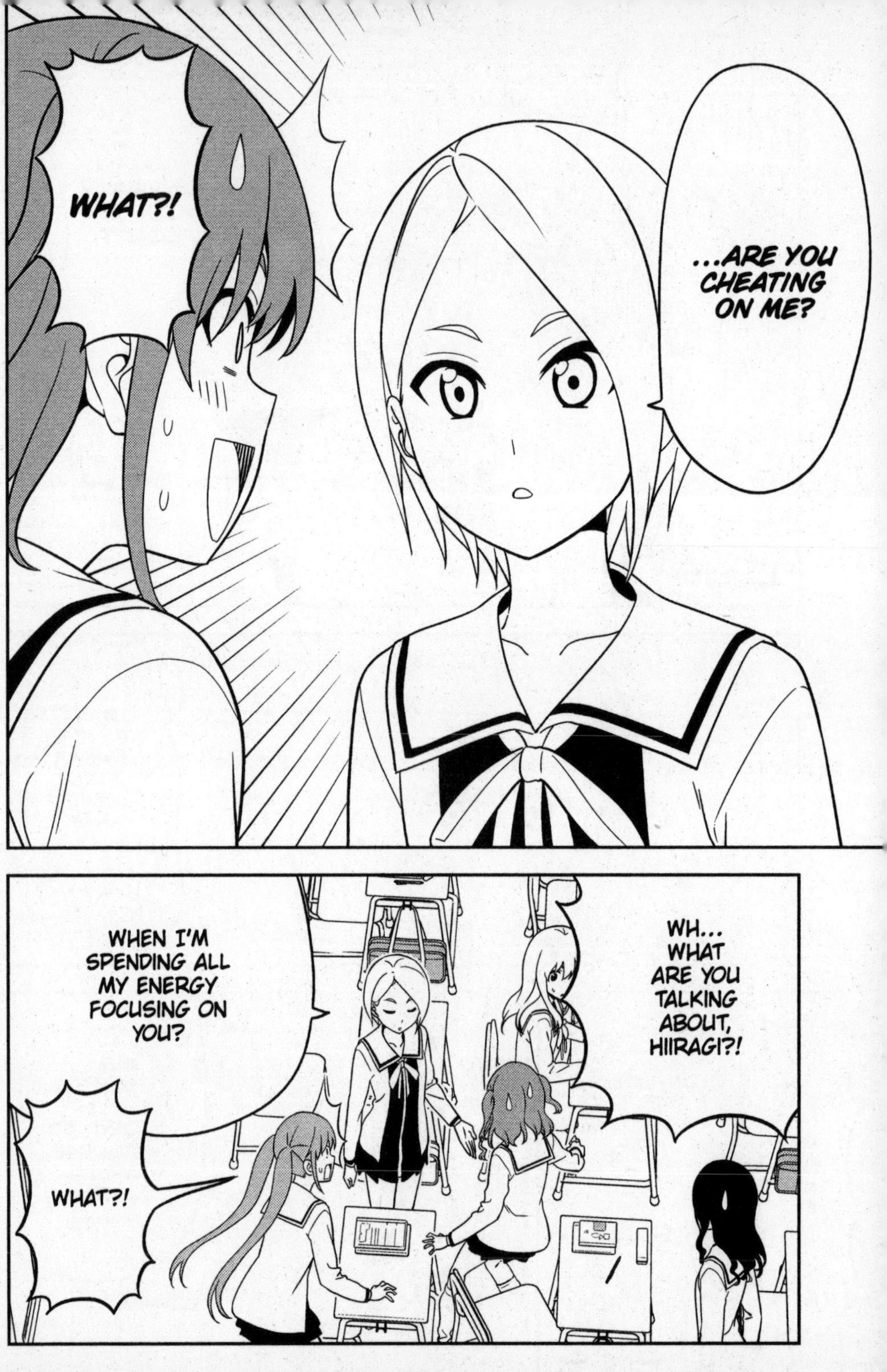
...ARE YOU CHEATING ON ME?
WHAT?!
WH... WHAT ARE YOU TALKING ABOUT, HIIRAGI?!
WHEN I'M SPENDING ALL MY ENERGY FOCUSING ON YOU?
WHAT?!

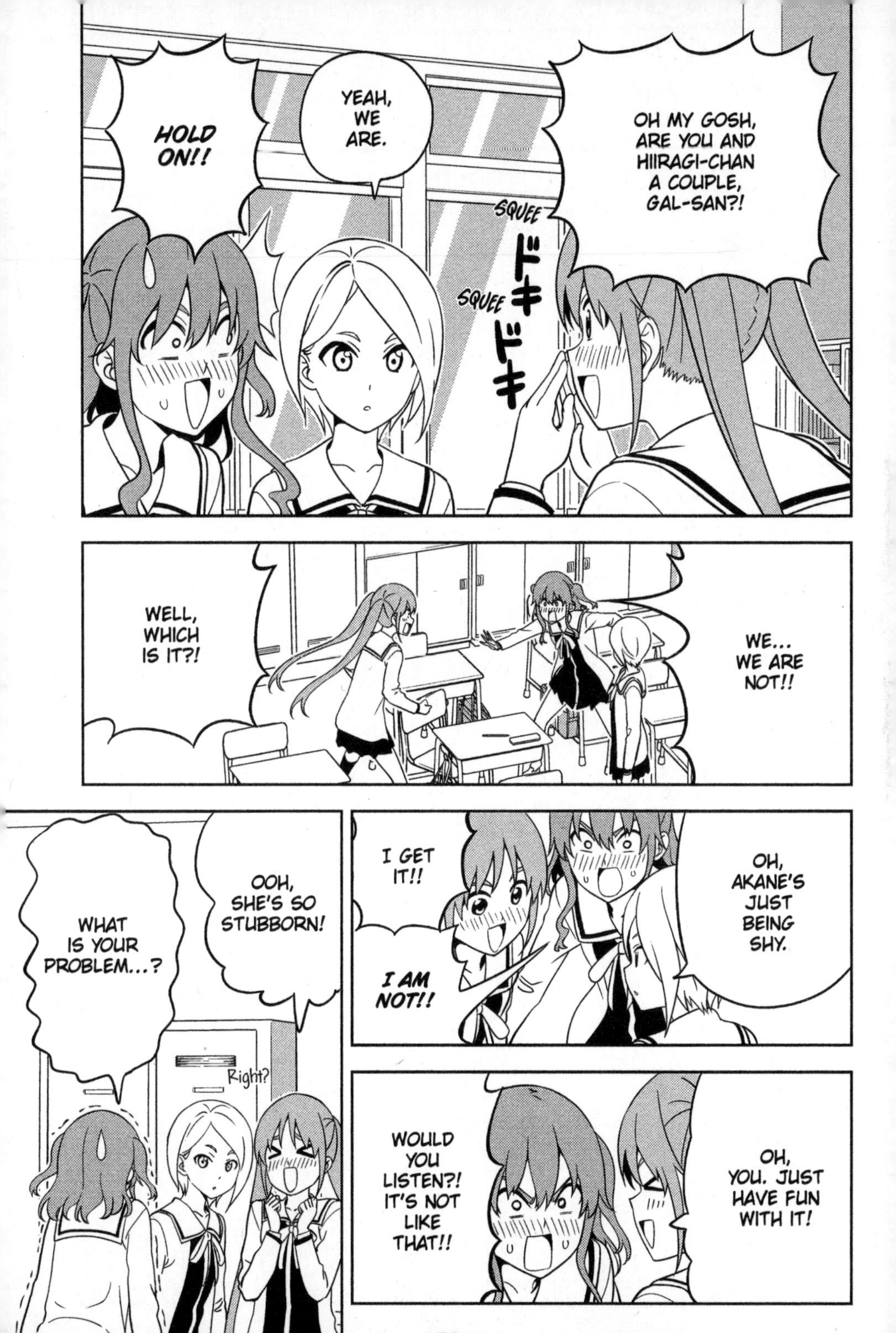
OH MY GOSH, ARE YOU AND HIIRAGI-CHAN A COUPLE, GAL-SAN?!
SQUEE
ドキ
SQUEE
ドキ
YEAH, WE ARE.
HOLD ON!!
WE... WE ARE NOT!!
WELL, WHICH IS IT?!
OH, AKANE'S JUST BEING SHY.
I GET IT!!
I AM NOT!!
OH, YOU. JUST HAVE FUN WITH IT!
WOULD YOU LISTEN?! IT'S NOT LIKE THAT!!
OOH, SHE'S SO STUBBORN!
Right?
WHAT IS YOUR PROBLEM...?

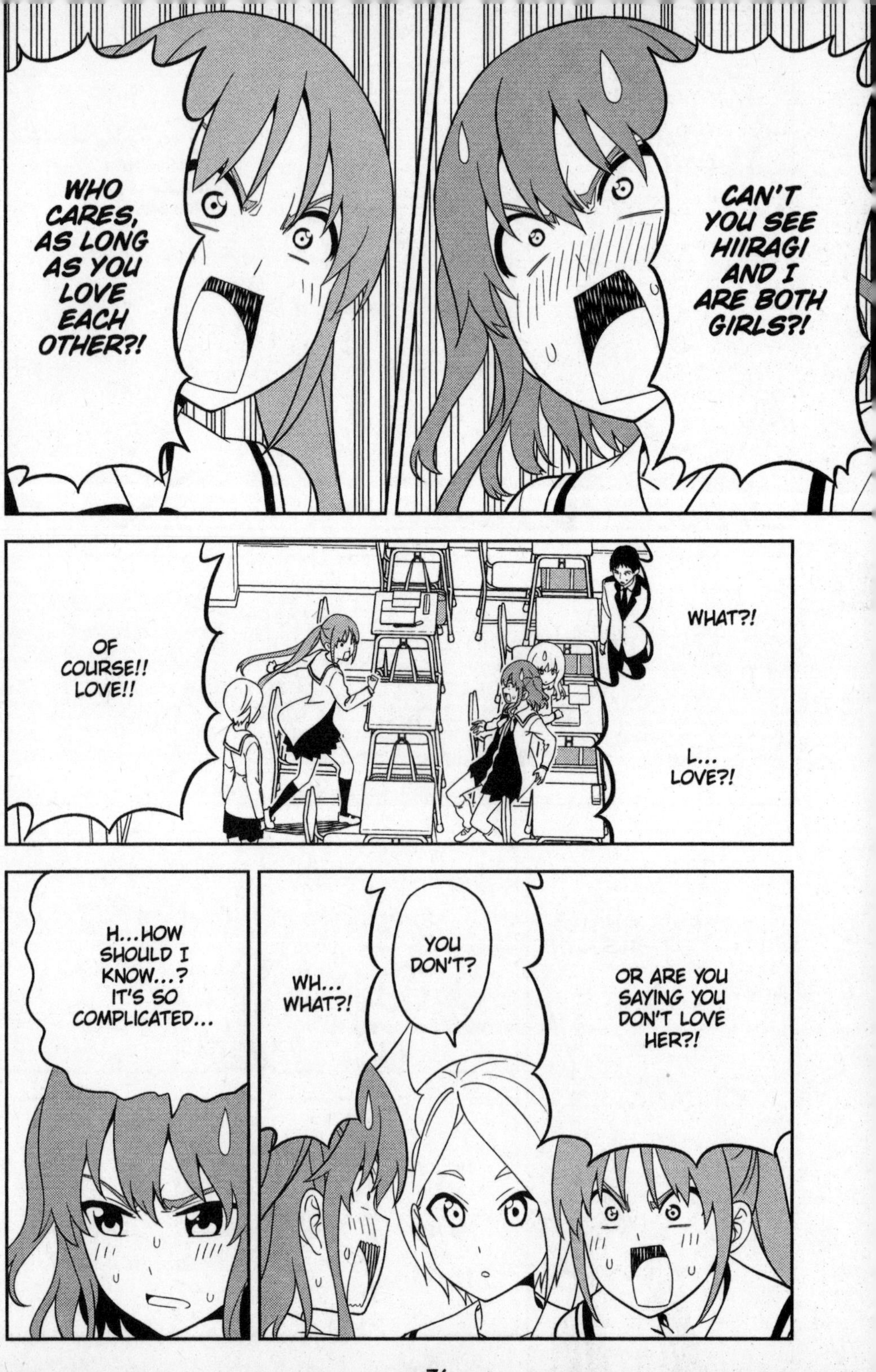
CAN'T YOU SEE HIIRAGI AND I ARE BOTH GIRLS?!
WHO CARES, AS LONG AS YOU LOVE EACH OTHER?!
WHAT?!
L... LOVE?!
OF COURSE!! LOVE!!
OR ARE YOU SAYING YOU DON'T LOVE HER?!
YOU DON'T?
WH... WHAT?!
H...HOW SHOULD I KNOW...? IT'S SO COMPLICATED...

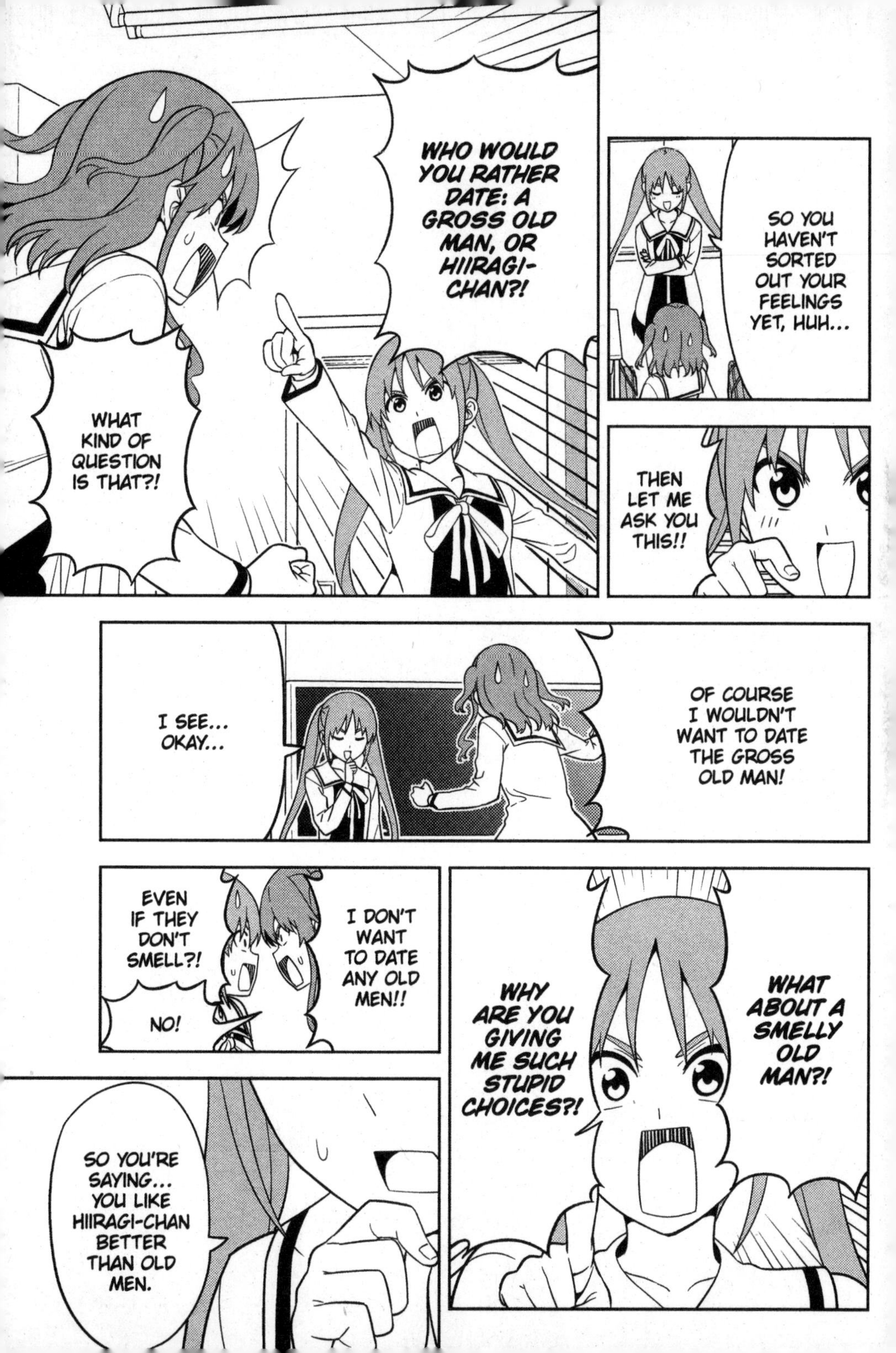

SO YOU HAVEN'T SORTED OUT YOUR FEELINGS YET, HUH...
THEN LET ME ASK YOU THIS!!
WHO WOULD YOU RATHER DATE: A GROSS OLD MAN, OR HIIRAGI-CHAN?!
WHAT KIND OF QUESTION IS THAT?!
OF COURSE I WOULDN'T WANT TO DATE THE GROSS OLD MAN!
I SEE... OKAY...
WHAT ABOUT A SMELLY OLD MAN?!
WHY ARE YOU GIVING ME SUCH STUPID CHOICES?!
I DON'T WANT TO DATE ANY OLD MEN!!
EVEN IF THEY DON'T SMELL?!
NO!
SO YOU'RE SAYING... YOU LIKE HIIRAGI-CHAN BETTER THAN OLD MEN.

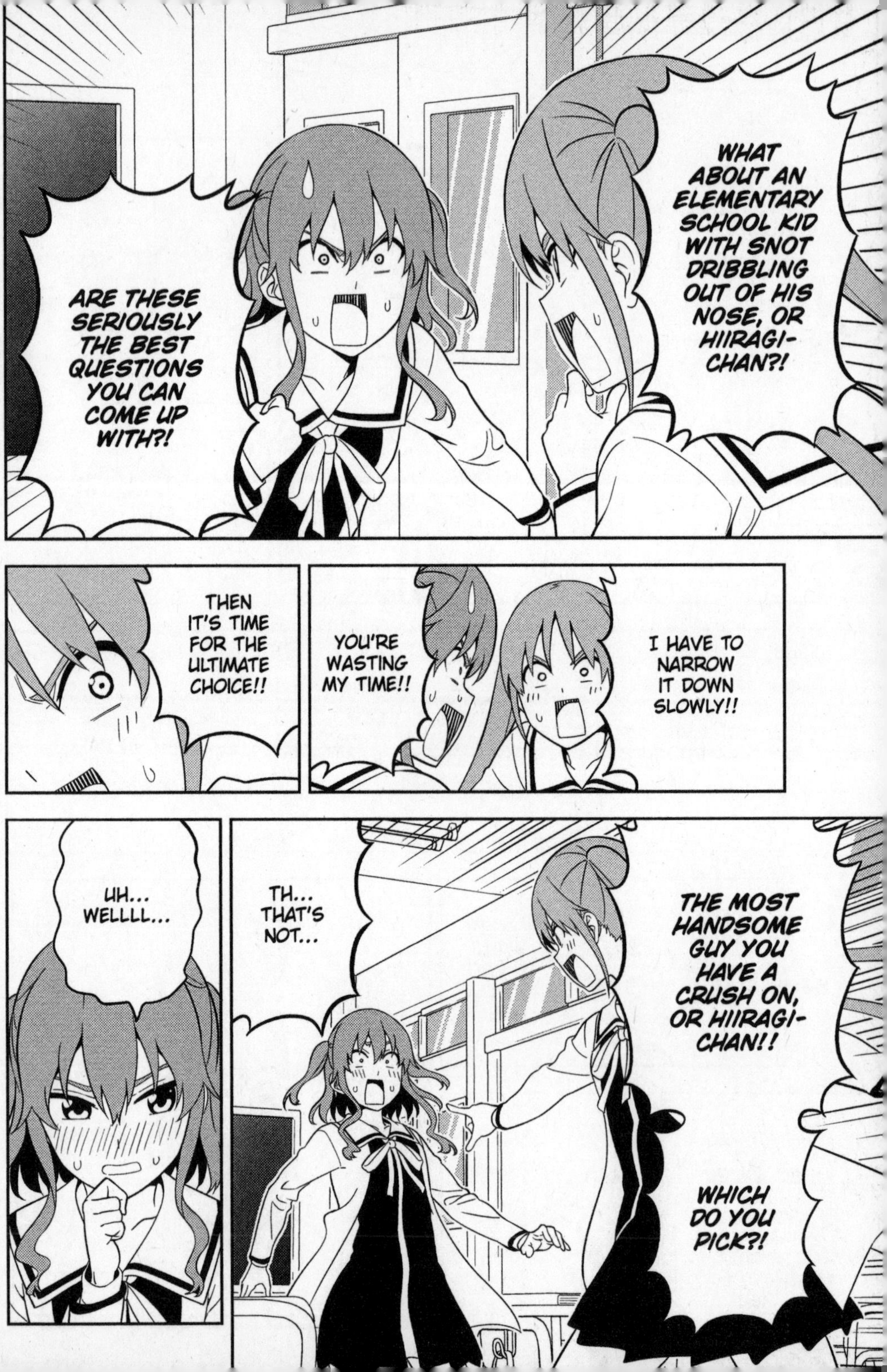
WHAT ABOUT AN ELEMENTARY SCHOOL KID WITH SNOT DRIBBLING OUT OF HIS NOSE, OR HIIRAGI-CHAN?!
ARE THESE SERIOUSLY THE BEST QUESTIONS YOU CAN COME UP WITH?!
I HAVE TO NARROW IT DOWN SLOWLY!!
YOU'RE WASTING MY TIME!!
THEN IT'S TIME FOR THE ULTIMATE CHOICE!!
THE MOST HANDSOME GUY YOU HAVE A CRUSH ON, OR HIIRAGI-CHAN!!
WHICH DO YOU PICK?!
TH... THAT'S NOT...
UH... WELLLL...

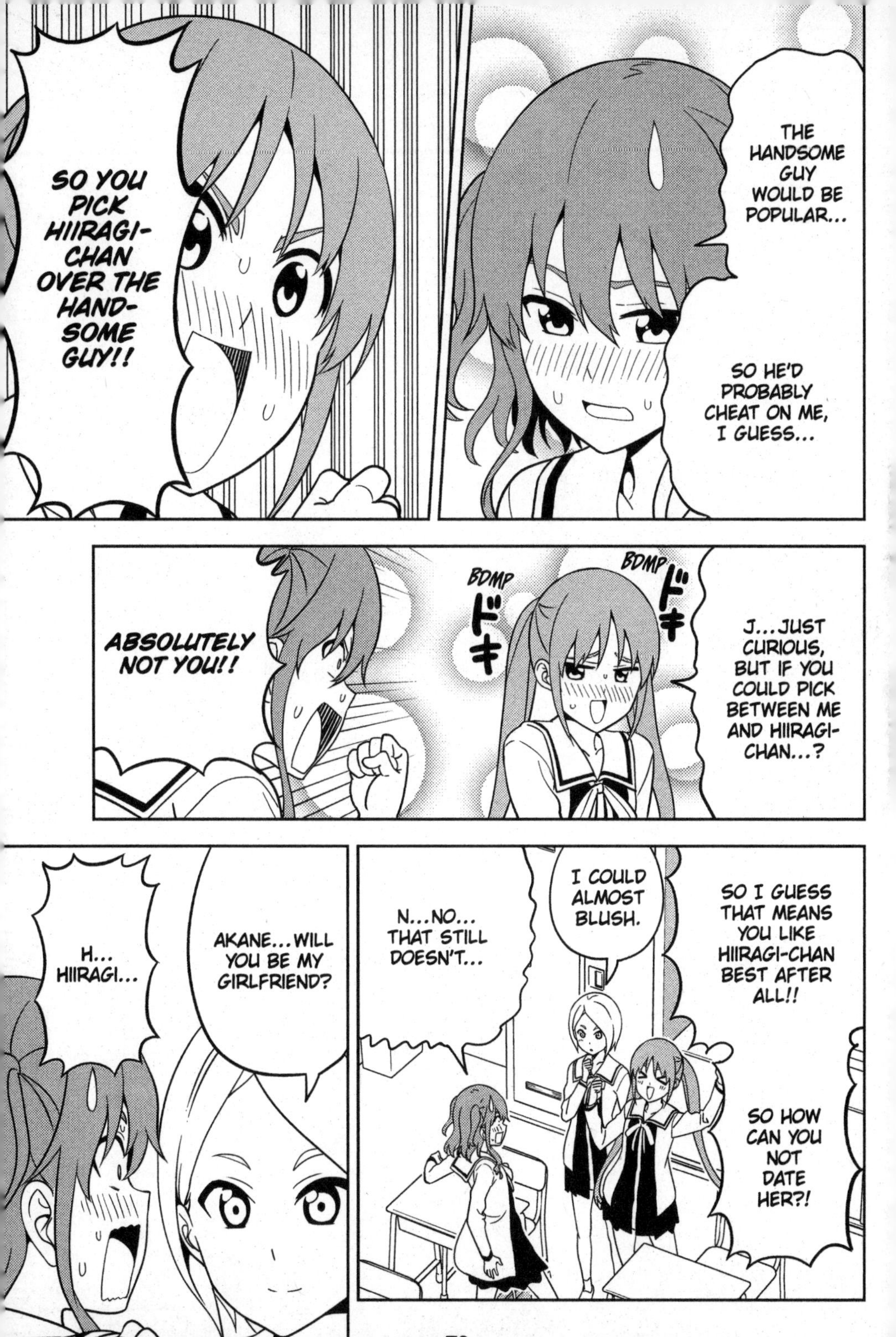
THE HANDSOME GUY WOULD BE POPULAR...
SO HE'D PROBABLY CHEAT ON ME, I GUESS...
SO YOU PICK HIIRAGI-CHAN OVER THE HAND-SOME GUY!!
J...JUST CURIOUS, BUT IF YOU COULD PICK BETWEEN ME AND HIIRAGI-CHAN...?
BDMP ドキ
BDMP ドキ
ABSOLUTELY NOT YOU!!
SO I GUESS THAT MEANS YOU LIKE HIIRAGI-CHAN BEST AFTER ALL!!
SO HOW CAN YOU NOT DATE HER?!
I COULD ALMOST BLUSH.
N...NO... THAT STILL DOESN'T...
AKANE...WILL YOU BE MY GIRLFRIEND?
H... HIIRAGI...

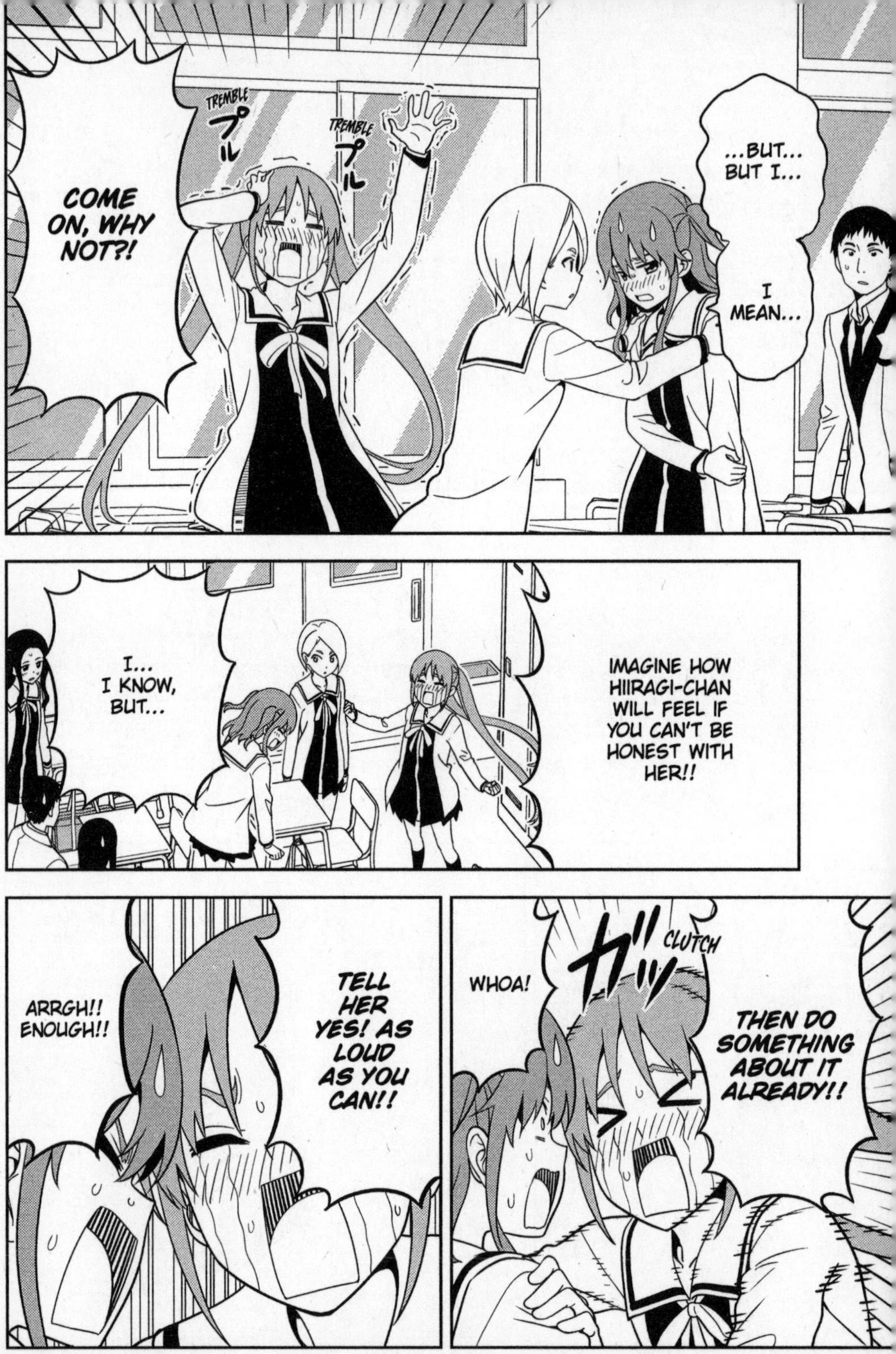

...BUT... BUT I...
I MEAN...
TREMBLE プル
TREMBLE プル
COME ON, WHY NOT?!
IMAGINE HOW HIIRAGI-CHAN WILL FEEL IF YOU CAN'T BE HONEST WITH HER!!
I... I KNOW, BUT...
THEN DO SOMETHING ABOUT IT ALREADY!!
ガッ CLUTCH
WHOA!
TELL HER YES! AS LOUD AS YOU CAN!!
ARRGH!! ENOUGH!!

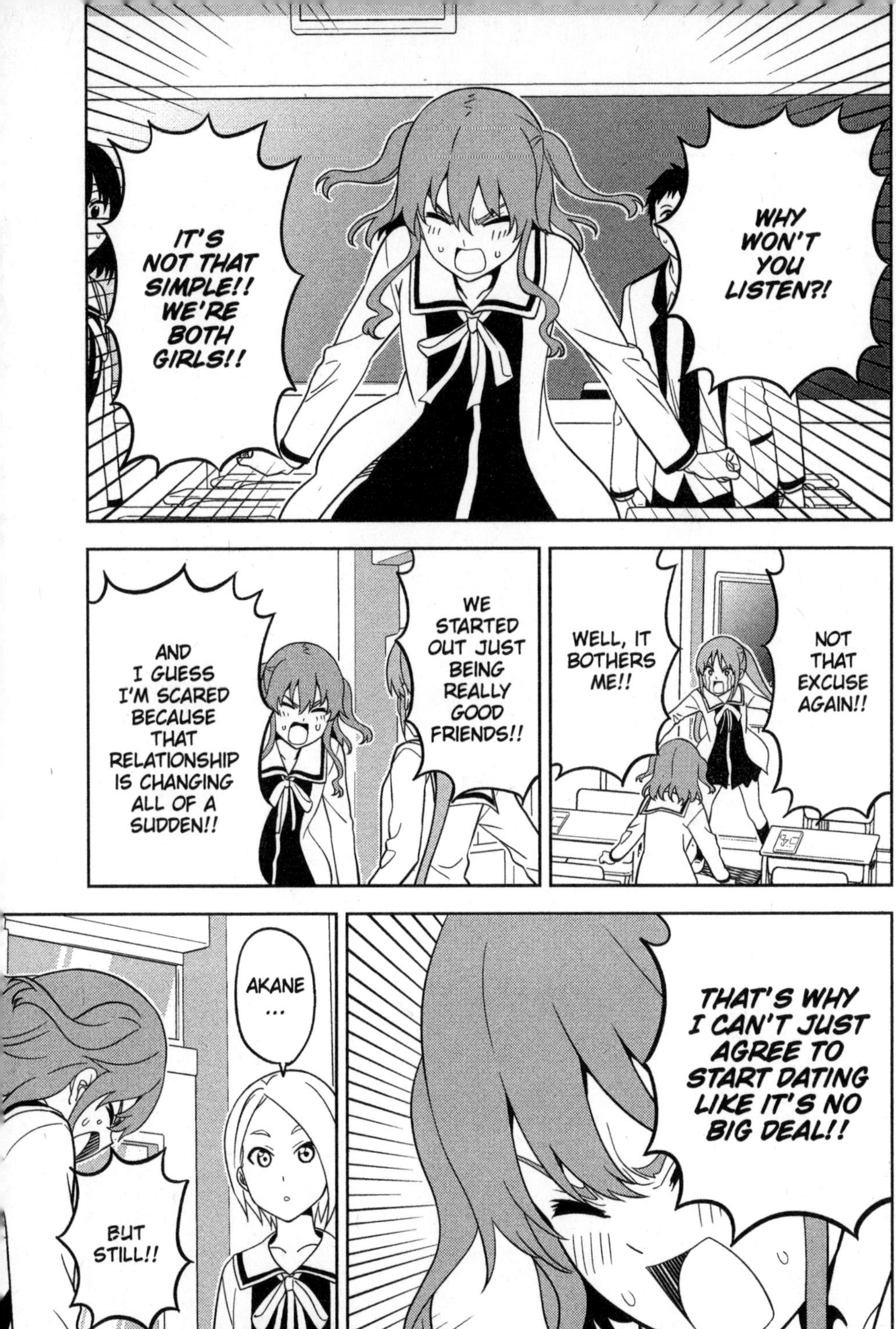
WHY WON'T YOU LISTEN?!
IT'S NOT THAT SIMPLE!! WE'RE BOTH GIRLS!!
NOT THAT EXCUSE AGAIN!!
WELL, IT BOTHERS ME!!
WE STARTED OUT JUST BEING REALLY GOOD FRIENDS!!
AND I GUESS I'M SCARED BECAUSE THAT RELATIONSHIP IS CHANGING ALL OF A SUDDEN!!
THAT'S WHY I CAN'T JUST AGREE TO START DATING LIKE IT'S NO BIG DEAL!!
AKANE ...
BUT STILL!!

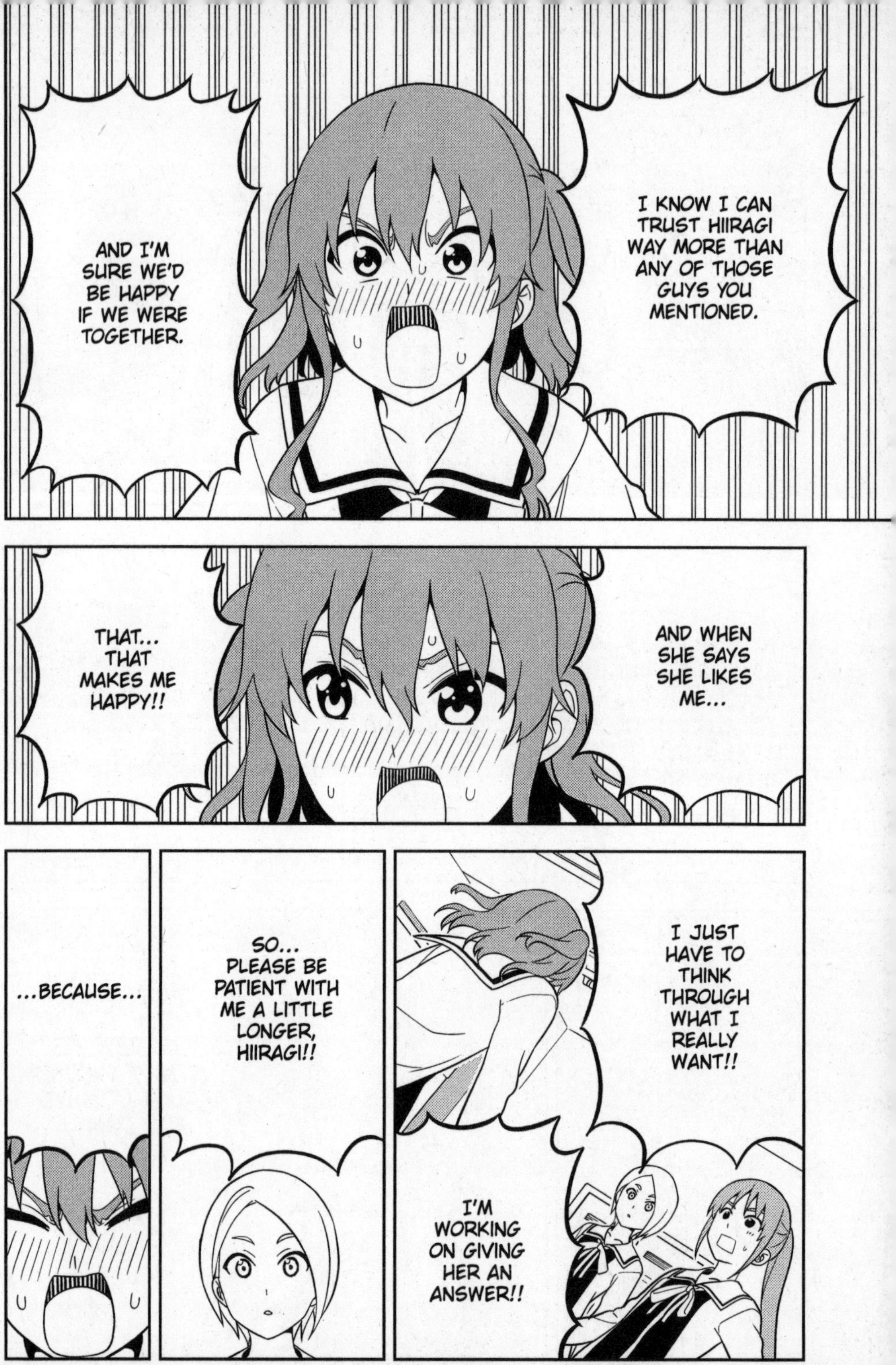
I KNOW I CAN TRUST HIIRAGI WAY MORE THAN ANY OF THOSE GUYS YOU MENTIONED.
AND I'M SURE WE'D BE HAPPY IF WE WERE TOGETHER.
AND WHEN SHE SAYS SHE LIKES ME...
THAT... THAT MAKES ME HAPPY!!
I JUST HAVE TO THINK THROUGH WHAT I REALLY WANT!!
I'M WORKING ON GIVING HER AN ANSWER!!
SO... PLEASE BE PATIENT WITH ME A LITTLE LONGER, HIIRAGI!!
...BECAUSE...

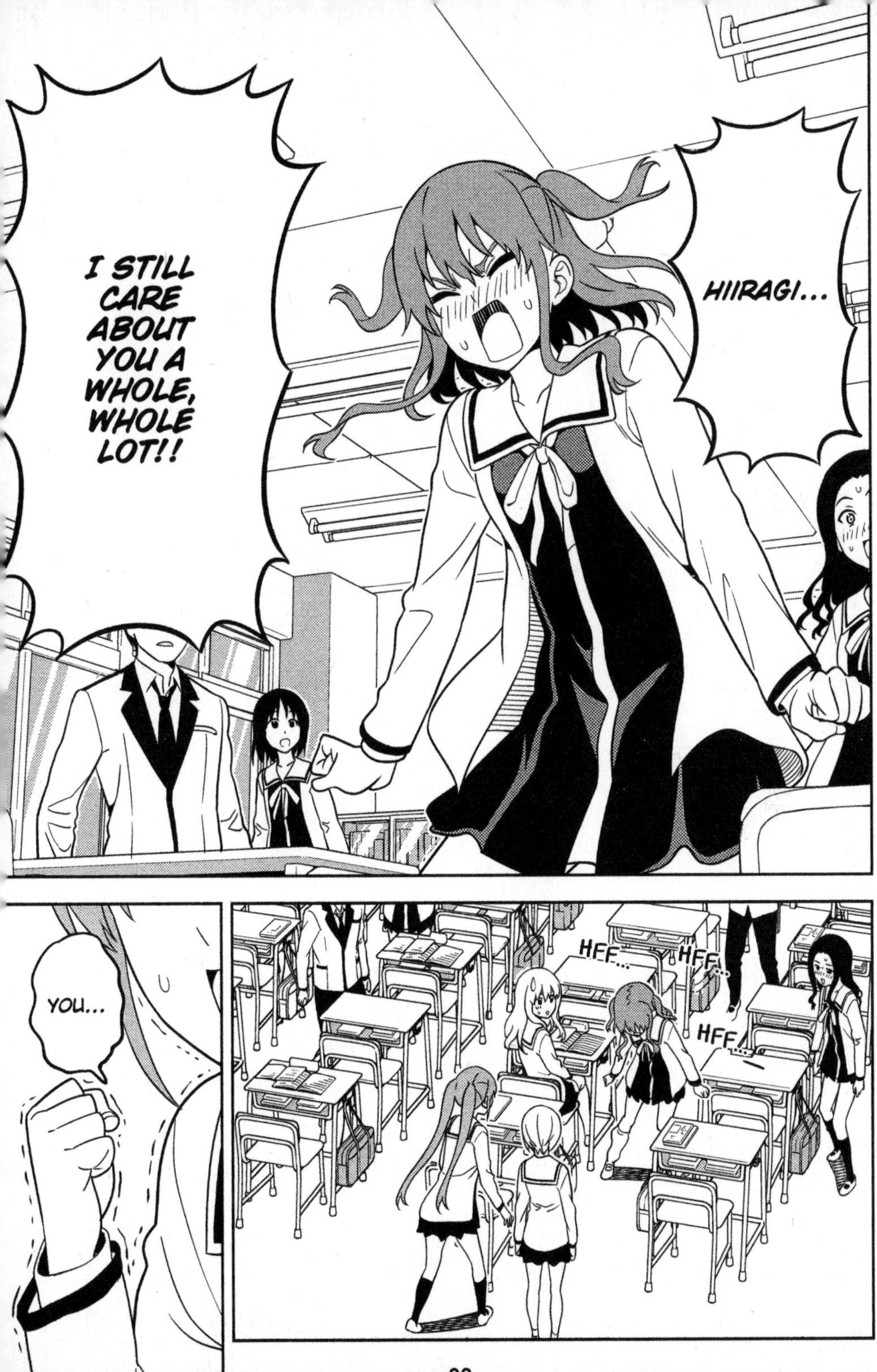
HIIRAGI...
I STILL CARE ABOUT YOU A WHOLE, WHOLE LOT!!
HFF...
HFF...
HFF...
YOU...

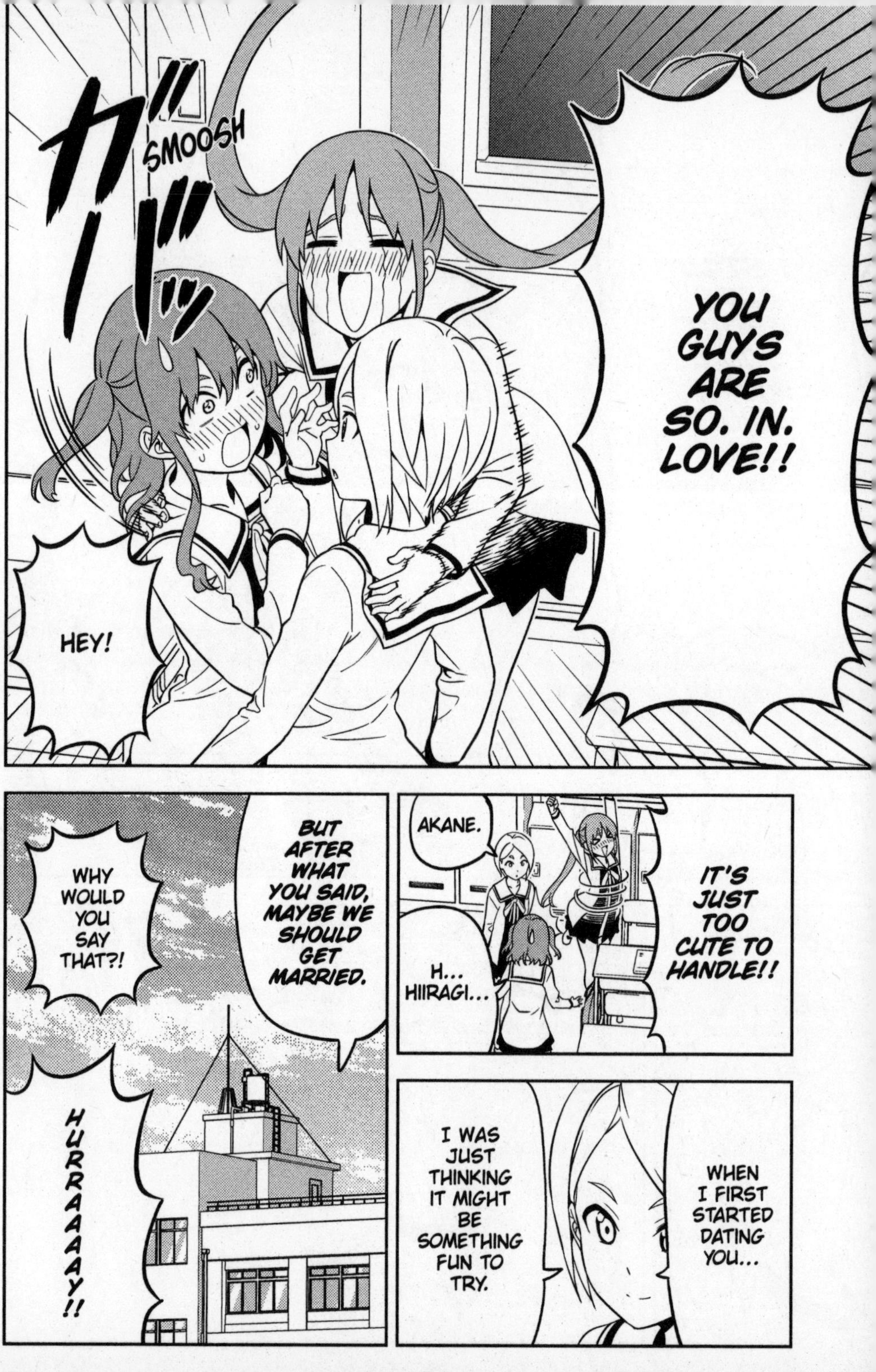
YOU GUYS ARE SO. IN. LOVE!!
SMOOSH
HEY!
IT'S JUST TOO CUTE TO HANDLE!!
AKANE.
H... HIIRAGI...
WHEN I FIRST STARTED DATING YOU...
I WAS JUST THINKING IT MIGHT BE SOMETHING FUN TO TRY.
BUT AFTER WHAT YOU SAID, MAYBE WE SHOULD GET MARRIED.
WHY WOULD YOU SAY THAT?!
HURRAAAAAY!!

The Approval of a Friend

C... CAN YOU BELIEVE HIIRAGI...?
HUH, SHIINA?!
UH... WELL ...
I... HOPE YOU TWO WILL BE HAPPY TO-GETH-ER...
ドキドキ
JITTER JITTER
NOT YOU, TOO!!

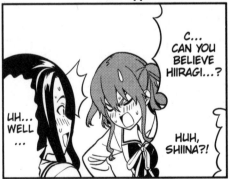

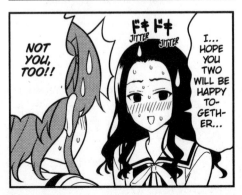

Aho-Girl

\ˈahôˌgərl\ *Japanese, noun.*
A clueless girl.

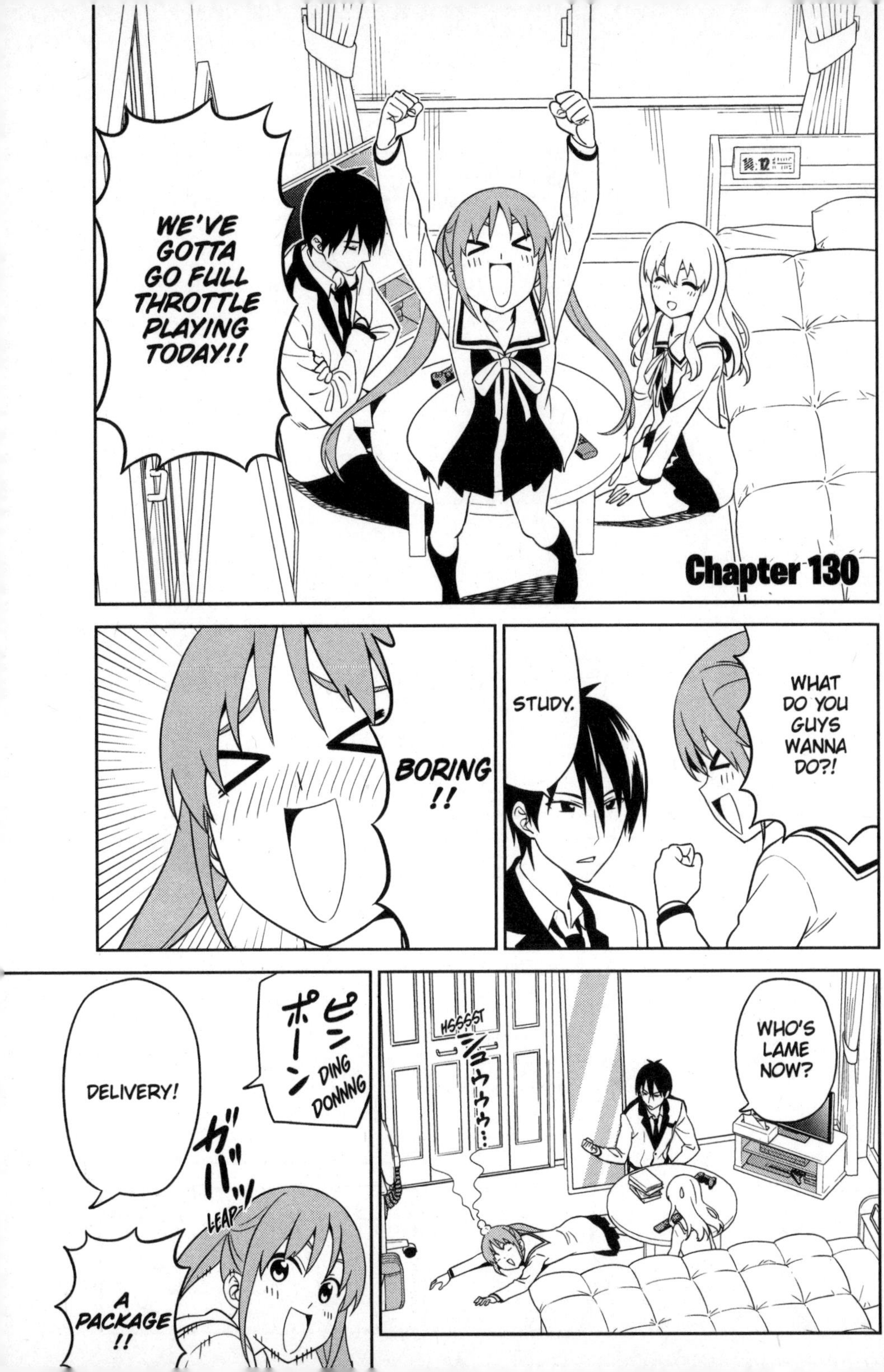
WE'VE GOTTA GO FULL THROTTLE PLAYING TODAY!!
Chapter 130
WHAT DO YOU GUYS WANNA DO?!
STUDY.
BORING!!
WHO'S LAME NOW?
シュウウウ…
HSSSST
ピンポーン
DING DONNNG
DELIVERY!
ガバッ
LEAP!
A PACKAGE!!

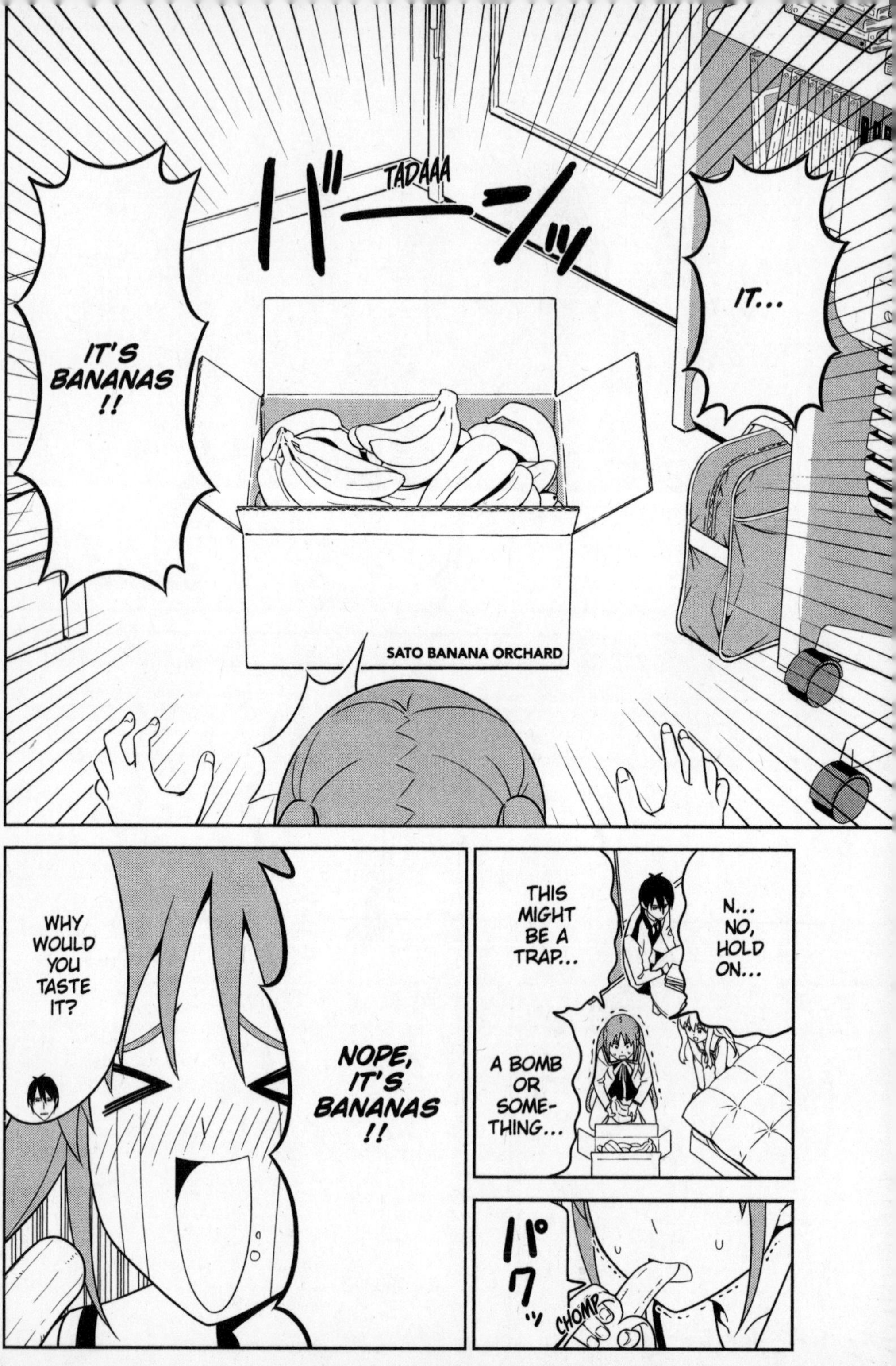
IT...
TADAAA
IT'S BANANAS !!
SATO BANANA ORCHARD
N... NO, HOLD ON...
THIS MIGHT BE A TRAP...
A BOMB OR SOME-THING...
CHOMP
NOPE, IT'S BANANAS !!
WHY WOULD YOU TASTE IT?

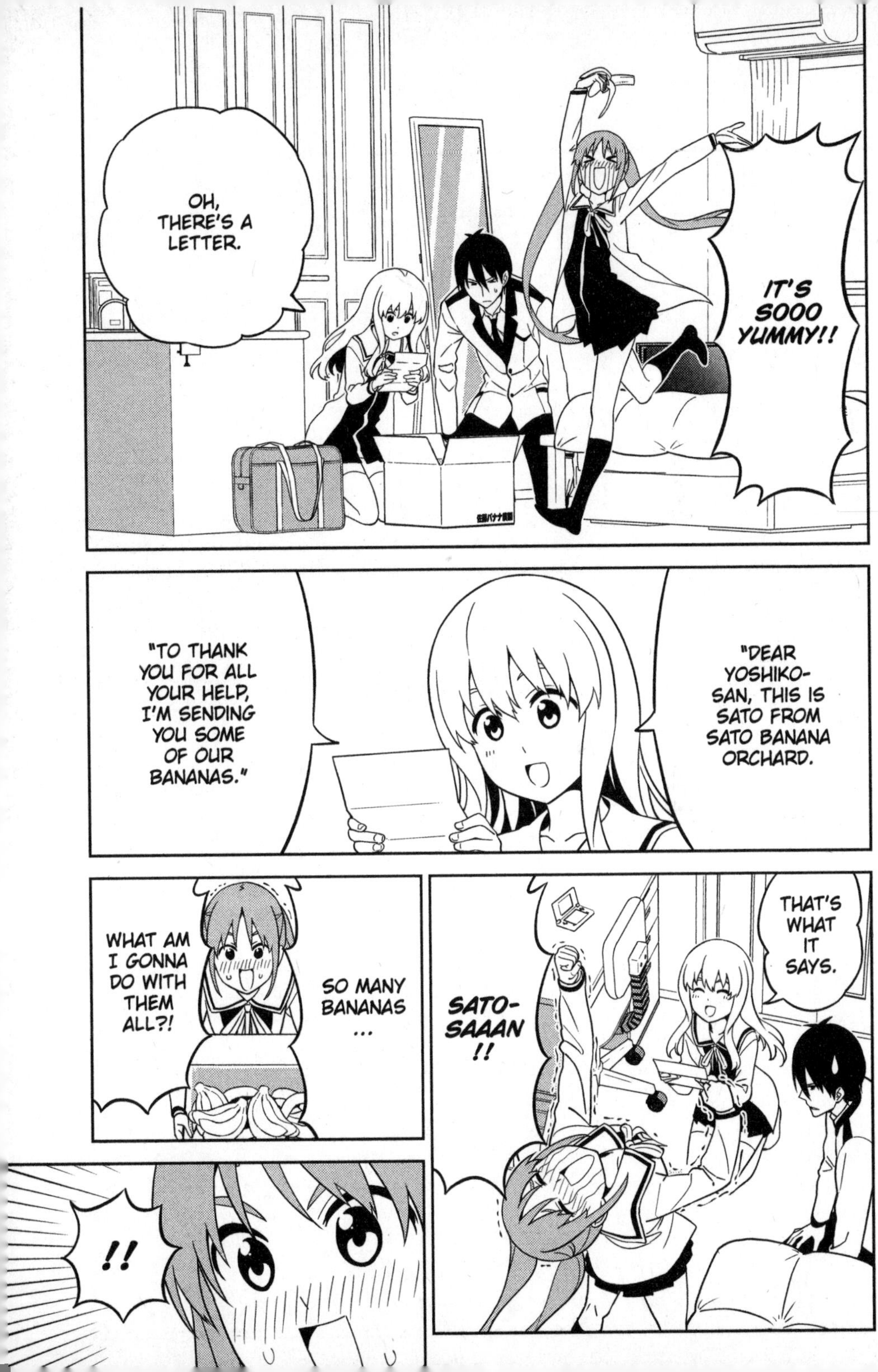
IT'S SOOO YUMMY!!
OH, THERE'S A LETTER.
"DEAR YOSHIKO-SAN, THIS IS SATO FROM SATO BANANA ORCHARD.
"TO THANK YOU FOR ALL YOUR HELP, I'M SENDING YOU SOME OF OUR BANANAS."
THAT'S WHAT IT SAYS.
SATO-SAAAN!!
SO MANY BANANAS...
WHAT AM I GONNA DO WITH THEM ALL?!
!!

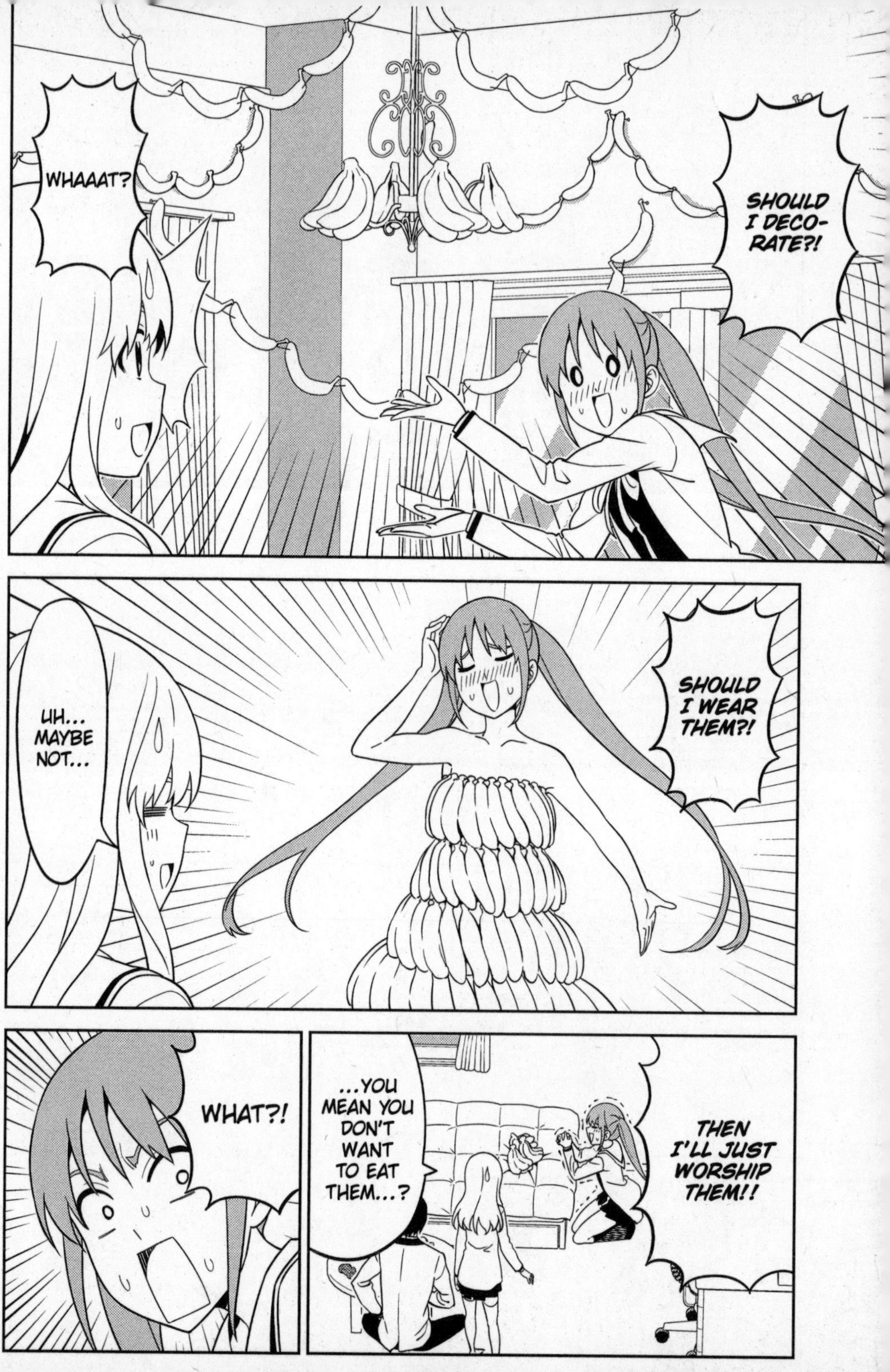
SHOULD I DECO-RATE?!
WHAAAT?
SHOULD I WEAR THEM?!
UH... MAYBE NOT...
THEN I'LL JUST WORSHIP THEM!!
...YOU MEAN YOU DON'T WANT TO EAT THEM...?
WHAT?!

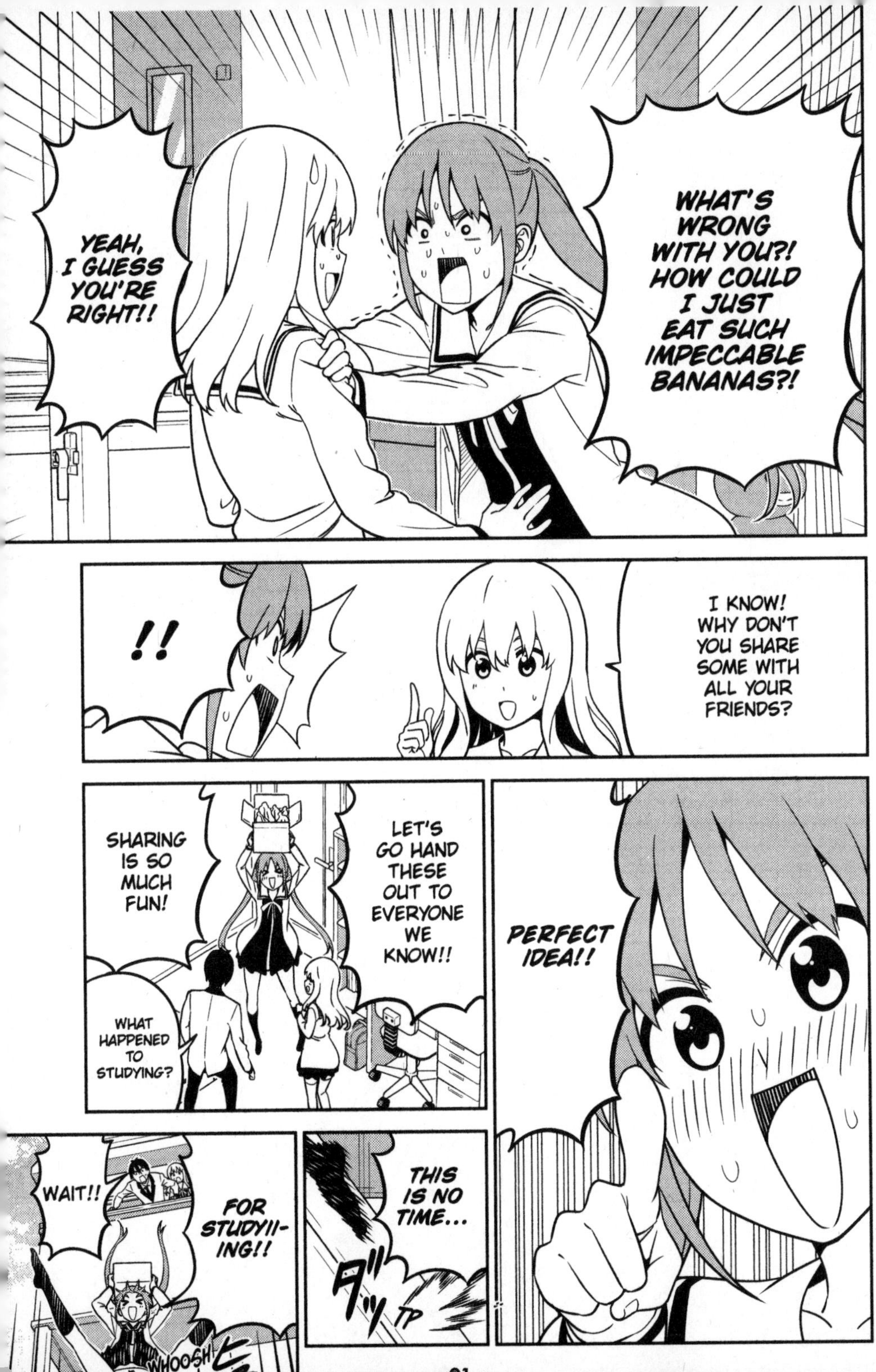

WHAT'S WRONG WITH YOU?! HOW COULD I JUST EAT SUCH IMPECCABLE BANANAS?!
YEAH, I GUESS YOU'RE RIGHT!!
I KNOW! WHY DON'T YOU SHARE SOME WITH ALL YOUR FRIENDS?
!!
PERFECT IDEA!!
LET'S GO HAND THESE OUT TO EVERYONE WE KNOW!!
SHARING IS SO MUCH FUN!
WHAT HAPPENED TO STUDYING?
THIS IS NO TIME...
TP
FOR STUDYII-ING!!
WAIT!!
WHOOSH!

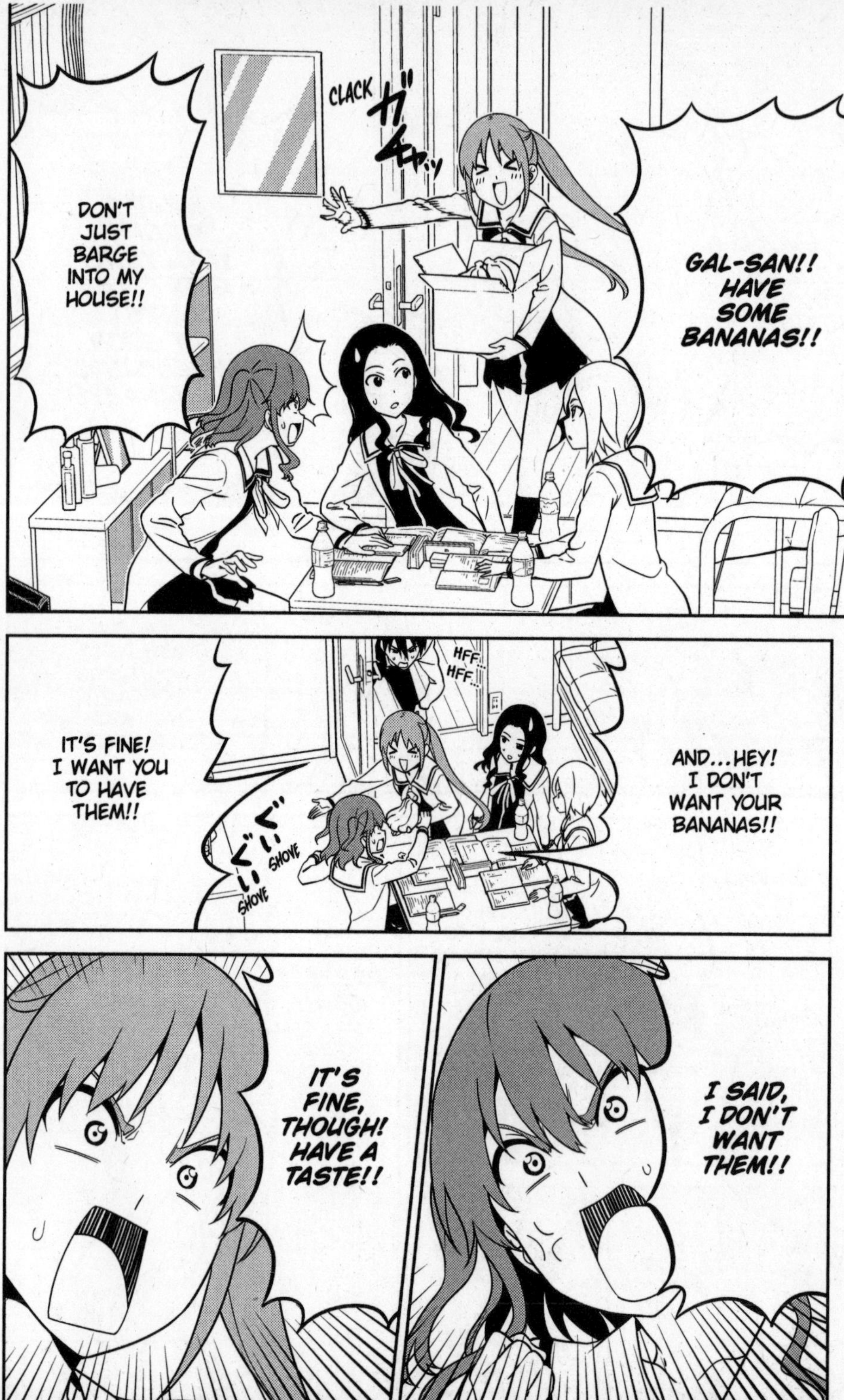
CLACK
GAL-SAN!! HAVE SOME BANANAS!!
DON'T JUST BARGE INTO MY HOUSE!!
AND...HEY! I DON'T WANT YOUR BANANAS!!
HFF... HFF...
IT'S FINE! I WANT YOU TO HAVE THEM!!
SHOVE
SHOVE
I SAID, I DON'T WANT THEM!!
IT'S FINE, THOUGH! HAVE A TASTE!!

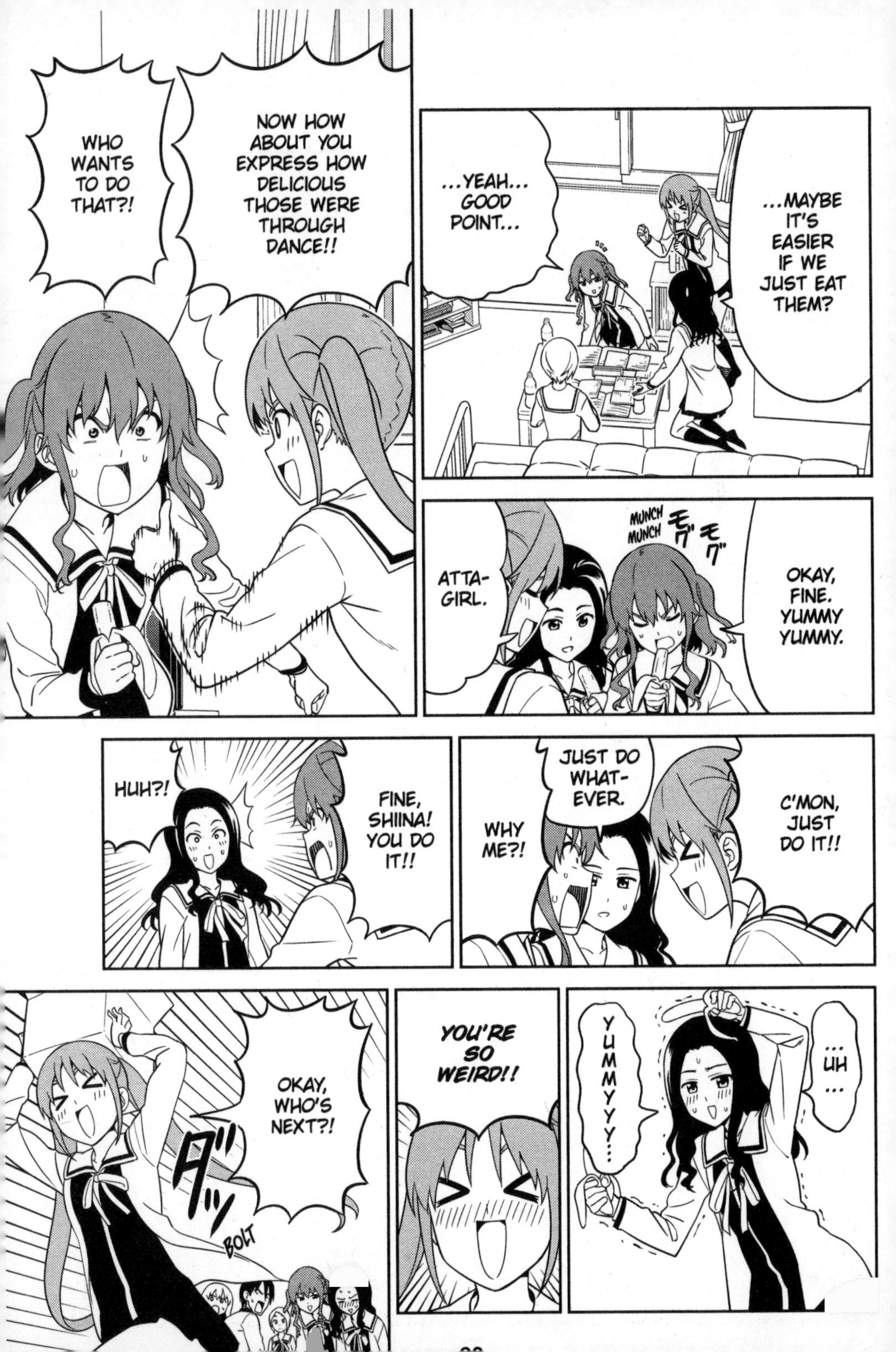
...MAYBE IT'S EASIER IF WE JUST EAT THEM?
...YEAH... GOOD POINT...
MUNCH MUNCH モグ モグ
OKAY, FINE. YUMMY YUMMY.
ATTA-GIRL.
NOW HOW ABOUT YOU EXPRESS HOW DELICIOUS THOSE WERE THROUGH DANCE!!
WHO WANTS TO DO THAT?!
C'MON, JUST DO IT!!
JUST DO WHAT-EVER.
WHY ME?!
FINE, SHIINA! YOU DO IT!!
HUH?!
...UH...
YUMMYYYY...
YOU'RE SO WEIRD!!
OKAY, WHO'S NEXT?!
ダッ
BOLT

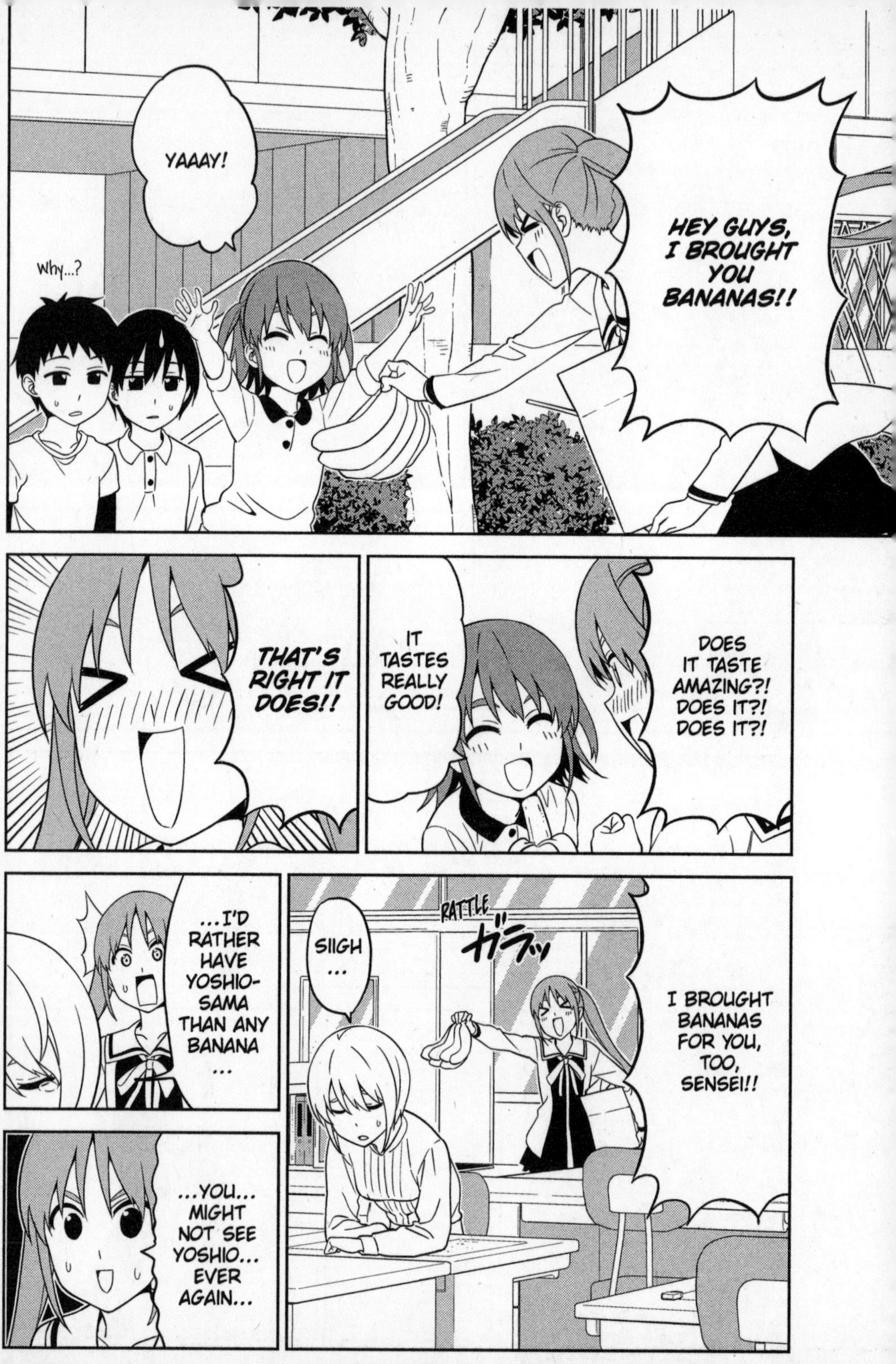
HEY GUYS, I BROUGHT YOU BANANAS!!
YAAAY!
Why...?
DOES IT TASTE AMAZING?! DOES IT?! DOES IT?!
IT TASTES REALLY GOOD!
THAT'S RIGHT IT DOES!!
I BROUGHT BANANAS FOR YOU, TOO, SENSEI!!
RATTLE
ガラッ
SIIGH ...
...I'D RATHER HAVE YOSHIO-SAMA THAN ANY BANANA ...
...YOU... MIGHT NOT SEE YOSHIO... EVER AGAIN...

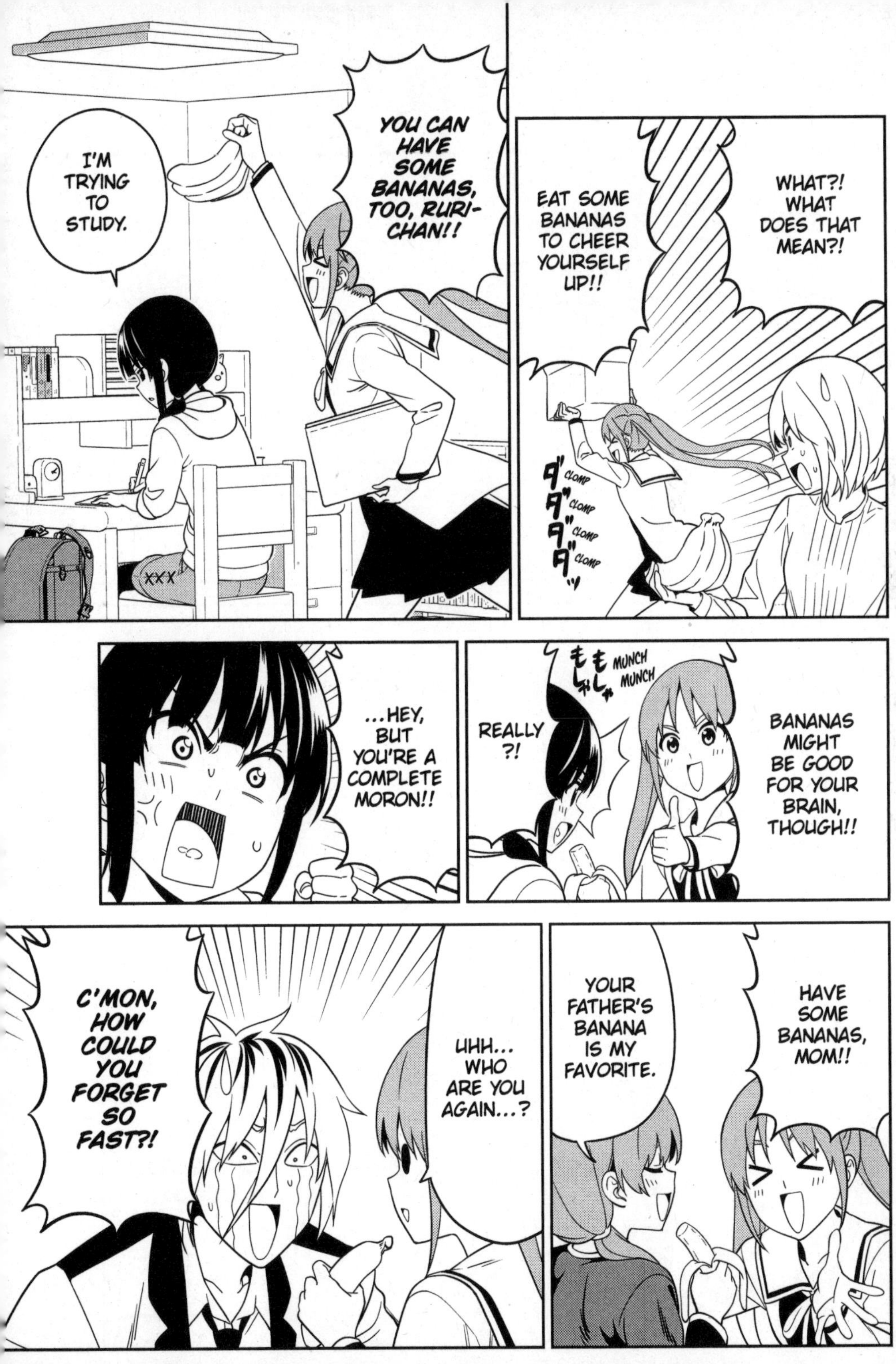
WHAT?! WHAT DOES THAT MEAN?!
EAT SOME BANANAS TO CHEER YOURSELF UP!!
ダ CLOMP ダ CLOMP ダ CLOMP ダ CLOMP ダッ
YOU CAN HAVE SOME BANANAS, TOO, RURI-CHAN!!
I'M TRYING TO STUDY.
BANANAS MIGHT BE GOOD FOR YOUR BRAIN, THOUGH!!
もしゃ MUNCH もしゃ MUNCH
REALLY ?!
...HEY, BUT YOU'RE A COMPLETE MORON!!
HAVE SOME BANANAS, MOM!!
YOUR FATHER'S BANANA IS MY FAVORITE.
UHH... WHO ARE YOU AGAIN...?
C'MON, HOW COULD YOU FORGET SO FAST?!

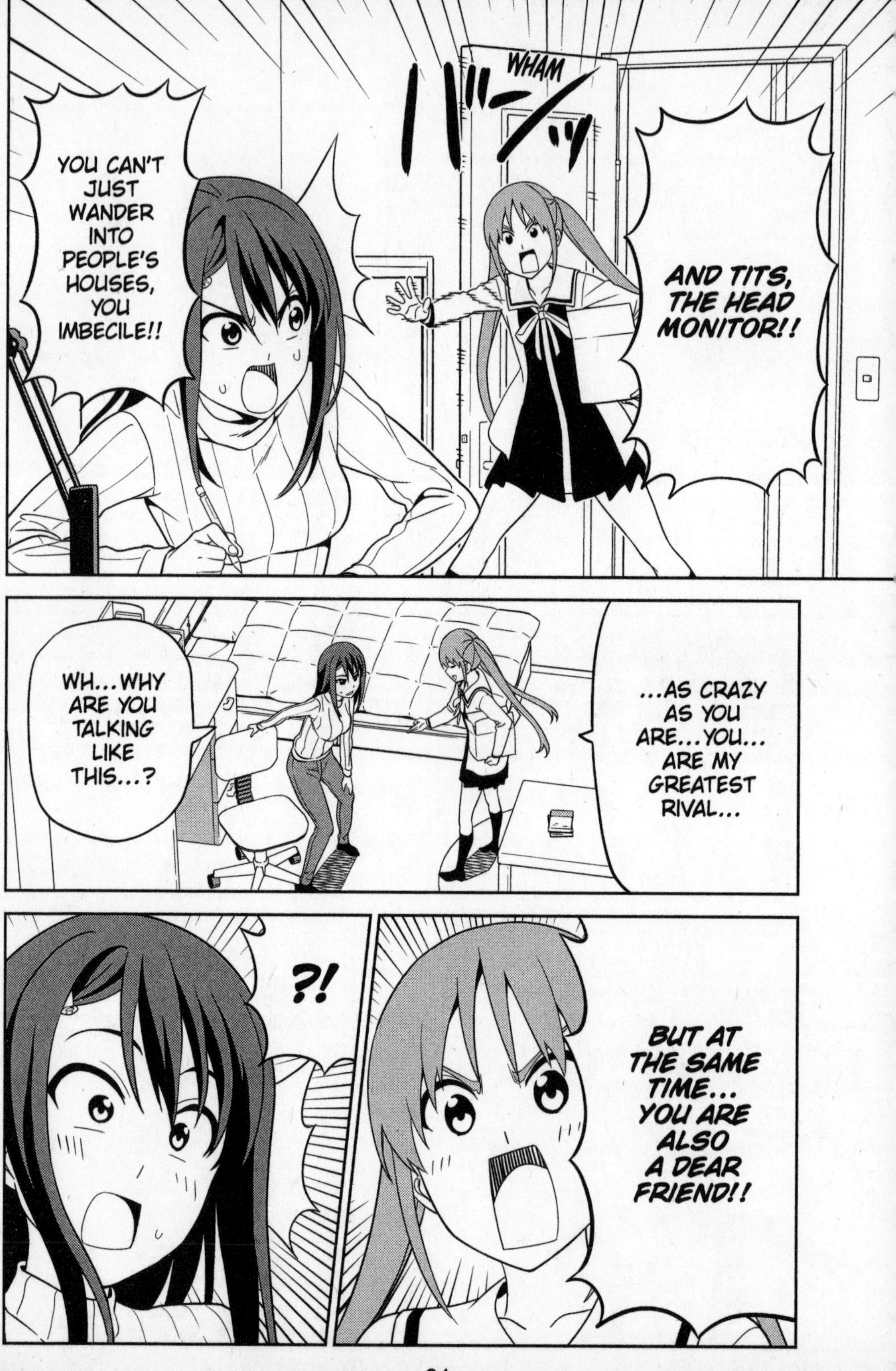
WHAM
バーンッ
AND TITS, THE HEAD MONITOR!!
YOU CAN'T JUST WANDER INTO PEOPLE'S HOUSES, YOU IMBECILE!!
...AS CRAZY AS YOU ARE...YOU... ARE MY GREATEST RIVAL...
WH...WHY ARE YOU TALKING LIKE THIS...?
BUT AT THE SAME TIME... YOU ARE ALSO A DEAR FRIEND!!
?!

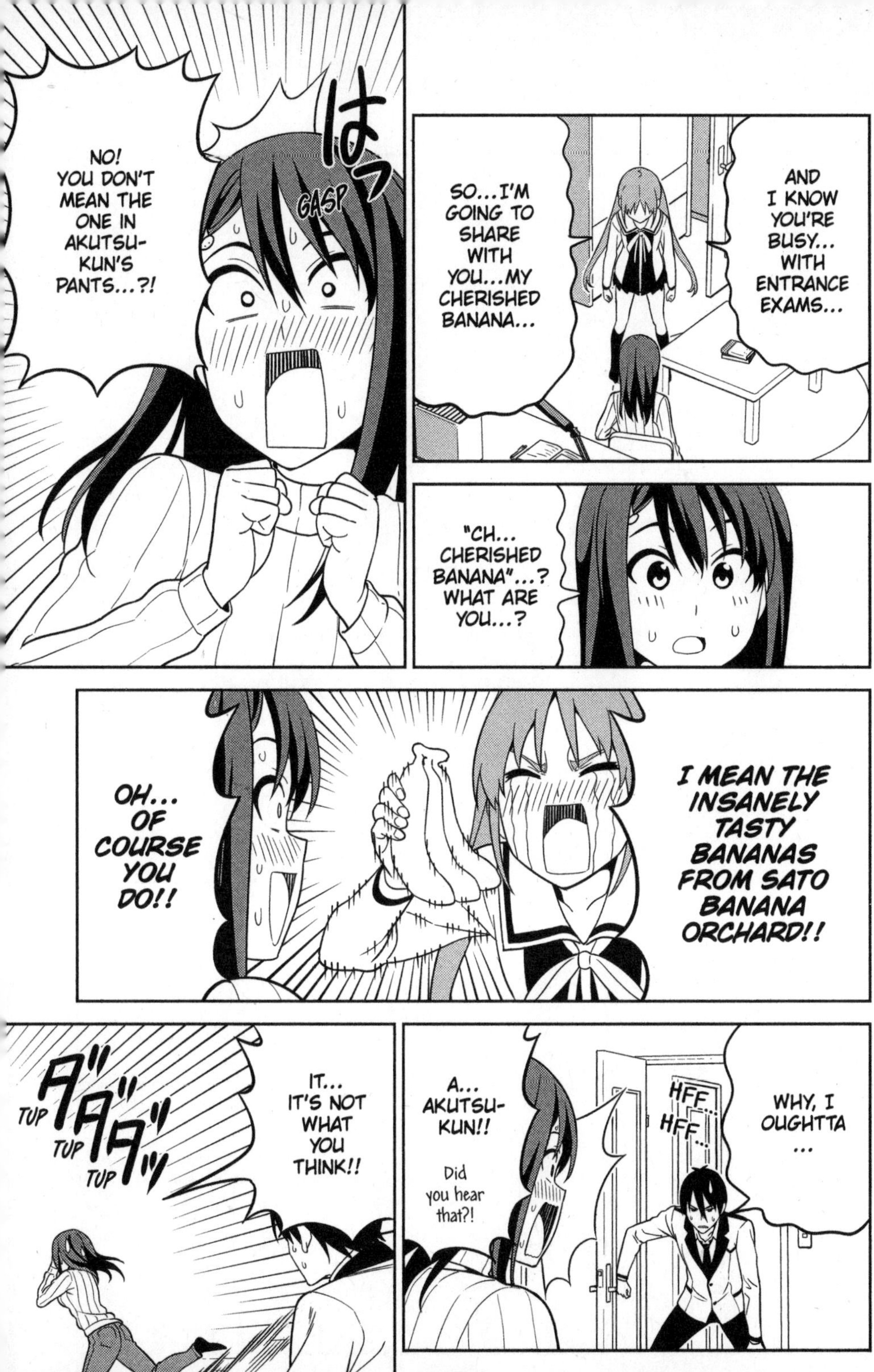
AND I KNOW YOU'RE BUSY... WITH ENTRANCE EXAMS...
SO...I'M GOING TO SHARE WITH YOU...MY CHERISHED BANANA...
"CH... CHERISHED BANANA"...? WHAT ARE YOU...?
はっ
GASP
NO! YOU DON'T MEAN THE ONE IN AKUTSU-KUN'S PANTS...?!
I MEAN THE INSANELY TASTY BANANAS FROM SATO BANANA ORCHARD!!
OH... OF COURSE YOU DO!!
WHY, I OUGHTTA ...
HFF... HFF...
A... AKUTSU-KUN!!
Did you hear that?!
IT... IT'S NOT WHAT YOU THINK!!
ダッ ダッ ダッ
TUP TUP TUP

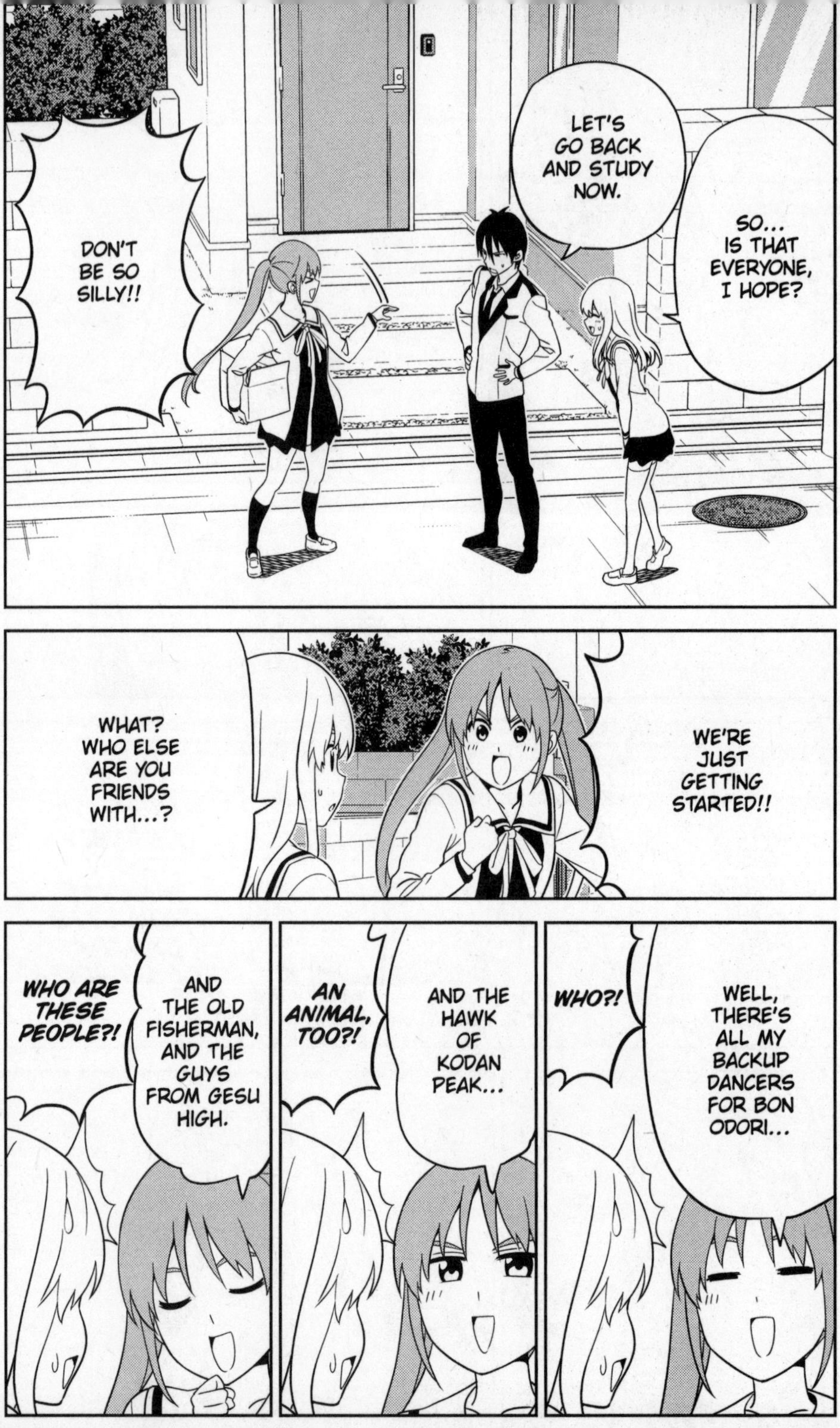
SO... IS THAT EVERYONE, I HOPE?
LET'S GO BACK AND STUDY NOW.
DON'T BE SO SILLY!!
WE'RE JUST GETTING STARTED!!
WHAT? WHO ELSE ARE YOU FRIENDS WITH...?
WELL, THERE'S ALL MY BACKUP DANCERS FOR BON ODORI...
WHO?!
AND THE HAWK OF KODAN PEAK...
AN ANIMAL, TOO?!
AND THE OLD FISHERMAN, AND THE GUYS FROM GESU HIGH.
WHO ARE THESE PEOPLE?!

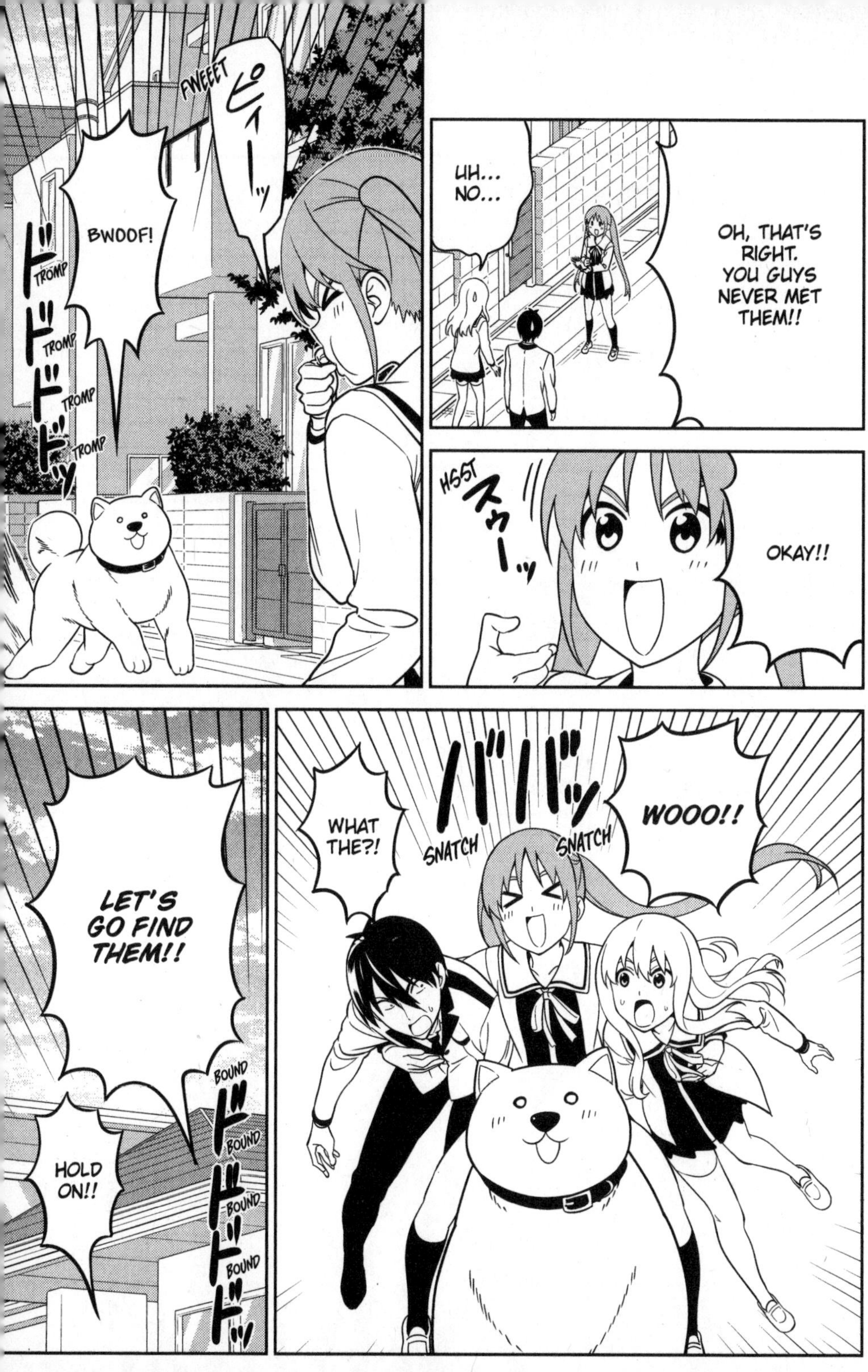

OH, THAT'S RIGHT. YOU GUYS NEVER MET THEM!!
UH... NO...
HSST
スゥーッ
OKAY!!
FWEEET
ピィーーッ
BWOOF!
ドドドドッ
TROMP TROMP TROMP TROMP
WOOO!!
SNATCH
ババッ
SNATCH
WHAT THE?!
LET'S GO FIND THEM!!
BOUND BOUND BOUND BOUND
ドドドドッ
HOLD ON!!

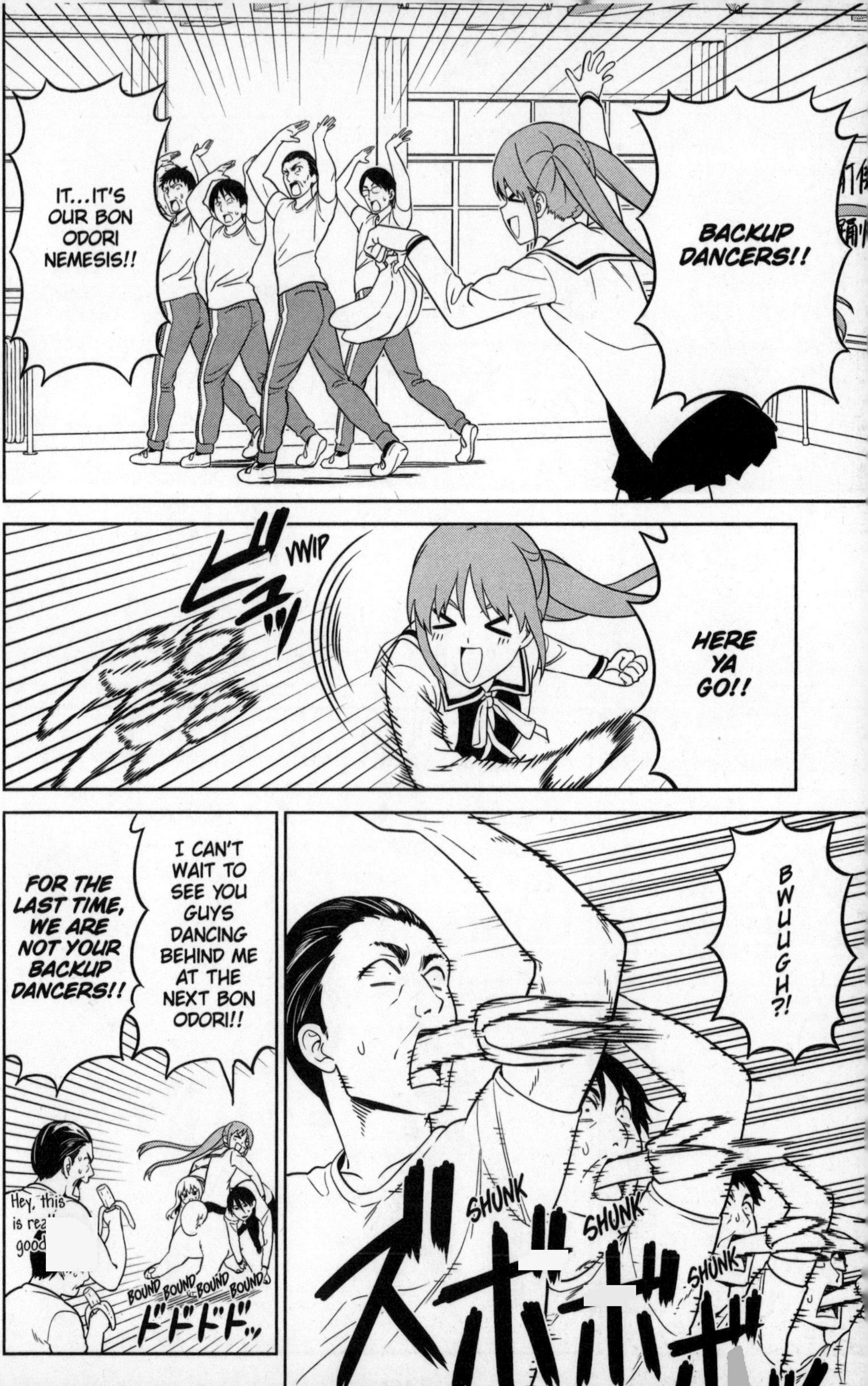
BACKUP DANCERS!!
IT...IT'S OUR BON ODORI NEMESIS!!
VWIP
HERE YA GO!!
BWUUGH?!
SHUNK
SHUNK
SHUNK
I CAN'T WAIT TO SEE YOU GUYS DANCING BEHIND ME AT THE NEXT BON ODORI!!
FOR THE LAST TIME, WE ARE NOT YOUR BACKUP DANCERS!!
Hey, this
BOUND BOUND BOUND BOUND

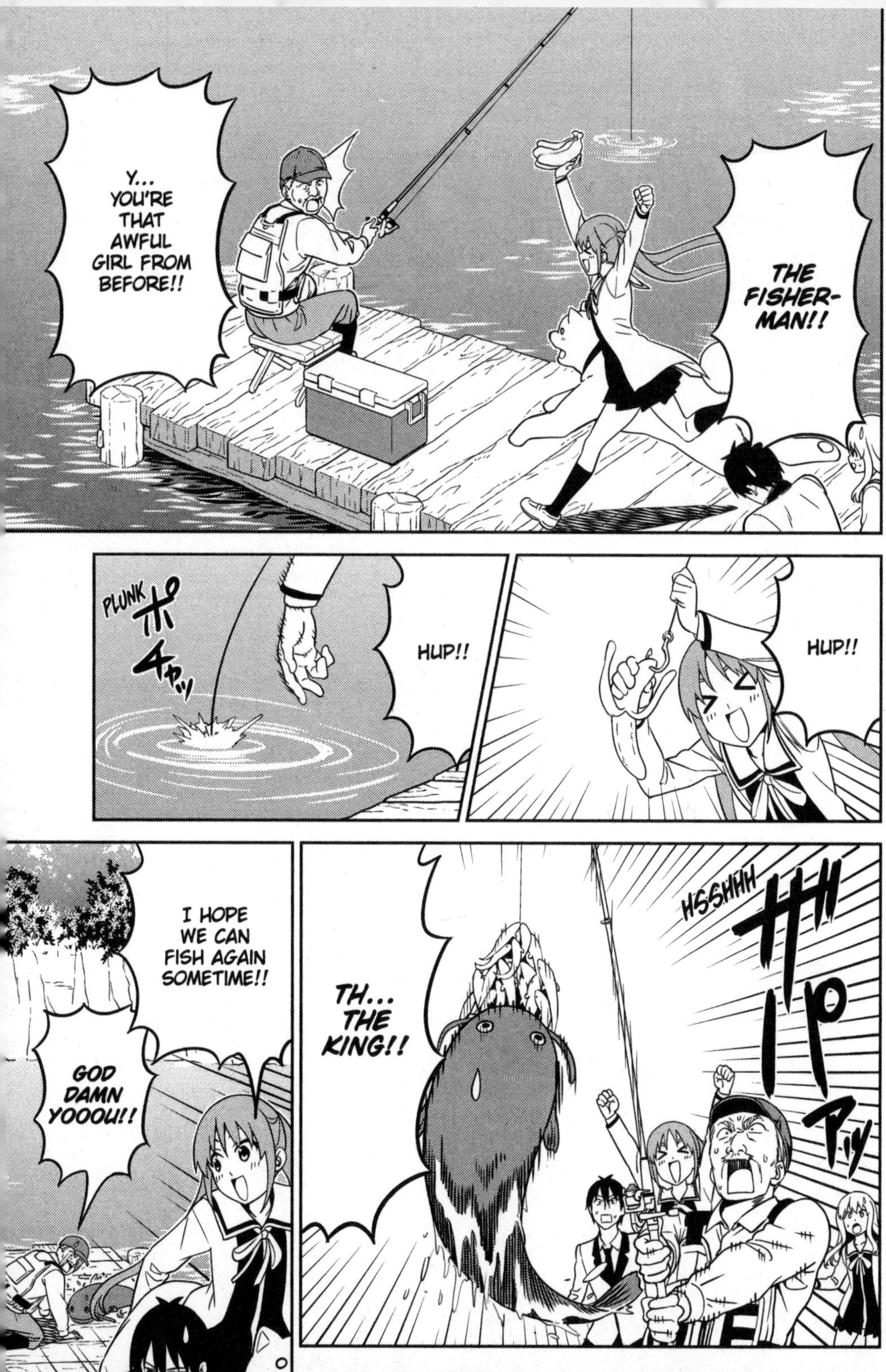
THE FISHER-MAN!!
Y... YOU'RE THAT AWFUL GIRL FROM BEFORE!!
HUP!!
HUP!!
PLUNK
HSSHHH
TH... THE KING!!
I HOPE WE CAN FISH AGAIN SOMETIME!!
GOD DAMN YOOOU!!

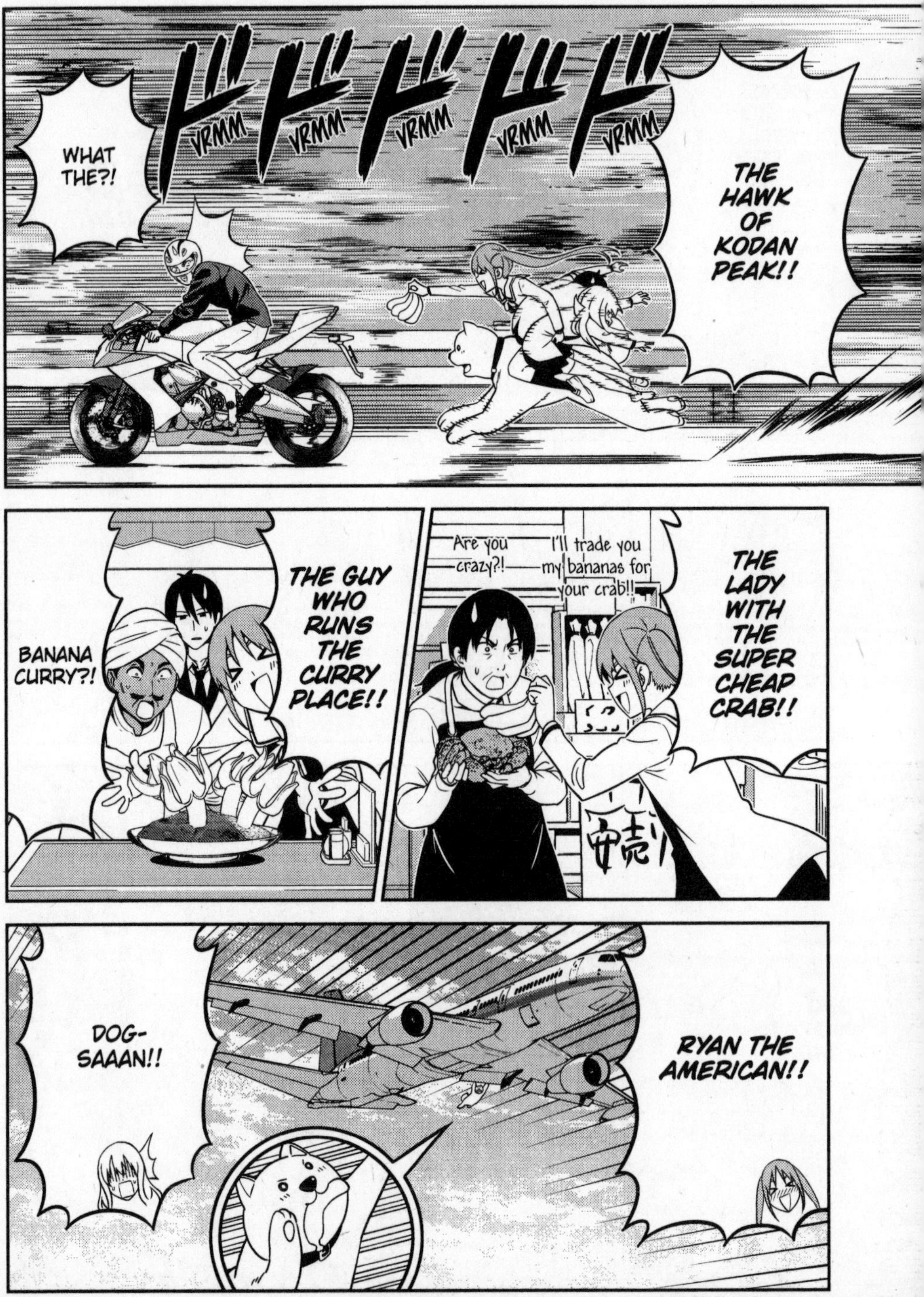
THE HAWK OF KODAN PEAK!!
ドドドドド
VRMM VRMM VRMM VRMM VRMM
WHAT THE?!
THE LADY WITH THE SUPER CHEAP CRAB!!
I'll trade you my bananas for your crab!!
Are you crazy?!
安売り
THE GUY WHO RUNS THE CURRY PLACE!!
BANANA CURRY?!
RYAN THE AMERICAN!!
DOG-SAAAN!!

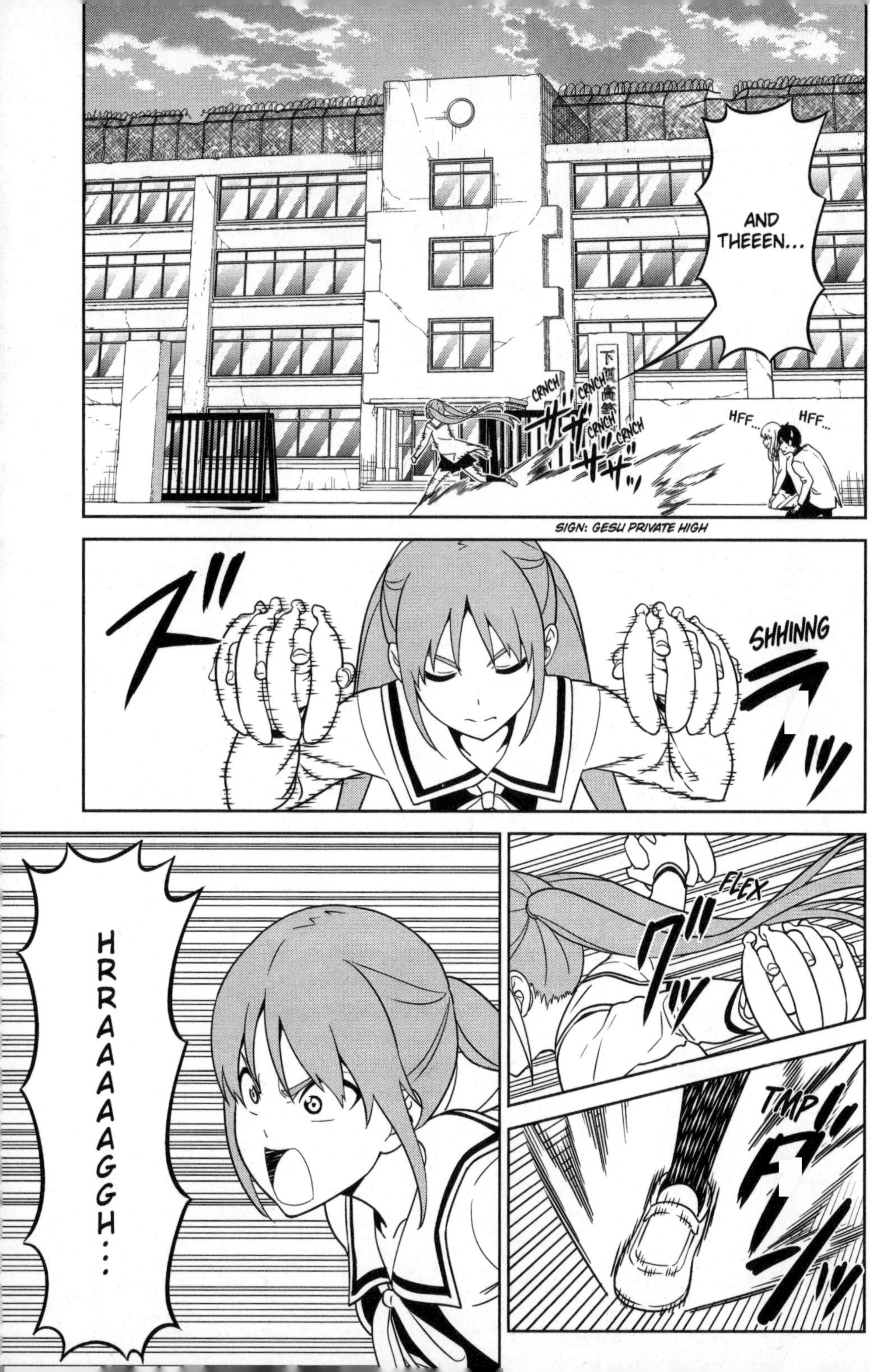
AND THEEEN...
CRNCH
CRNCH
CRNCH
CRNCH
HFF...
HFF...
SIGN: GESU PRIVATE HIGH
SHHINNG
FLEX
TMP
HRRAAAAAAGGH...

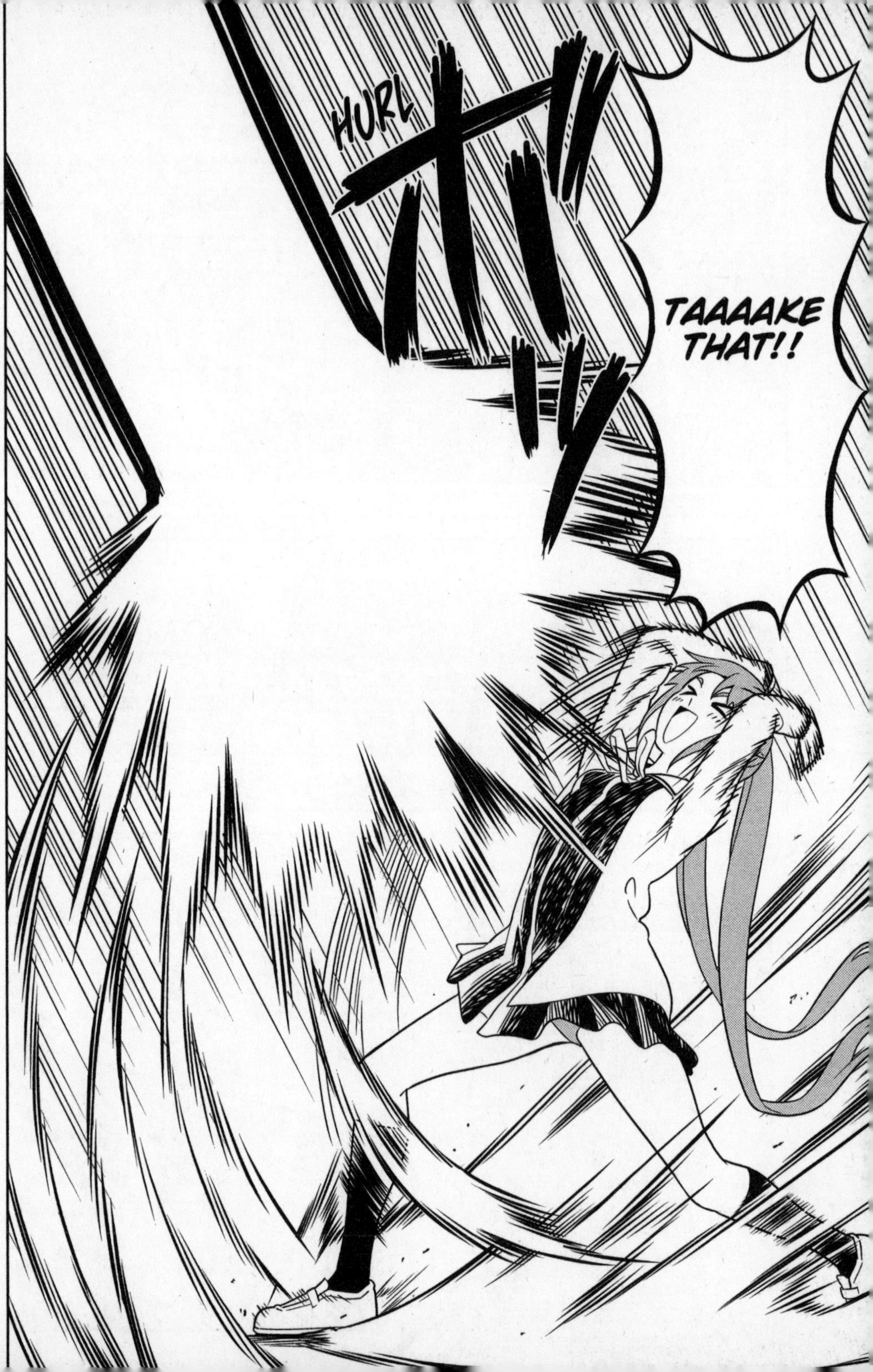
TAAAAKE THAT!!
HURL

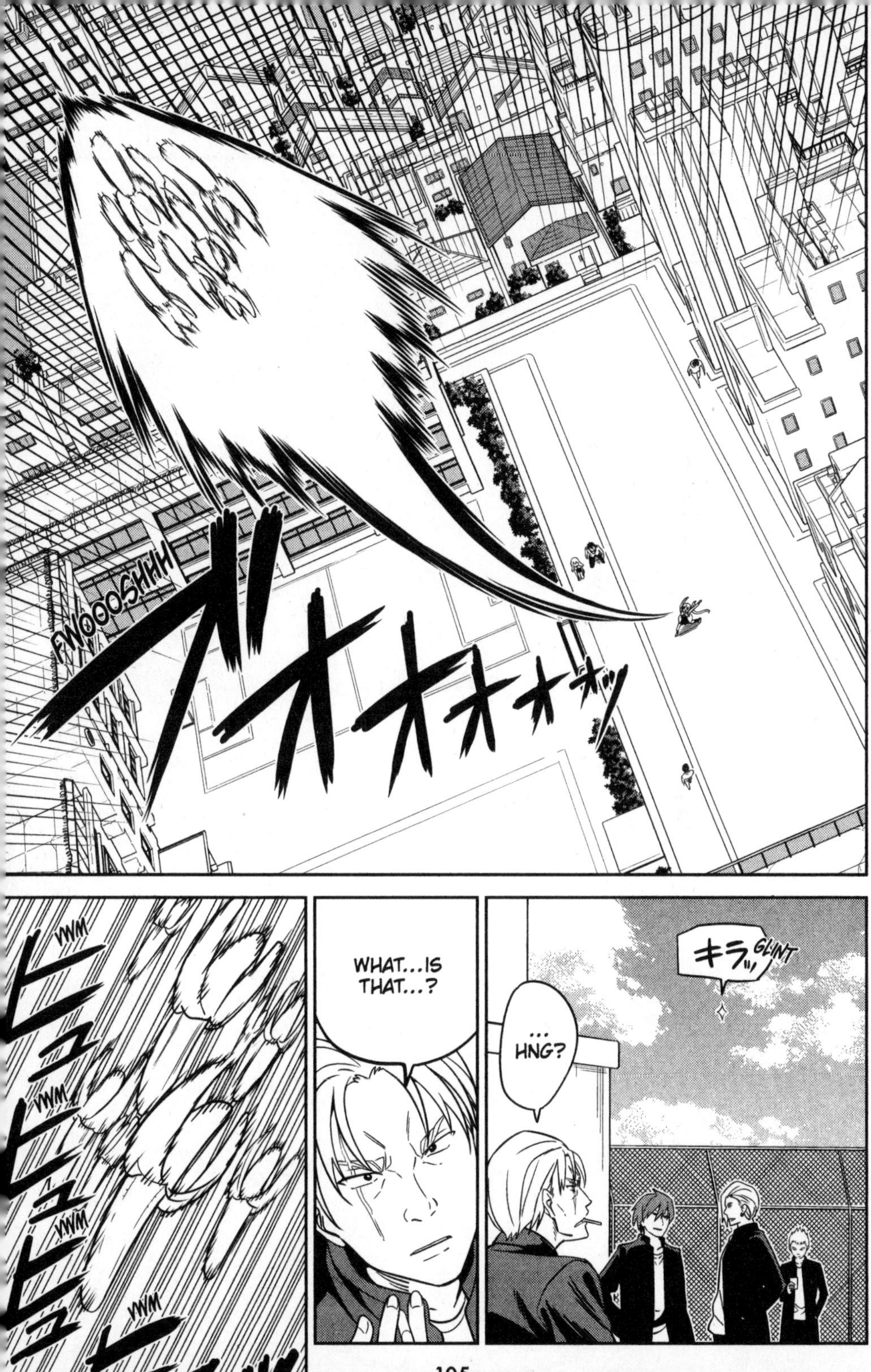

FWOOOSHHH
キラッ
GLINT
... HNG?
WHAT... IS THAT...?
VWM
VWM
VWM
VWM

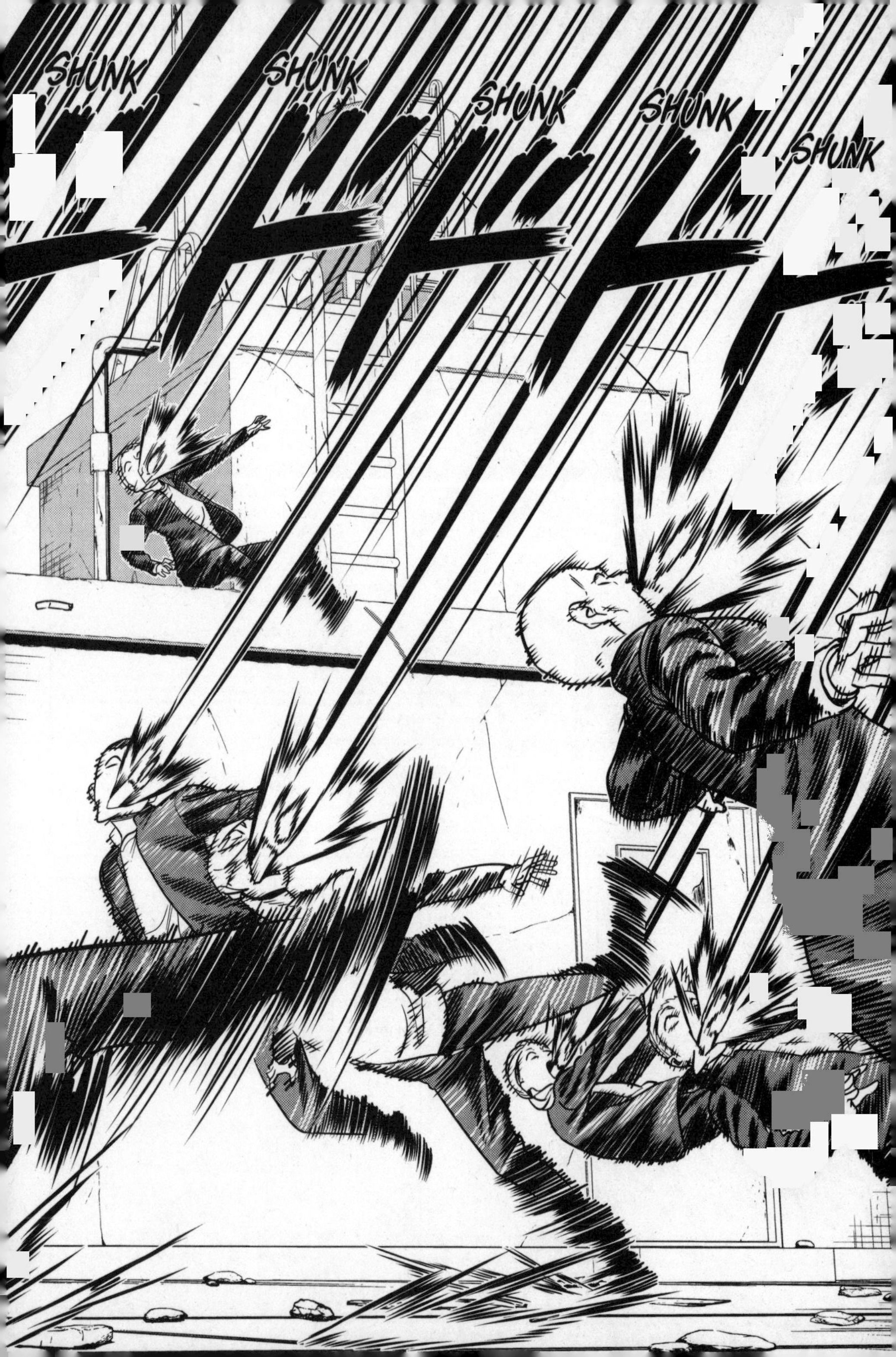
SHUNK
SHUNK
SHUNK
SHUNK
SHUNK

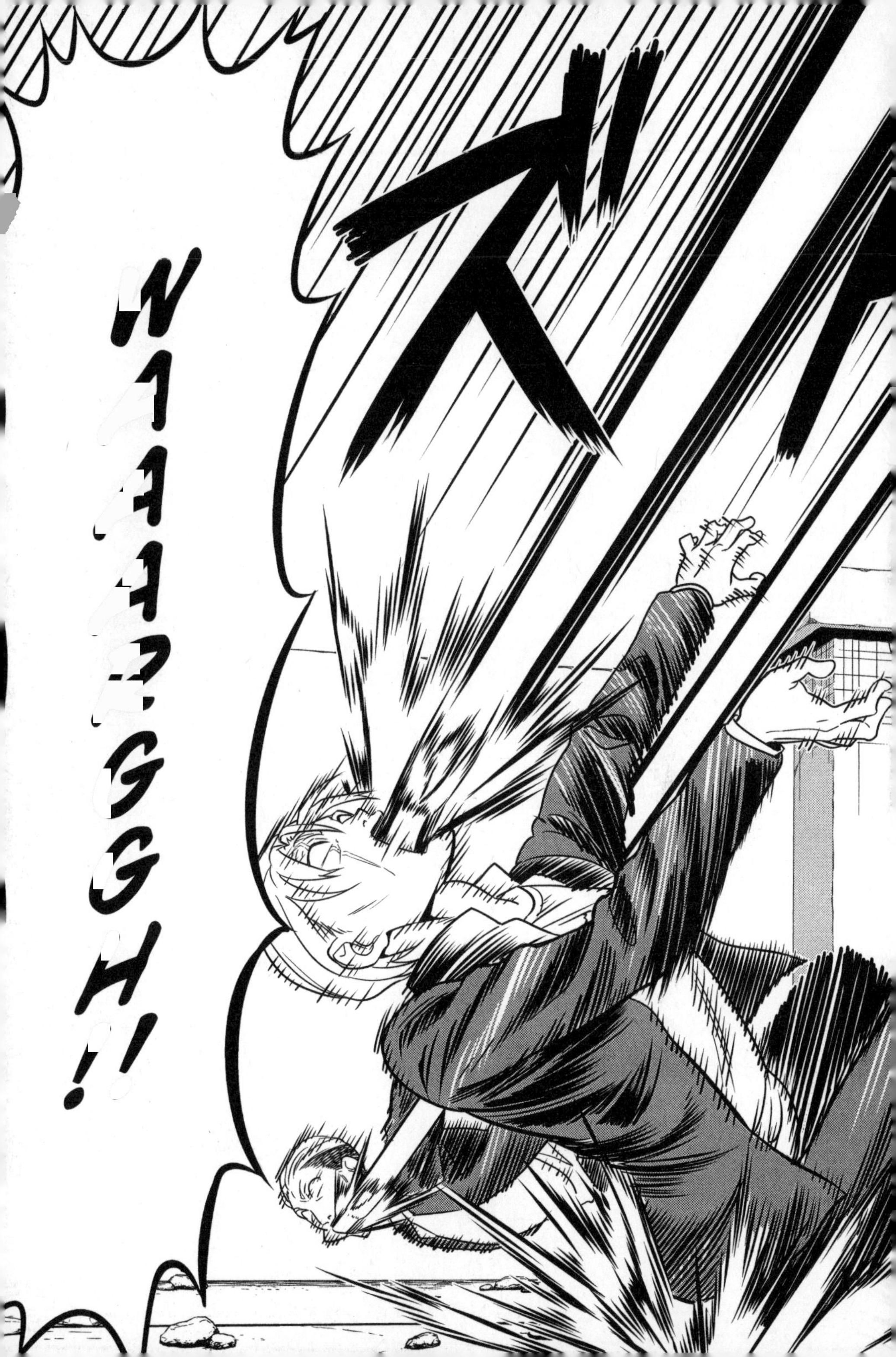
WAAARGGH!!

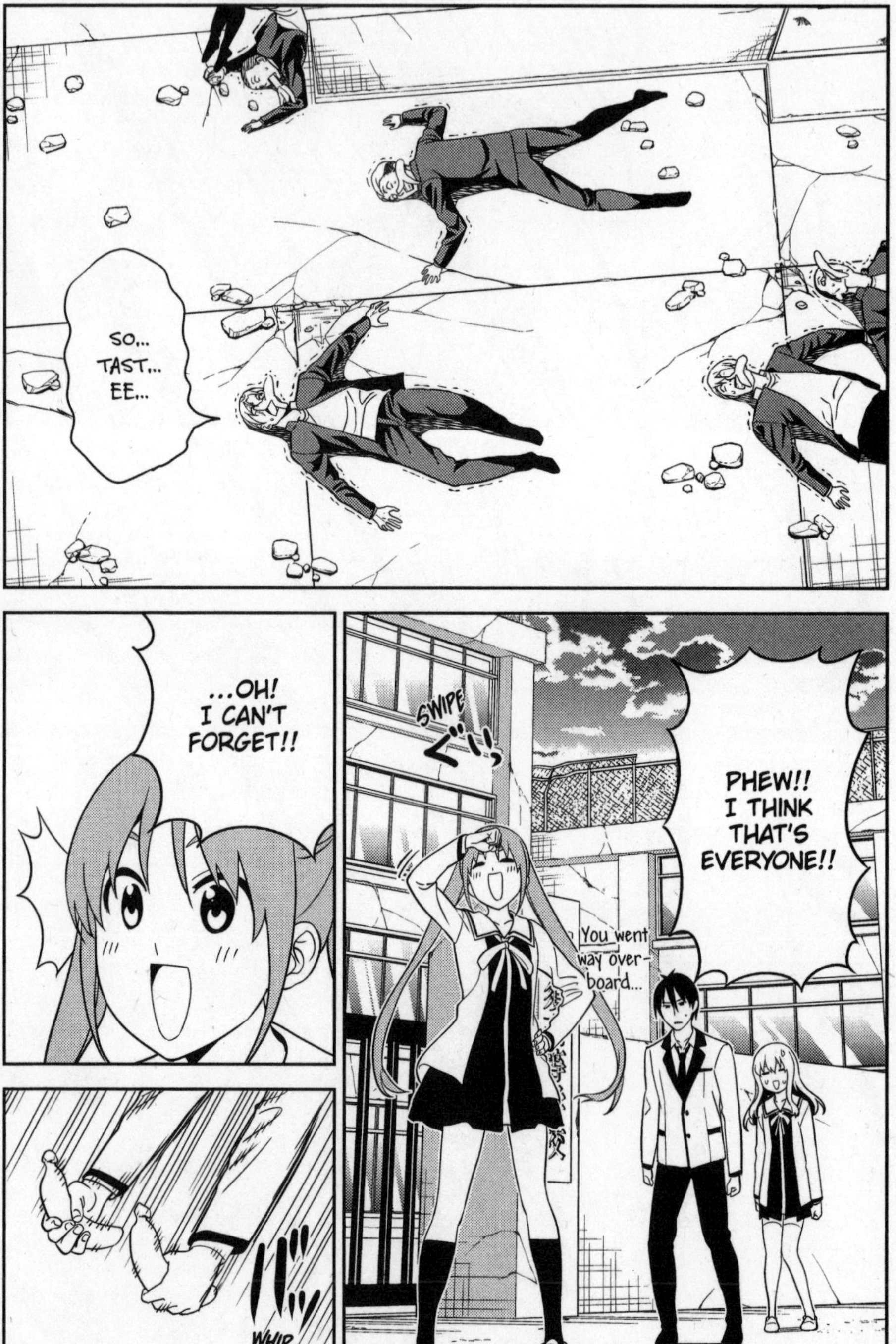
SO... TAST... EE...
PHEW!! I THINK THAT'S EVERYONE!!
SWIPE
You went way over-board...
...OH! I CAN'T FORGET!!
WHIP

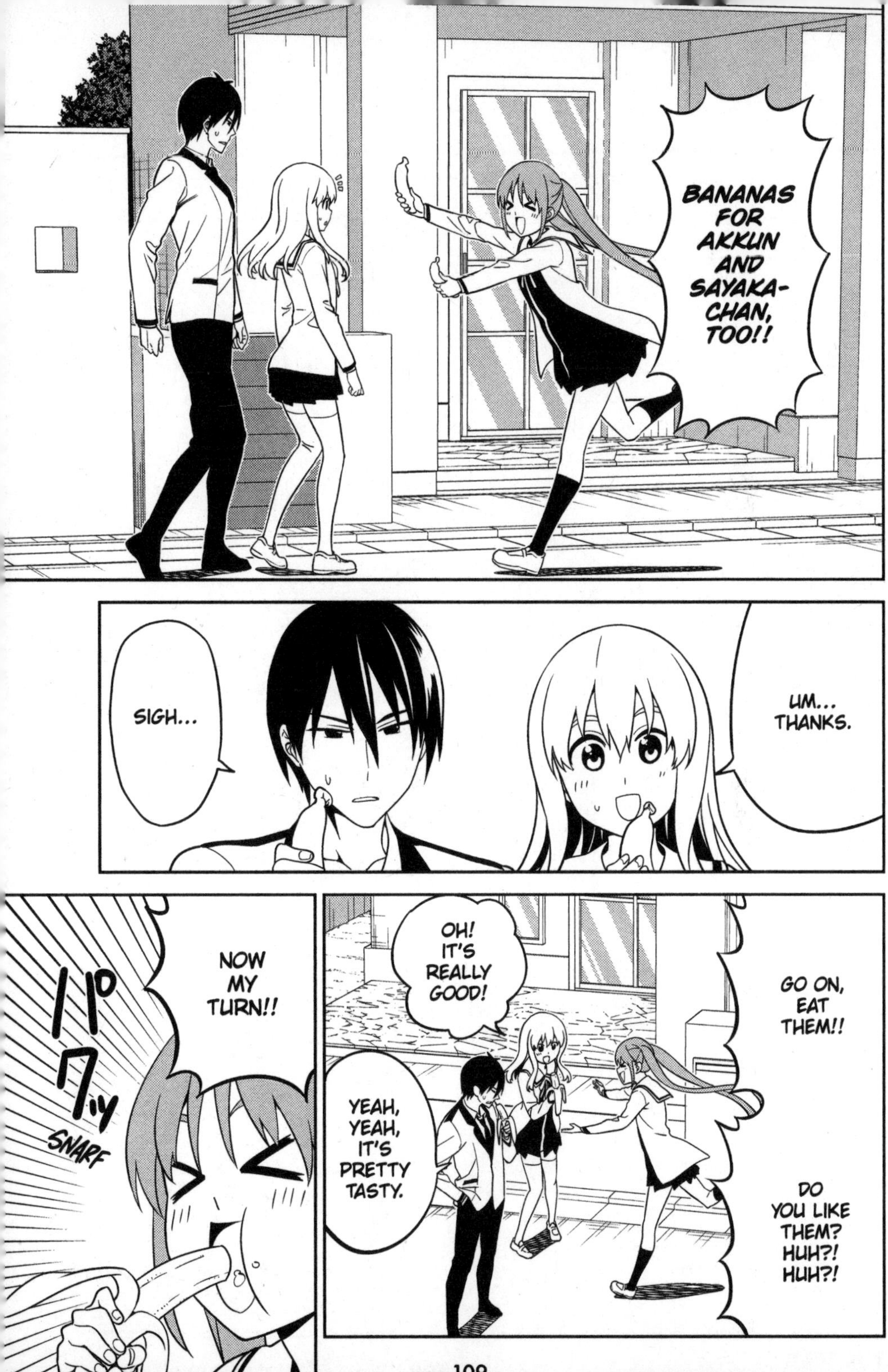
BANANAS FOR AKKUN AND SAYAKA-CHAN, TOO!!
UM... THANKS.
SIGH...
GO ON, EAT THEM!!
OH! IT'S REALLY GOOD!
DO YOU LIKE THEM? HUH?! HUH?!
YEAH, YEAH, IT'S PRETTY TASTY.
NOW MY TURN!!
パクッ
SNARF

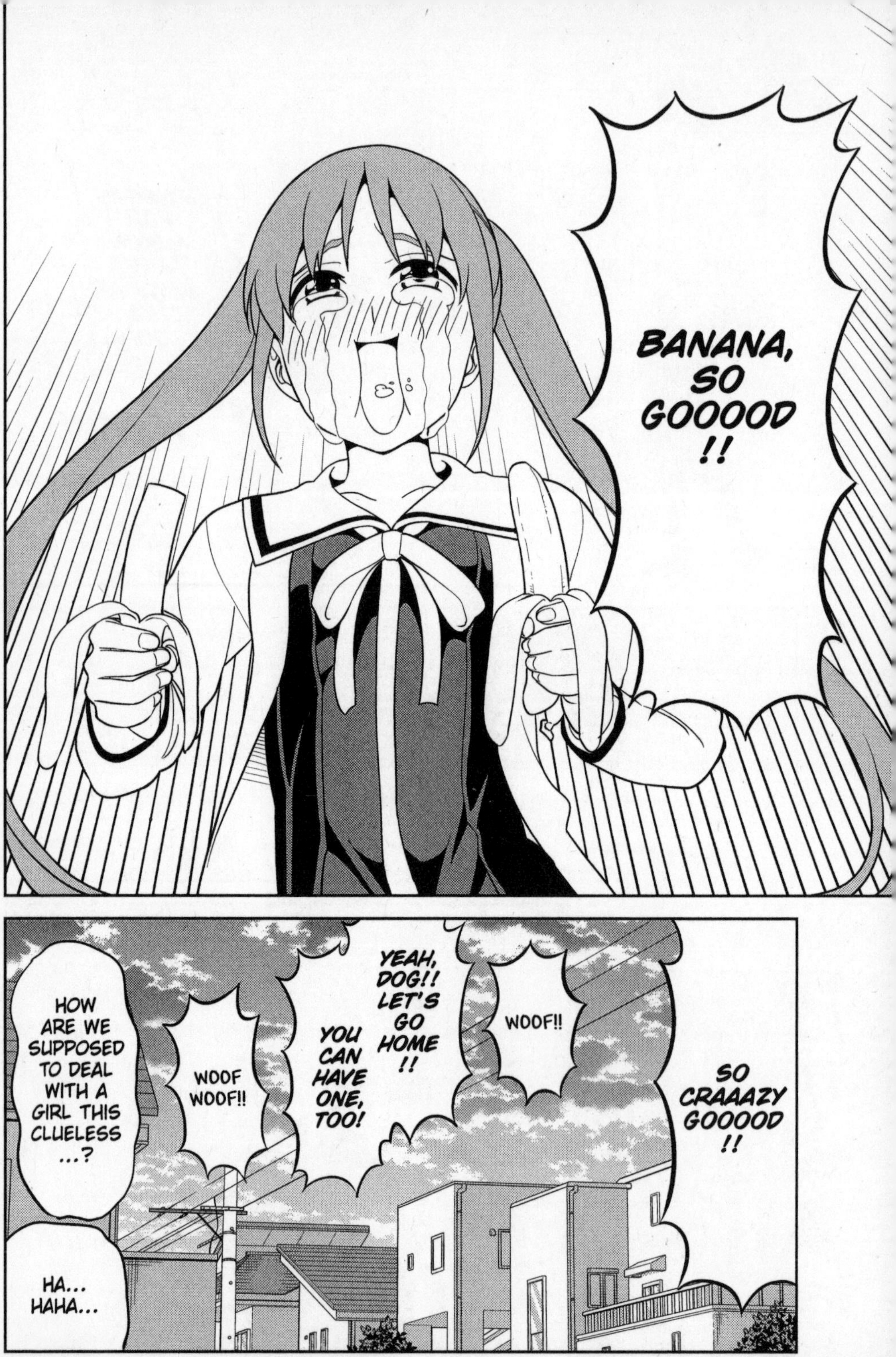
BANANA, SO GOOOOD!!
SO CRAAAZY GOOOOD!!
WOOF!!
YEAH, DOG!! LET'S GO HOME!!
YOU CAN HAVE ONE, TOO!
WOOF WOOF!!
HOW ARE WE SUPPOSED TO DEAL WITH A GIRL THIS CLUELESS ...?
HA... HAHA...

THE END!

(Somewhere, there's always)

Aho-Girl

\'ahô,gərl\ *Japanese, noun.*

A clueless girl.

Aho-Girl

\ˈahôˌgərl \ *Japanese, noun.*
A clueless girl.

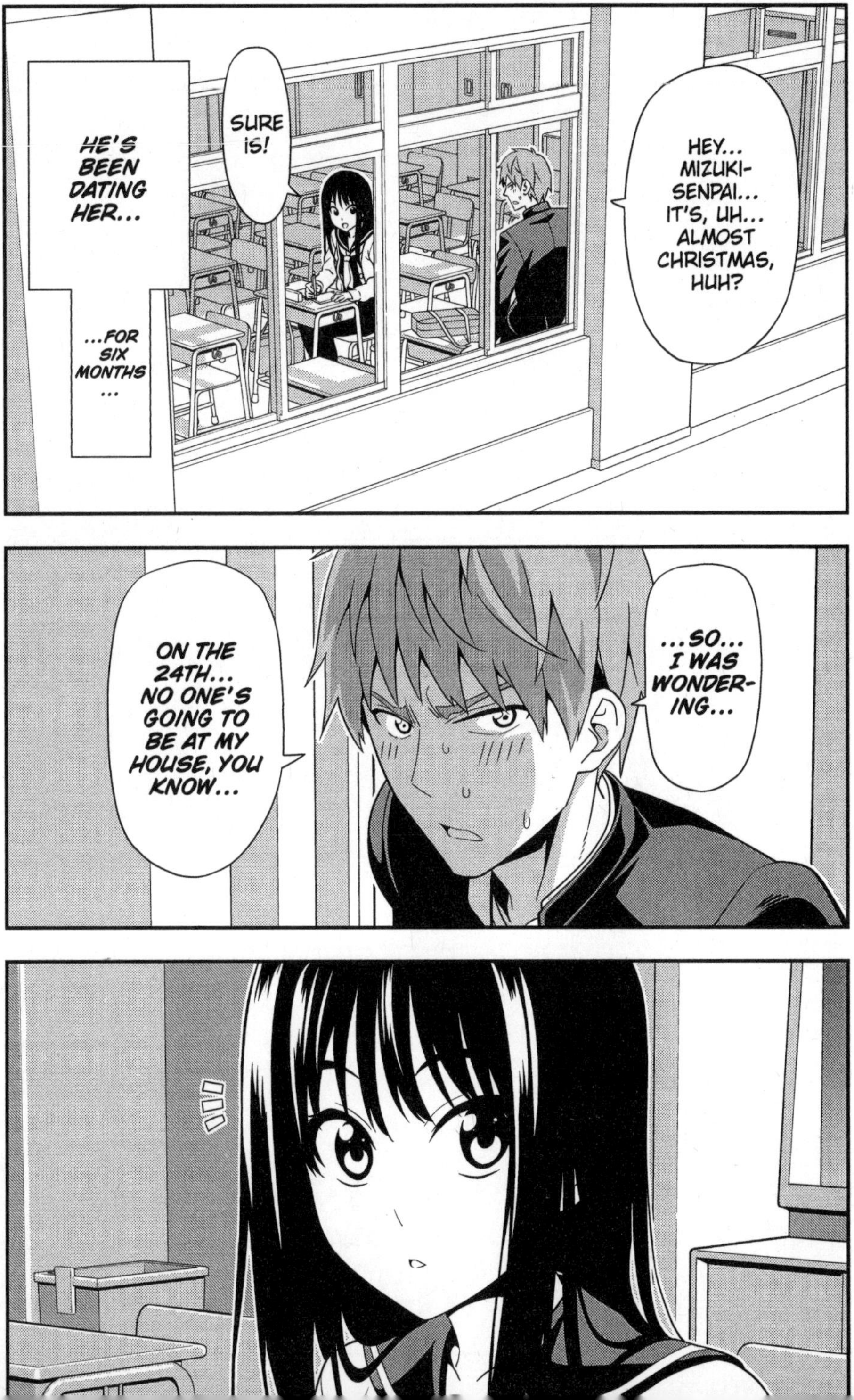
HEY... MIZUKI-SENPAI... IT'S, UH... ALMOST CHRISTMAS, HUH?
SURE IS!
HE'S BEEN DATING HER...
...FOR SIX MONTHS...
...SO... I WAS WONDERING...
ON THE 24TH... NO ONE'S GOING TO BE AT MY HOUSE, YOU KNOW...

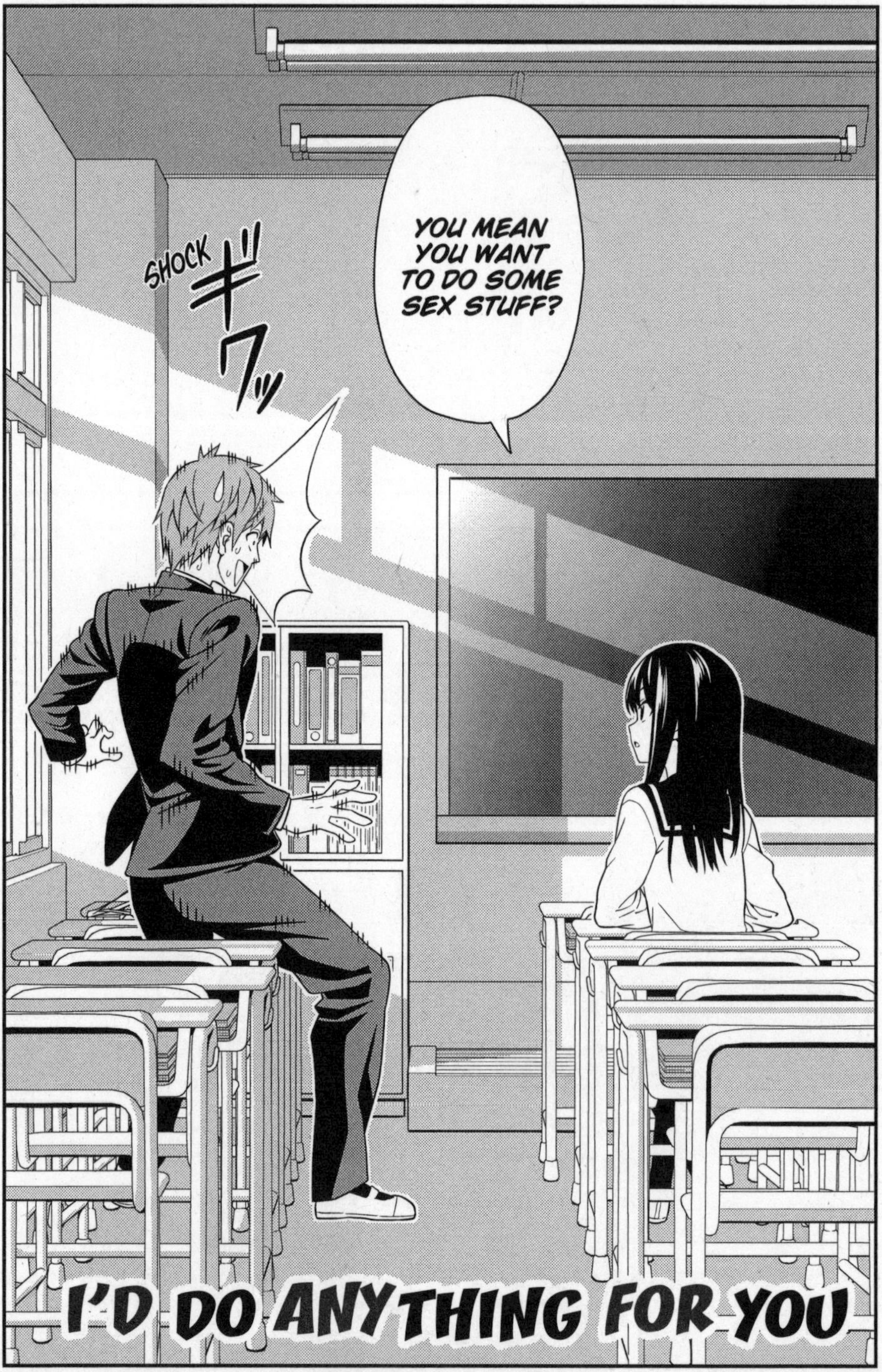
YOU MEAN YOU WANT TO DO SOME SEX STUFF?
SHOCK
ギクッ
I'D DO ANYTHING FOR YOU

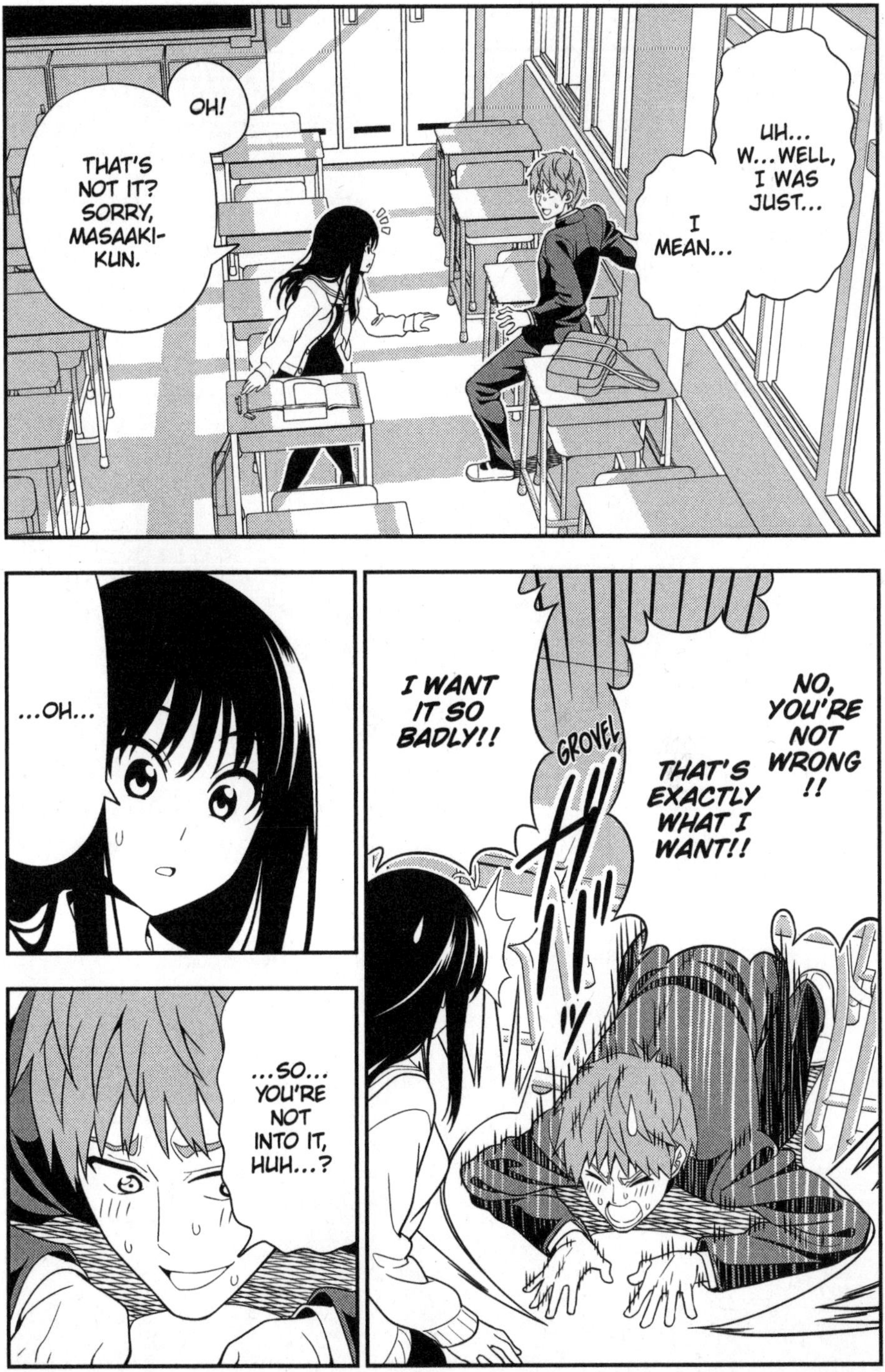
UH... W...WELL, I WAS JUST...
I MEAN...
OH!
THAT'S NOT IT? SORRY, MASAAKI-KUN.
NO, YOU'RE NOT WRONG!!
THAT'S EXACTLY WHAT I WANT!!
GROVEL
I WANT IT SO BADLY!!
...OH...
...SO... YOU'RE NOT INTO IT, HUH...?

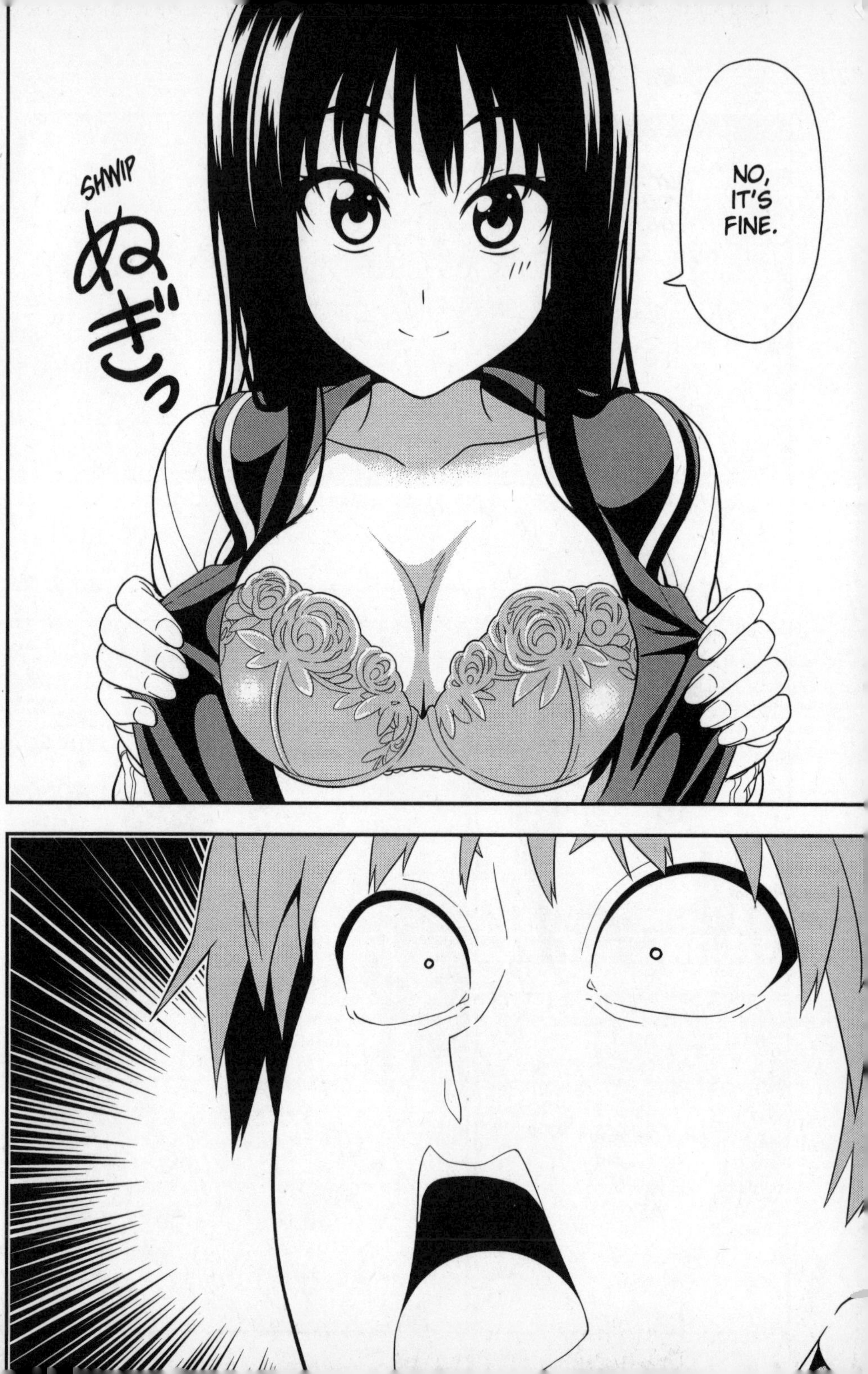
NO, IT'S FINE.
SHWIP
ぬぎっ

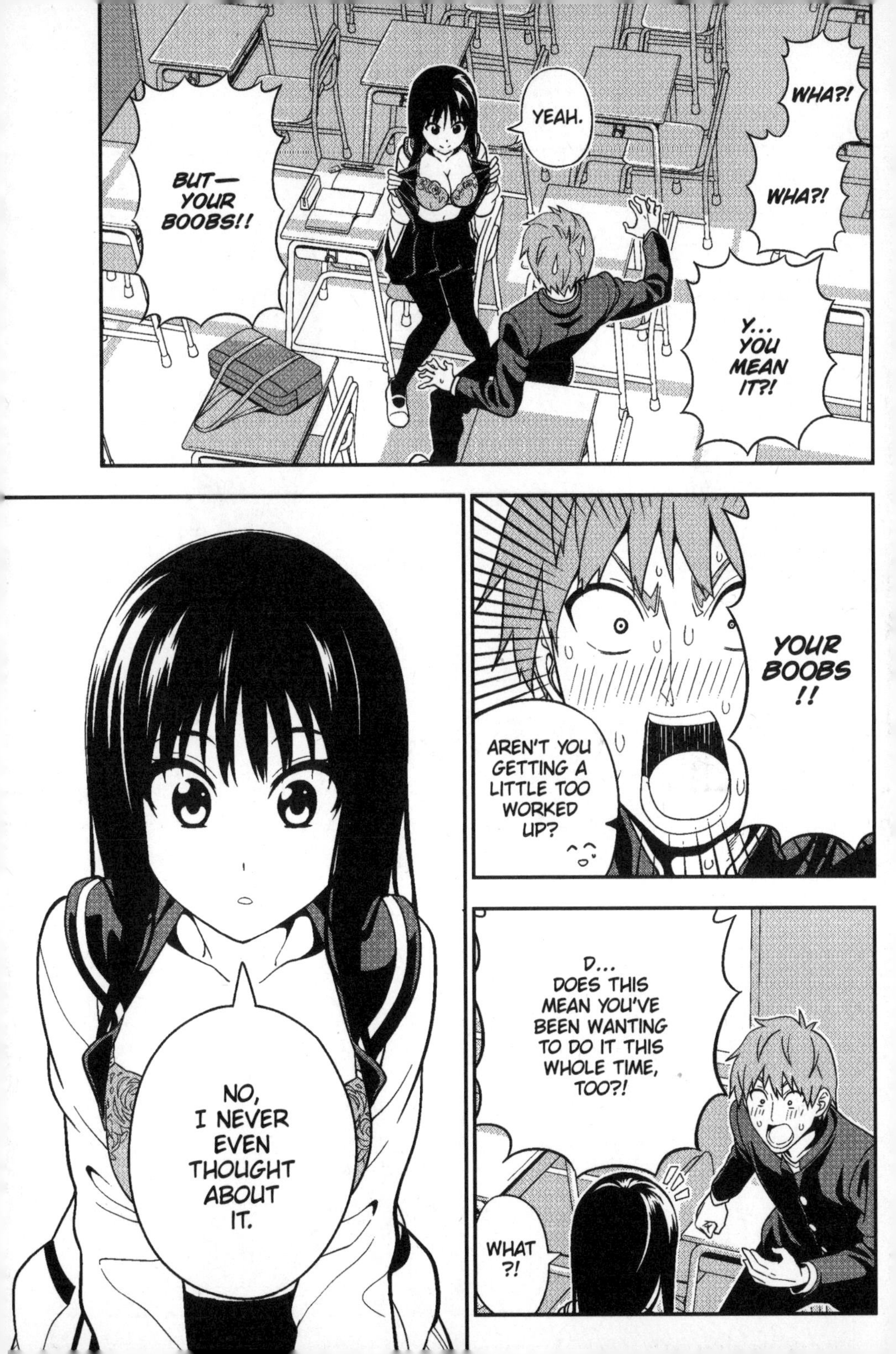
WHA?!
WHA?!
Y... YOU MEAN IT?!
YEAH.
BUT— YOUR BOOBS!!
YOUR BOOBS !!
AREN'T YOU GETTING A LITTLE TOO WORKED UP?
D... DOES THIS MEAN YOU'VE BEEN WANTING TO DO IT THIS WHOLE TIME, TOO?!
WHAT ?!
NO, I NEVER EVEN THOUGHT ABOUT IT.

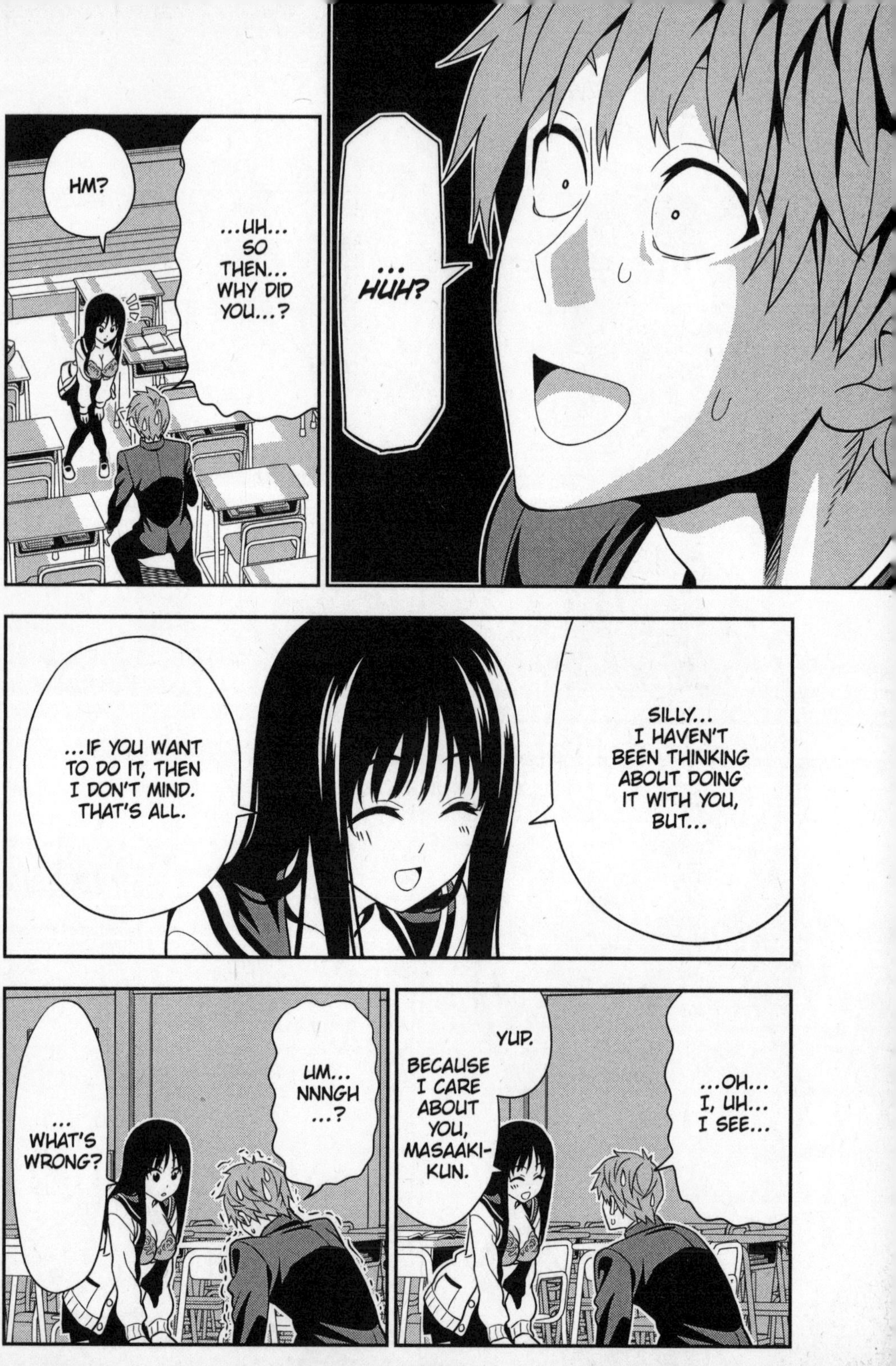
...HUH?
...UH... SO THEN... WHY DID YOU...?
HM?
SILLY... I HAVEN'T BEEN THINKING ABOUT DOING IT WITH YOU, BUT...
...IF YOU WANT TO DO IT, THEN I DON'T MIND. THAT'S ALL.
...OH... I, UH... I SEE...
YUP.
BECAUSE I CARE ABOUT YOU, MASAAKI-KUN.
UM... NNNGH ...?
... WHAT'S WRONG?

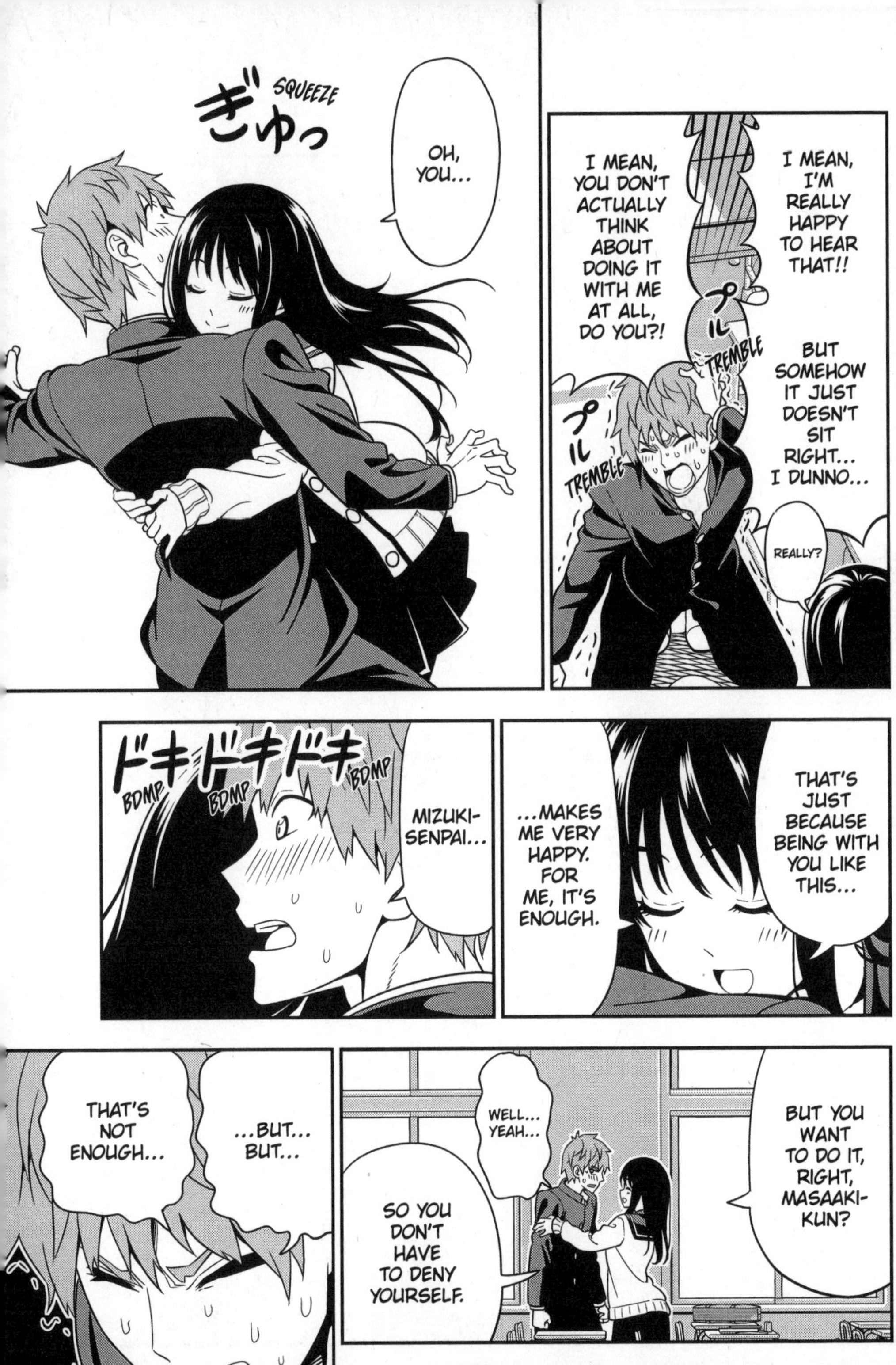
I MEAN, I'M REALLY HAPPY TO HEAR THAT!!
BUT SOMEHOW IT JUST DOESN'T SIT RIGHT... I DUNNO...
I MEAN, YOU DON'T ACTUALLY THINK ABOUT DOING IT WITH ME AT ALL, DO YOU?!
プル TREMBLE
プル TREMBLE
REALLY?
OH, YOU...
ぎゅっ SQUEEZE
THAT'S JUST BECAUSE BEING WITH YOU LIKE THIS...
...MAKES ME VERY HAPPY. FOR ME, IT'S ENOUGH.
MIZUKI-SENPAI...
ドキドキドキ BDMP BDMP BDMP
BUT YOU WANT TO DO IT, RIGHT, MASAAKI-KUN?
WELL... YEAH...
SO YOU DON'T HAVE TO DENY YOURSELF.
...BUT... BUT...
THAT'S NOT ENOUGH...

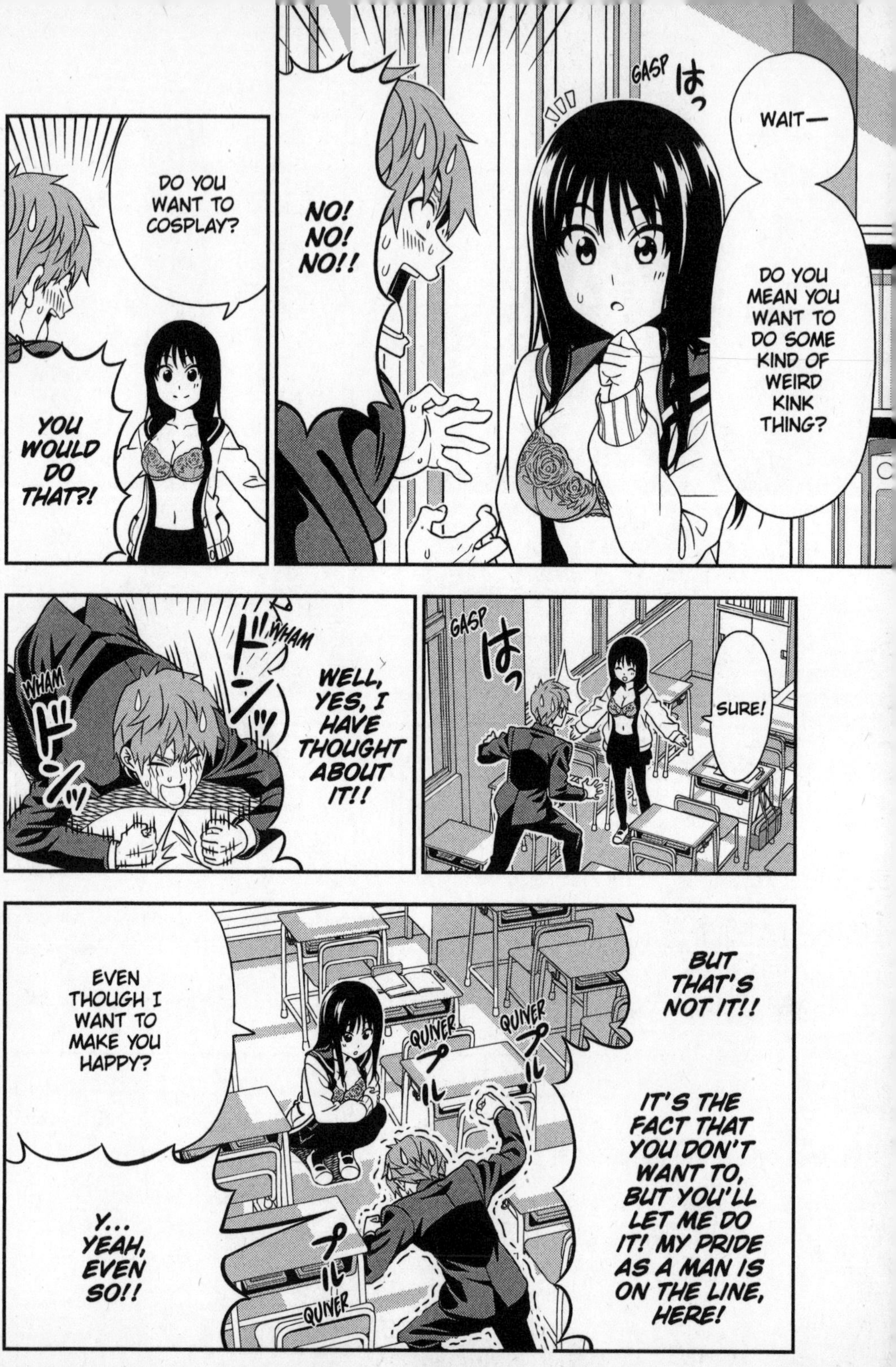

GASP はっ
WAIT—
DO YOU MEAN YOU WANT TO DO SOME KIND OF WEIRD KINK THING?
NO! NO! NO!!
DO YOU WANT TO COSPLAY?
YOU WOULD DO THAT?!
GASP はっ
SURE!
WHAM ドンッ
WELL, YES, I HAVE THOUGHT ABOUT IT!!
WHAM ドンッ
BUT THAT'S NOT IT!!
IT'S THE FACT THAT YOU DON'T WANT TO, BUT YOU'LL LET ME DO IT! MY PRIDE AS A MAN IS ON THE LINE, HERE!
QUIVER プル
QUIVER プル
EVEN THOUGH I WANT TO MAKE YOU HAPPY?
QUIVER プル
Y... YEAH, EVEN SO!!

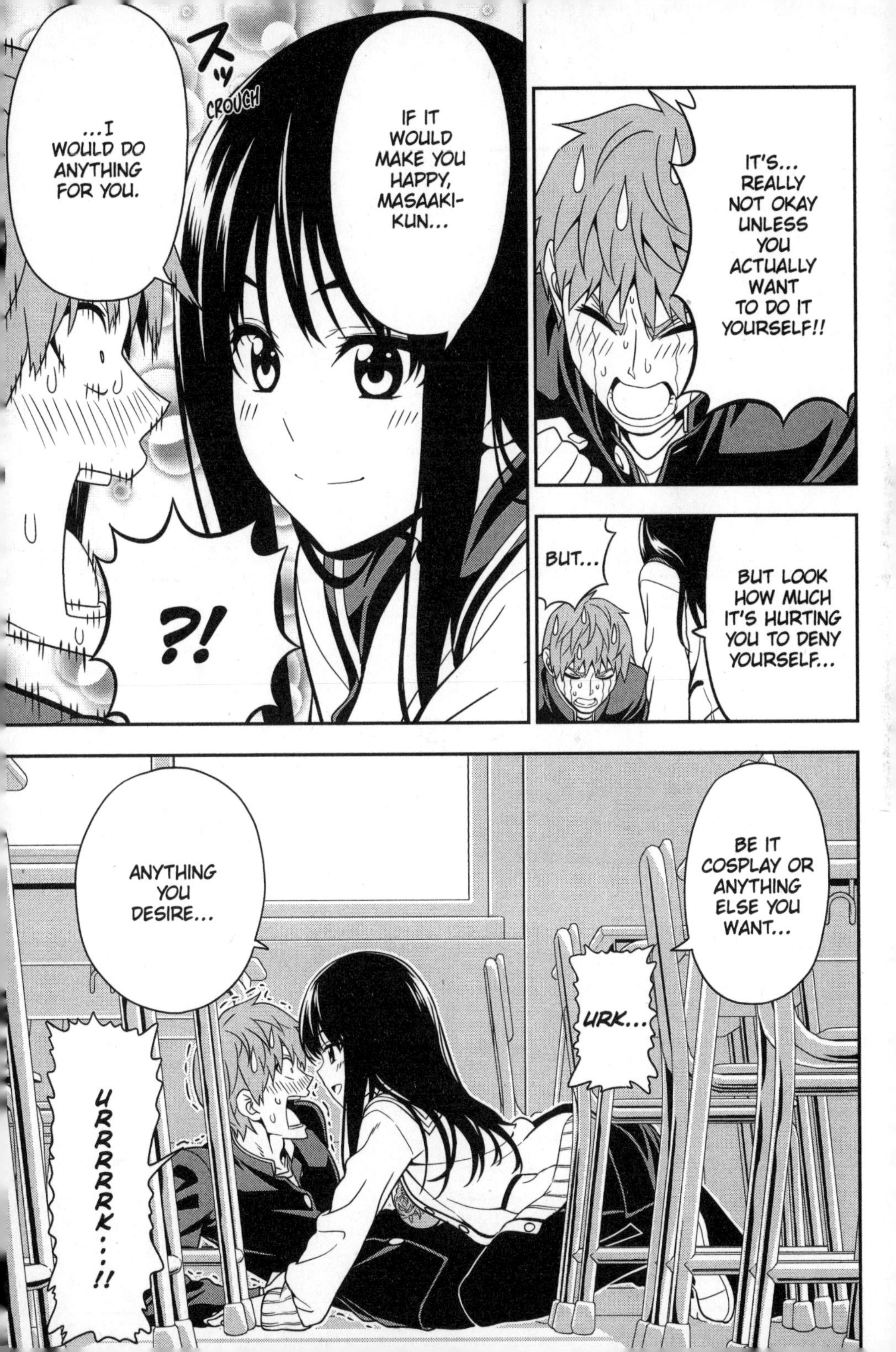
IT'S... REALLY NOT OKAY UNLESS YOU ACTUALLY WANT TO DO IT YOURSELF!!
BUT LOOK HOW MUCH IT'S HURTING YOU TO DENY YOURSELF...
BUT...
IF IT WOULD MAKE YOU HAPPY, MASAAKI-KUN...
CROUCH
...I WOULD DO ANYTHING FOR YOU.
?!
BE IT COSPLAY OR ANYTHING ELSE YOU WANT...
URK...
ANYTHING YOU DESIRE...
URRRRRK...!!

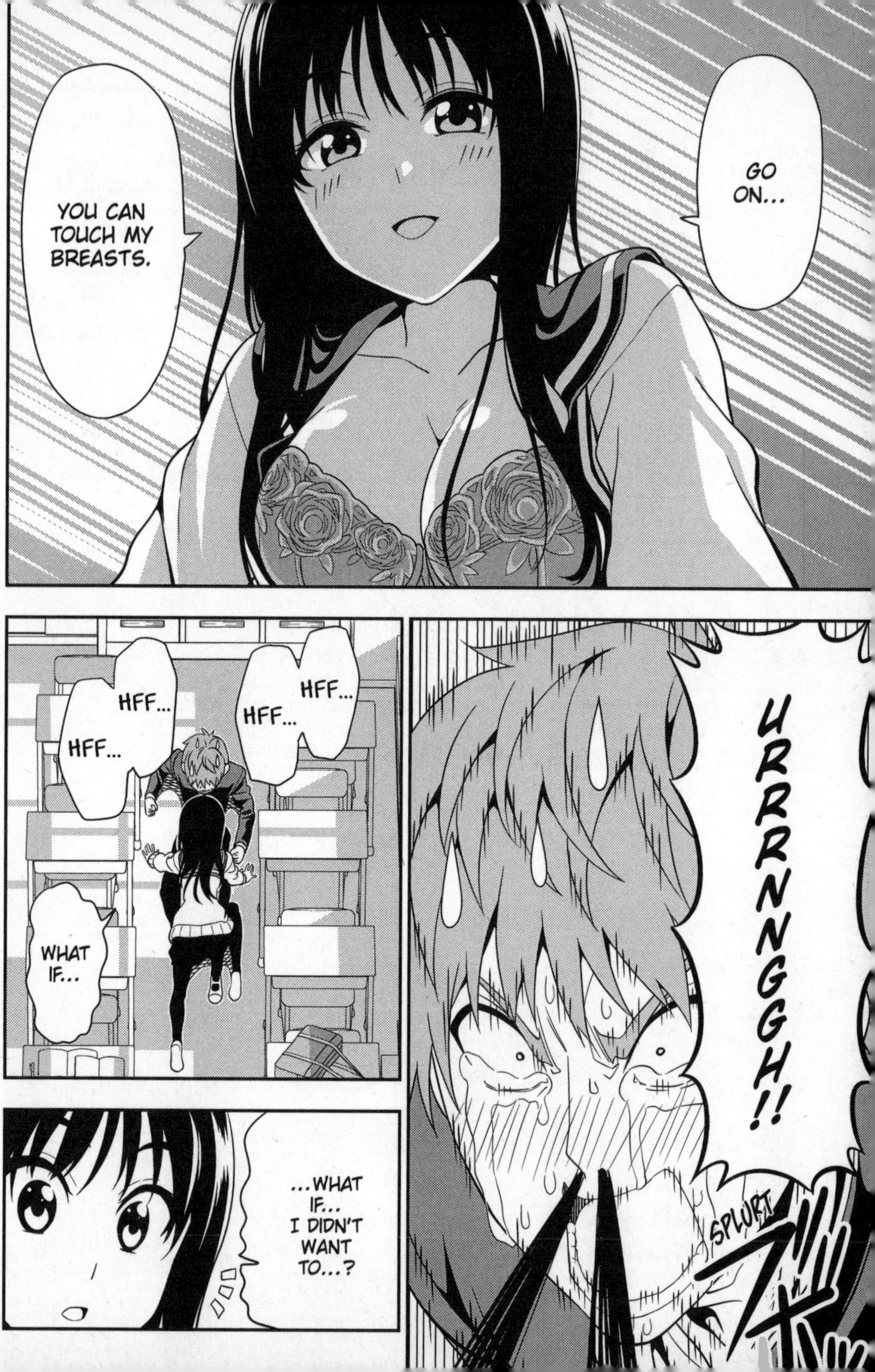
GO ON...
YOU CAN TOUCH MY BREASTS.
URRRNNGGH!!
SPLURT
HFF... HFF...
HFF... HFF...
WHAT IF...
...WHAT IF... I DIDN'T WANT TO...?

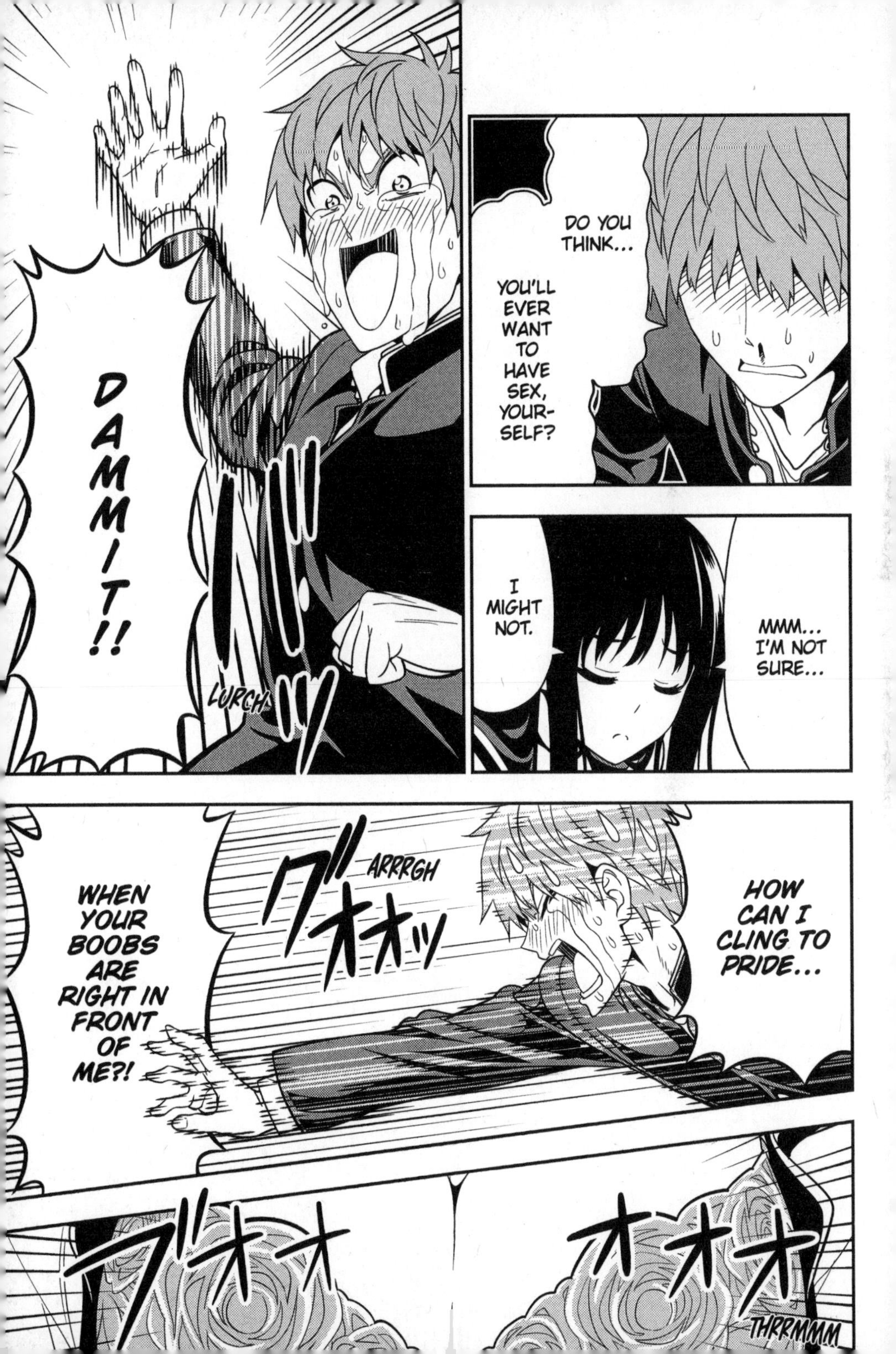
DO YOU THINK...
YOU'LL EVER WANT TO HAVE SEX, YOUR-SELF?
MMM... I'M NOT SURE...
I MIGHT NOT.
DAMMIT!!
LURCH
HOW CAN I CLING TO PRIDE...
グオオッ
ARRRGH
WHEN YOUR BOOBS ARE RIGHT IN FRONT OF ME?!
ブオオ
オオオ
THRRMMM

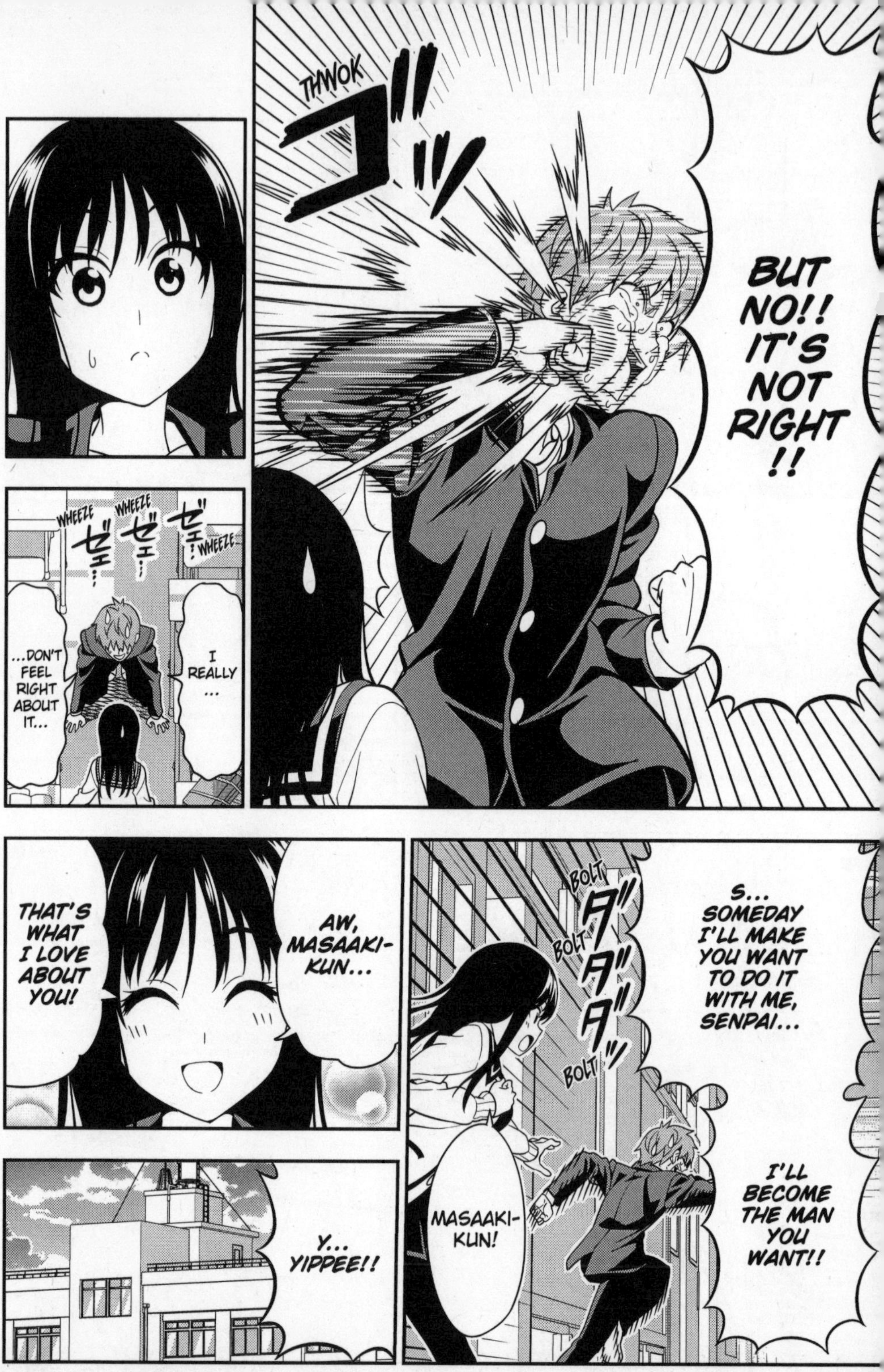
BUT NO!! IT'S NOT RIGHT!!
THWOK
WHEEZE
WHEEZE
WHEEZE
I REALLY...
...DON'T FEEL RIGHT ABOUT IT...
S... SOMEDAY I'LL MAKE YOU WANT TO DO IT WITH ME, SENPAI...
BOLT
BOLT
BOLT
I'LL BECOME THE MAN YOU WANT!!
MASAAKI-KUN!
AW, MASAAKI-KUN...
THAT'S WHAT I LOVE ABOUT YOU!
Y... YIPPEE!!

THE END!

THE DRAMA OF HOW HIROYUKI BECAME A MANGA-KA – FINAL CHAPTER

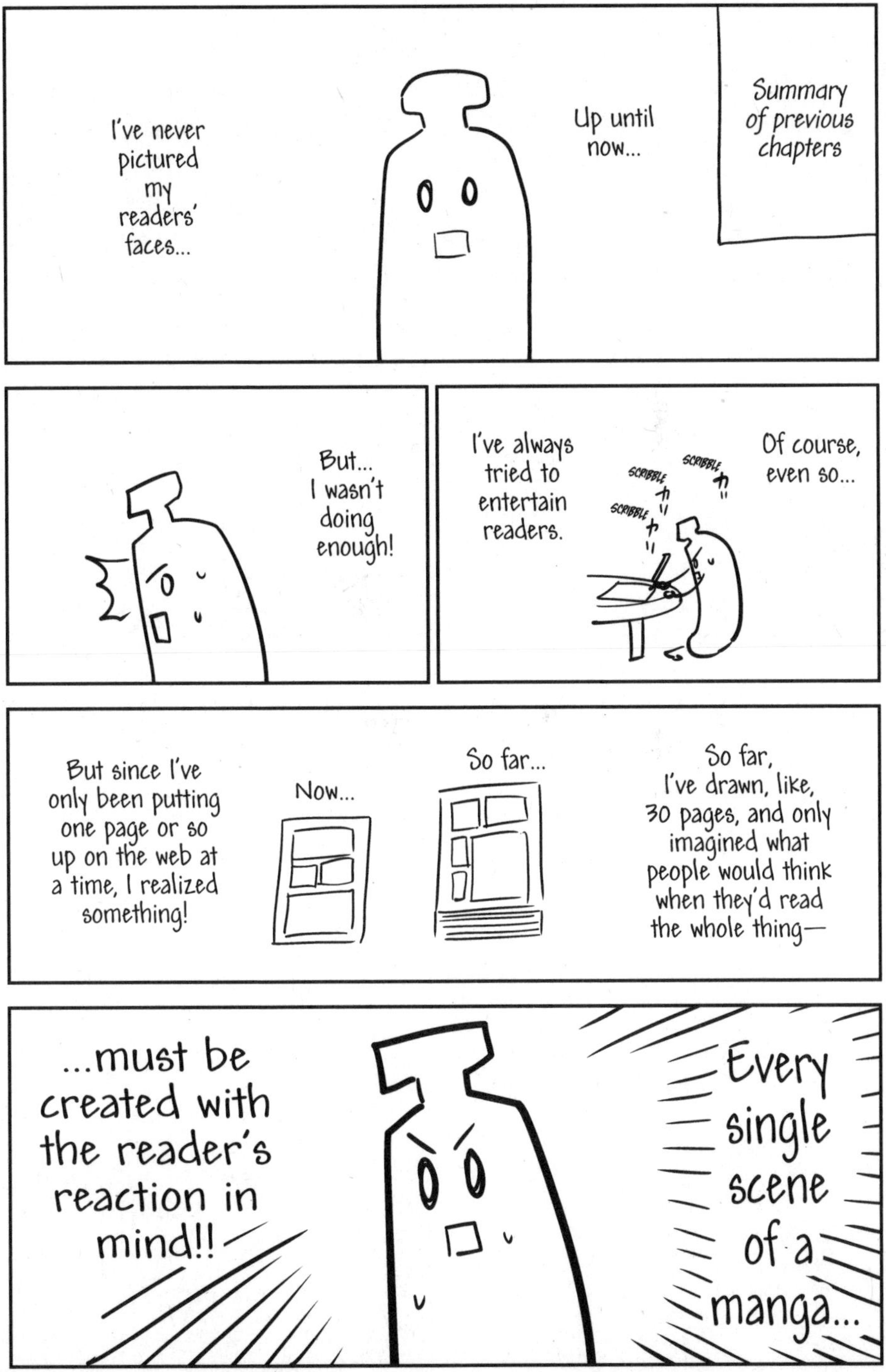
Summary of previous chapters
Up until now...
I've never pictured my readers' faces...
Of course, even so...
I've always tried to entertain readers.
SCRIBBLE
SCRIBBLE
SCRIBBLE
But... I wasn't doing enough!
So far, I've drawn, like, 30 pages, and only imagined what people would think when they'd read the whole thing—
So far...
Now...
But since I've only been putting one page or so up on the web at a time, I realized something!
Every single scene of a manga...
...must be created with the reader's reaction in mind!!

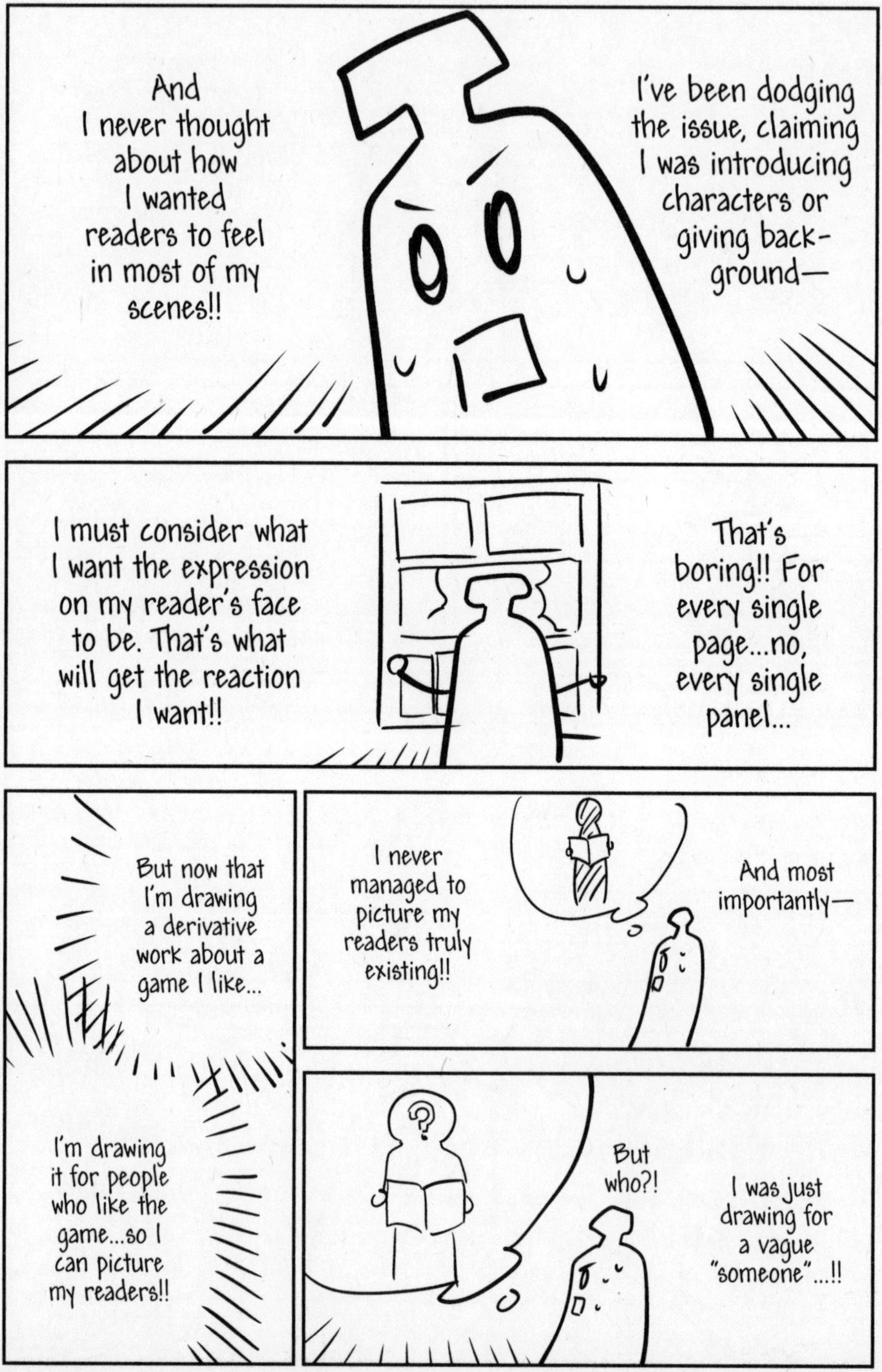
I've been dodging the issue, claiming I was introducing characters or giving back-ground—
And I never thought about how I wanted readers to feel in most of my scenes!!
That's boring!! For every single page...no, every single panel...
I must consider what I want the expression on my reader's face to be. That's what will get the reaction I want!!
And most importantly—
I never managed to picture my readers truly existing!!
I was just drawing for a vague "someone"...!!
But who?!
But now that I'm drawing a derivative work about a game I like...
I'm drawing it for people who like the game...so I can picture my readers!!

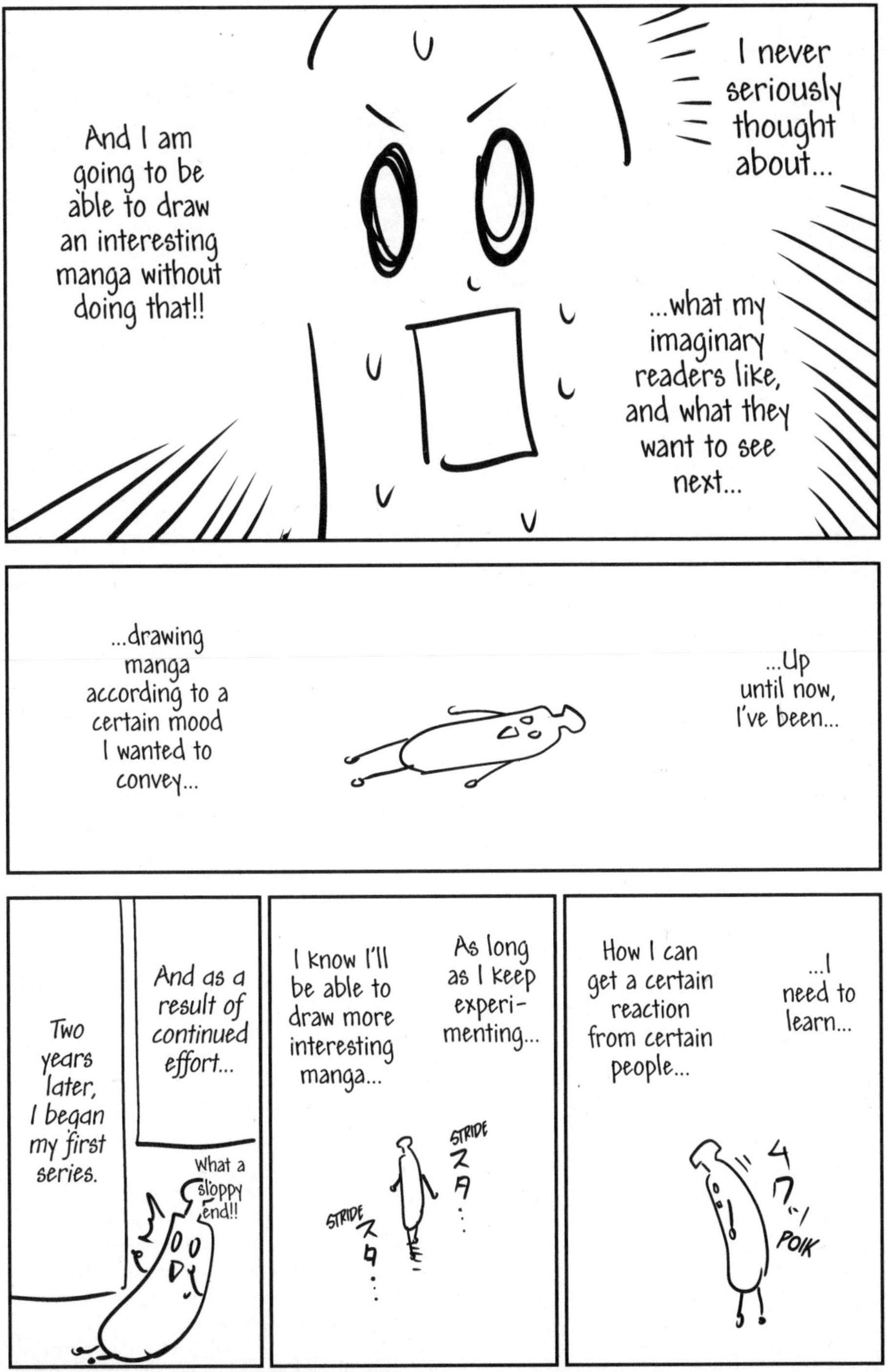
I never seriously thought about...
...what my imaginary readers like, and what they want to see next...
And I am going to be able to draw an interesting manga without doing that!!
...Up until now, I've been...
...drawing manga according to a certain mood I wanted to convey...
...I need to learn...
How I can get a certain reaction from certain people...
ムク
POIK
As long as I keep experimenting...
I know I'll be able to draw more interesting manga...
STRIDE
スタ...
STRIDE
スタ...
And as a result of continued effort...
Two years later, I began my first series.
What a sloppy end!!

THE END

Translation Notes

Page 2

"Aggravated straight man"

This is an explanatory gloss of the Japanese term "*tsukkomi.*" The *tsukkomi* and *boke* duo are a common trope in *manzai*-style stand-up comedy routines. The boke, like Yoshiko, draws over-the-top and just plain stupid conclusions to the *tsukkomi*'s set-ups. The *tsukkomi* tries to remain calm and reasonable during the act, but is invariably pushed into extreme and sometimes violent reactions out of his frustration.

Page 3

"Gals"

The term "gal" (Japanese *gyaru*) refers to a broad segment of popular youth culture in Japan that began in the mid-1990s. The term encompasses many distinct subcultures with different stereotyped behaviors (such as extreme tanning, bleached-white hair, or casual dating in exchange for spending money) that are considered contrary to prevailing Japanese morality. In general, though, most people who are labeled by the term "gal" merely subscribe to a particular fashion aesthetic characterized by loose socks (the familiar slouchy socks that hang loose around the ankles), lightly bleached hair, extensive nail art or cell phone bangles, and school uniform skirts that are rolled up at the waist to be scandalously short.

"Head Monitor"

The head monitor's title in Japanese includes the word *fuuki*, which roughly translates to "moral order" or "discipline." She would not be merely checking for hall passes the way a hall monitor in a Western school might, and would be more broadly responsible for reporting anything in violation of the moral standards of the institution.

"G Cup"

Going by Japanese bra sizing conventions, the head monitor's "G cup" would be roughly equivalent to an American DDD.

Page 5

"Christmas date"

Although it has some of the trappings of Christmas in the West, and everyone knows the traditional religious and cultural stories surrounding the holiday (like baby Jesus, Santa Claus, and Rudolph), Christmas in Japan is celebrated more like how the West now celebrates New Year's Eve: as a time for friends and couples. (In contrast, in Japan, New Year's is when people go home to visit their families and participate in religious rituals and have a big meal.) In fact, Christmas Eve carries much the same weight as Valentine's Day does in the U.S., where people feel inordinate pressure to engage in romantic gestures, buy their girlfriends jewelry, and avoid the stigma of being alone.

Page 6

"Oh, holy night!!"

In the original Japanese, there is a written pun in the head monitor's speech, which replaces the character *sei* (holy) with the character for *sei* (sex).

Page 36

"Totally x6"

This is the name of a one-hit wonder girl supergroup, whose one hit is titled "*Kimi no Koto ga Suki Dakara*" ("It's Because I Love You").

Page 37

"Oneechan," "Oniichan"

Literally "older sister" and "older brother," respectively, these terms are also used to address teenage to early 30s-aged men and women not related to the speaker.

Page 54

"Everyone is different, everyone is"

This line comes from a children's poem titled "A Bird, a Bell, and Me" (*watashi to kotori to suzu*) written by Misuzu Kaneko. The short poem tells, in three stanzas, how the author wishes she could fly like a bird, but recognizes that she can run faster, and how she wishes she could make her body sing like a bell, but that she knows many more songs than a bell does, and concludes with the lines: "A bird, a bell, and me; everyone is different, everyone is good."

Page 58

"A gacha, a random generator that you have to pay for"

A gacha game is a mobile game that uses a monetization mechanic much like Ryuichi describes, where a player pays (either in-game currency or real-world money) to activate a random generator, which will provide some sort of game resource like equipment or a rare character. The name derives from the Japanese word for vending machines that sell toys in plastic capsules, or *gachapon*, where the user has no control over what toy they'll receive.

"¥300"

Equivalent to about $2.75 in US dollars.

Page 59

"¥300,000"

Equivalent to about $2,750 in US dollars.

"Banana curry?!"
In the original Japanese, the Indian chef's dialogue is written in katakana, the writing system primarily used for foreign loan words. This technique is used to indicate that the man is speaking with an accent.

Page 111
"Somewhere, there's always"
This is the title and refrain of a song (*itsudemo dokoka ni*) by Masatoshi Ono, the front man of various rock and heavy metal bands. Various lines of the song include "Somewhere, there's always a blue sky" and "Somewhere, there's always your dream waiting for you."

Page 112
"Until we meet again"
This is likely a reference to a song sung at Japanese graduations, thanking classmates and school staff for all the memories a student has gained during their time. The refrain reads "Until we meet again, until we meet again; goodbye. Thank you."

Page 113
"Hey…Mizuki-senpai…it's, uh…almost Christmas, huh?"
See note for page 5.

Page 60
"¥30,000"
Equivalent to about $275 in US dollars.

Page 69
"Akurtz-sama!!"
Ryuichi calls Akkun "Akutsu-kun," which would be the standard form of address between age peer boys, and has been referring to Akurtz without any suffix whatsoever, which is normal when speaking about a fictional character one has no emotional investment in. However, here Ryuichi starts using the honorific suffix "-sama." Such a choice is an over-the-top expression of respect or admiration, putting Akurtz on an almost god-like plane above Ryuichi.

Page 72
"If you think about it, micropayments might actually be"
Aoi Yuki, the voice actress who plays Yoshiko in the *Aho-Girl* anime, released a concert DVD with interviews in 2015, and in one interview Aoi was asked how much she spends on internet and mobile games. She replied, "Well, it's like food. So you make micropayments to something, but when the service ends, it disappears. A delicious meal disappears after you eat it, too. If you think about it, micropayments might actually be more worthwhile."

Page 98
Bon Odori
Dance performed at an Obon festival, which is an upbeat summer festival to commemorate the spirits of deceased family members and ancestors. The dance is traditional and differs by locale, and is usually performed for bystanders by an official group that has been practicing for weeks ahead of time. See Volume 3 for details.

"Hawk of Kodan Peak"
See Volume 3 for details.

"The old fisherman"
See Volume 5 for details.

"The guys from Gesu High"
See Volume 4 for details.

Page 102
"The lady with the super cheap crab!!"
See Volume 6 for details.

"The guy who runs the curry place!!"
See Volume 6 for details.

Aho-Girl
\ˈahô͵gərl \ *Japanese, noun.*
A clueless girl.

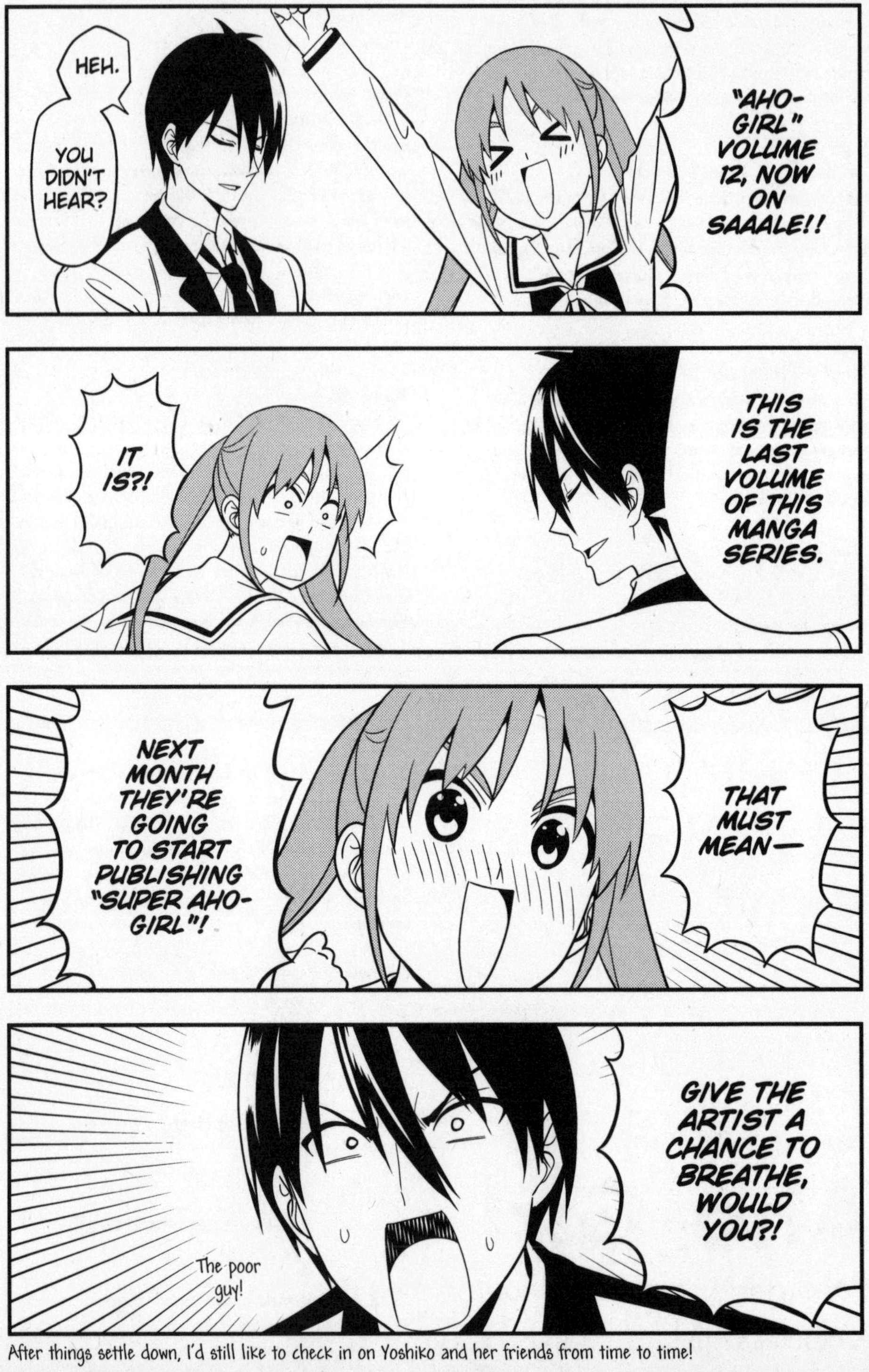
"AHO-GIRL" VOLUME 12, NOW ON SAAALE!!
HEH.
YOU DIDN'T HEAR?
THIS IS THE LAST VOLUME OF THIS MANGA SERIES.
IT IS?!
THAT MUST MEAN—
NEXT MONTH THEY'RE GOING TO START PUBLISHING "SUPER AHO-GIRL"!
GIVE THE ARTIST A CHANCE TO BREATHE, WOULD YOU?!
The poor guy!

After things settle down, I'd still like to check in on Yoshiko and her friends from time to time!

See you later!!

Again!!

Kinichiro Imamura isn't a bad guy, really, but on the first day of high school his narrow eyes and bleached blonde hair made him look so shifty that his classmates assumed the worst. Three years later, without any friends or fond memories, he isn't exactly feeling bittersweet about graduation. But after an accidental fall down a flight of stairs, Kinichiro wakes up three years in the past... on the first day of high school! School's starting again—but it's gonna be different this time around!

Vol. 1-3 now available in PRINT and DIGITAL! Vol. 4 coming August 2018!

Find out **MORE** by visiting:
kodanshacomics.com/MitsurouKubo

ABOUT MITSUROU KUBO

Mitsurou Kubo is a manga artist born in Nagasaki prefecture. Her series *3.3.7 Byoshi!!* (2001-2003), *Tokkyu!!* (2004-2008), and *Again!!* (2011-2014) were published in *Weekly Shonen Magazine*, and *Moteki* (2008-2010) was published in the seinen comics magazine *Evening*. After the publication of *Again!!* concluded, she met Sayo Yamamoto, director of the global smash-hit anime **Yuri!!! on ICE**. Working with Yamamoto, Kubo contributed the original concept, original character designs, and initial script for **Yuri!!! on ICE**. *Again!!* is her first manga to be published in English.

In love, there are
no save points.

KC
KODANSHA
COMICS

NOW AN
ANIME!

ヲタクに恋は難しい

WOTAKOI!
LOVE IS HARD FOR OTAKU
by FUJITA

Narumi has had it rough: Every boyfriend she's had dumped her
once they found out she was an otaku, so she's gone to great
lengths to hide it. At her new job, she bumps into Hirotaka, her
childhood friend and fellow otaku. When Hirotaka almost gets
her secret outed at work, she comes up with a plan to keep him
quiet. But he comes up with a counter-proposal:
Why doesn't she just date him instead?

"Far more entertaining than it ought to be... What kid doesn't want to think that every time they sneeze, a torpedo shoots out their nose?"

—Anime News Network

Strep throat! Hay fever! Influenza! The world is a dangerous place for a red blood cell just trying to get her deliveries finished. Fortunately, she's not alone. She's got a whole human body's worth of cells ready to help out! The mysterious white blood cell, the buff and brash killer T cell, the nerdy neuron, even the cute little platelets— everyone's got to come together if they want to keep you healthy!

Cells at Work!

はたらく細胞

By Akane Shimizu

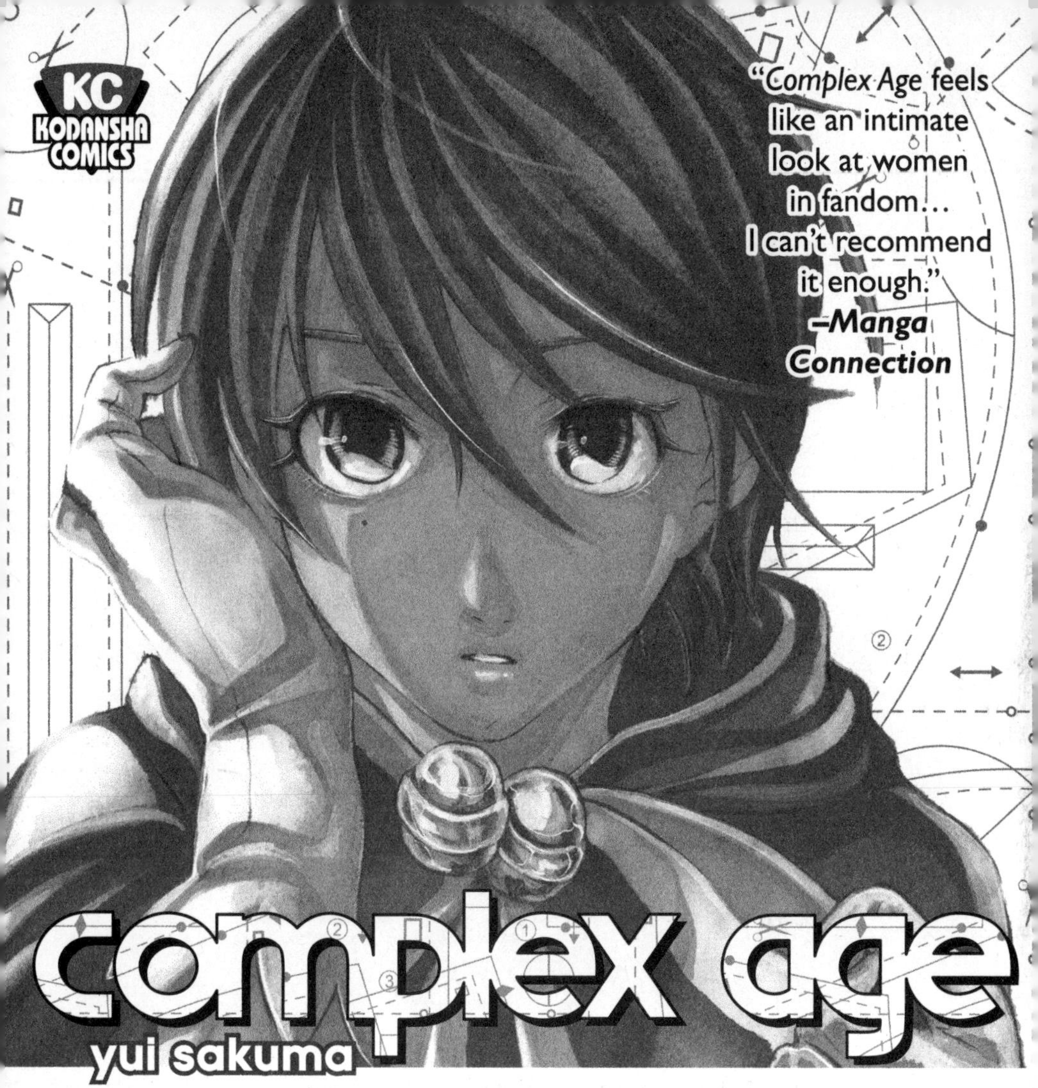
KC
KODANSHA COMICS
"Complex Age feels like an intimate look at women in fandom… I can't recommend it enough."
–Manga Connection
complex age
yui sakuma

26-year-old Nagisa Kataura has a secret. Transforming into her favorite anime and manga characters is her passion in life, and she's earned great respect amongst her fellow cospayers.

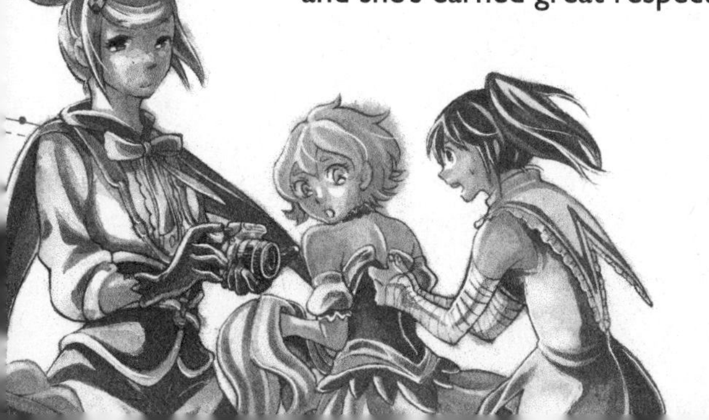

But to the rest of society, her hobby is a silly fantasy. As demands from both her office job and cosplaying begin to increase, she may one day have to make a tough choice—what's more important to her, cosplay or being "normal"?

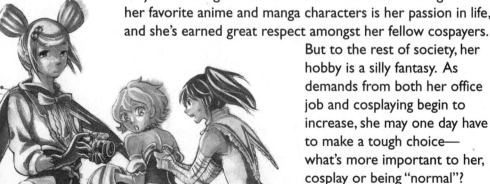

A new series from the creator of *Soul Eater*, the megahit manga and anime seen on Toonami!

"Fun and lively... a great start!"
-Adventures in Poor Taste

FIRE FORCE

By Atsushi Ohkubo

The city of Tokyo is plagued by a deadly phenomenon: spontaneous human combustion! Luckily, a special team is there to quench the inferno: The Fire Force! The fire soldiers at Special Fire Cathedral 8 are about to get a unique addition. Enter Shinra, a boy who possesses the power to run at the speed of a rocket, leaving behind the famous "devil's footprints" (and destroying his shoes in the process). Can Shinra and his colleagues discover the source of this strange epidemic before the city burns to ashes?

KC
KODANSHA
COMICS

Japan's most powerful spirit medium delves into the ghost world's greatest mysteries!

Story by Kyo Shirodaira, famed author of mystery fiction and creator of *Spiral*, *Blast of Tempest*, and *The Record of a Fallen Vampire*.

Both touched by spirits called yôkai, Kotoko and Kurô have gained unique superhuman powers. But to gain her powers Kotoko has given up an eye and a leg, and Kurô's personal life is in shambles. So when Kotoko suggests they team up to deal with renegades from the spirit world, Kurô doesn't have many other choices, but Kotoko might just have a few ulterior motives...

IN/SPECTRE

STORY BY KYO SHIRODAIRA
ART BY CHASHIBA KATASE

KODANSHA COMICS

New action series from Hiroyuki Takei, creator of the classic shonen franchise Shaman King!

In medieval Japan, a bell hanging on the collar is a sign that a cat has a master. Norachiyo's bell hangs from his katana sheath, but he is nonetheless a stray — a ronin. This one-eyed cat samurai travels across a dishonest world, cutting through pretense and deception with his blade.

NEKOGAHARA

STRAY CAT SAMURAI

By

Hiroyuki Takei

Based on the critically acclaimed classic horror manga

The first new *Parasyte* manga in over 20 years!

NEO Parasyte f

BY ASUMIKO NAKAMURA, EMA TOYAMA, MIKI RINNO, LALAKO KOJIMA, KAORI YUKI, BANKO KUZE, YUUKI OBATA, KASHIO, YUI KUROE, ASIA WATANABE, MIKIMAKI, HIKARU SURUGA, HAJIME SHINJO, RENJURO KINDAICHI, AND YURI NARUSHIMA

A collection of chilling new *Parasyte* stories from Japan's top shojo artists!

Parasites: shape-shifting aliens whose only purpose is to assimilate with and consume the human race... but do these monsters have a different side? A parasite becomes a prince to save his romance-obsessed female host from a dangerous stalker. Another hosts a cooking show, in which the real monsters are revealed. These and 13 more stories, from some of the greatest shojo manga artists alive today, together make up a chilling, funny, and entertaining tribute to one of manga's horror classics!

KC KODANSHA COMICS

"I'm pleasantly surprised to find modern shojo using cross-dressing as a dramatic device to deliver social commentary... Recommended."

-Otaku USA Magazine

The prince in his dark days

By Hico Yamanaka

A drunkard for a father, a household of poverty... For 17-year-old Atsuko, misfortune is all she knows and believes in. Until one day, a chance encounter with Itaru–the wealthy heir of a huge corporation–changes everything. The two look identical, uncannily so. When Itaru curiously goes missing, Atsuko is roped into being his stand in. There, in his shoes, Atsuko must parade like a prince in a palace. She encounters many new experiences, but at what cost...?

Princess Jellyfish

Akiko Higashimura

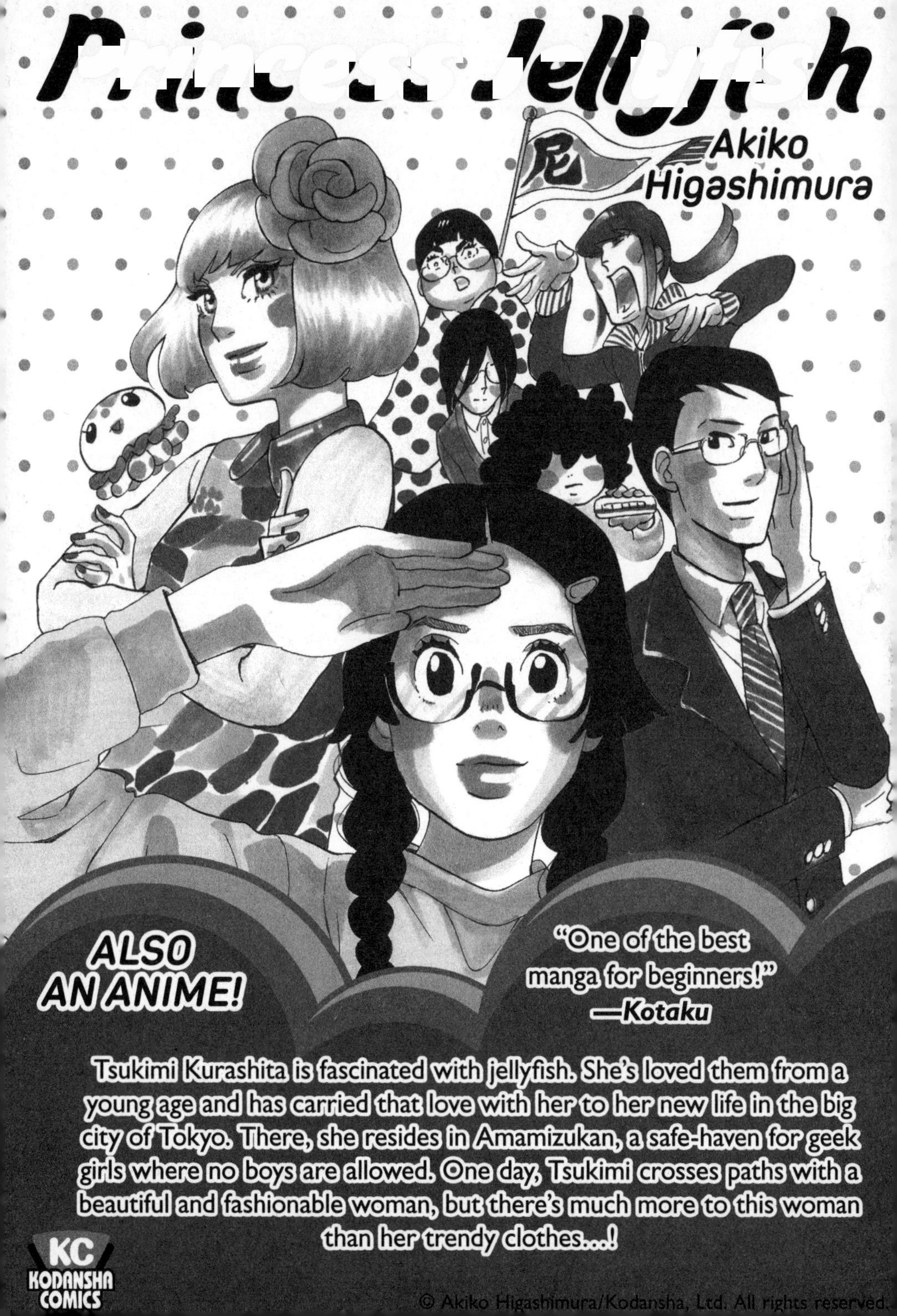

ALSO AN ANIME!

"One of the best manga for beginners!"
—*Kotaku*

Tsukimi Kurashita is fascinated with jellyfish. She's loved them from a young age and has carried that love with her to her new life in the big city of Tokyo. There, she resides in Amamizukan, a safe-haven for geek girls where no boys are allowed. One day, Tsukimi crosses paths with a beautiful and fashionable woman, but there's much more to this woman than her trendy clothes...!

KC KODANSHA COMICS

ANIME COMING OUT SUMMER 2018!

Mikami's middle age hasn't gone as he planned: He never found a girlfriend, he got stuck in a dead-end job, and he was abruptly stabbed to death in the street at 37. So when he wakes up in a new world straight out of a fantasy RPG, he's disappointed, but not exactly surprised to find that he's facing down a dragon, not as a knight or a wizard, but as a blind slime monster. But there are chances for even a slime to become a hero...

"A fun adventure that fantasy readers will relate to and enjoy." –*AiPT!*

THAT TIME I GOT REINCARNATED AS A SLIME

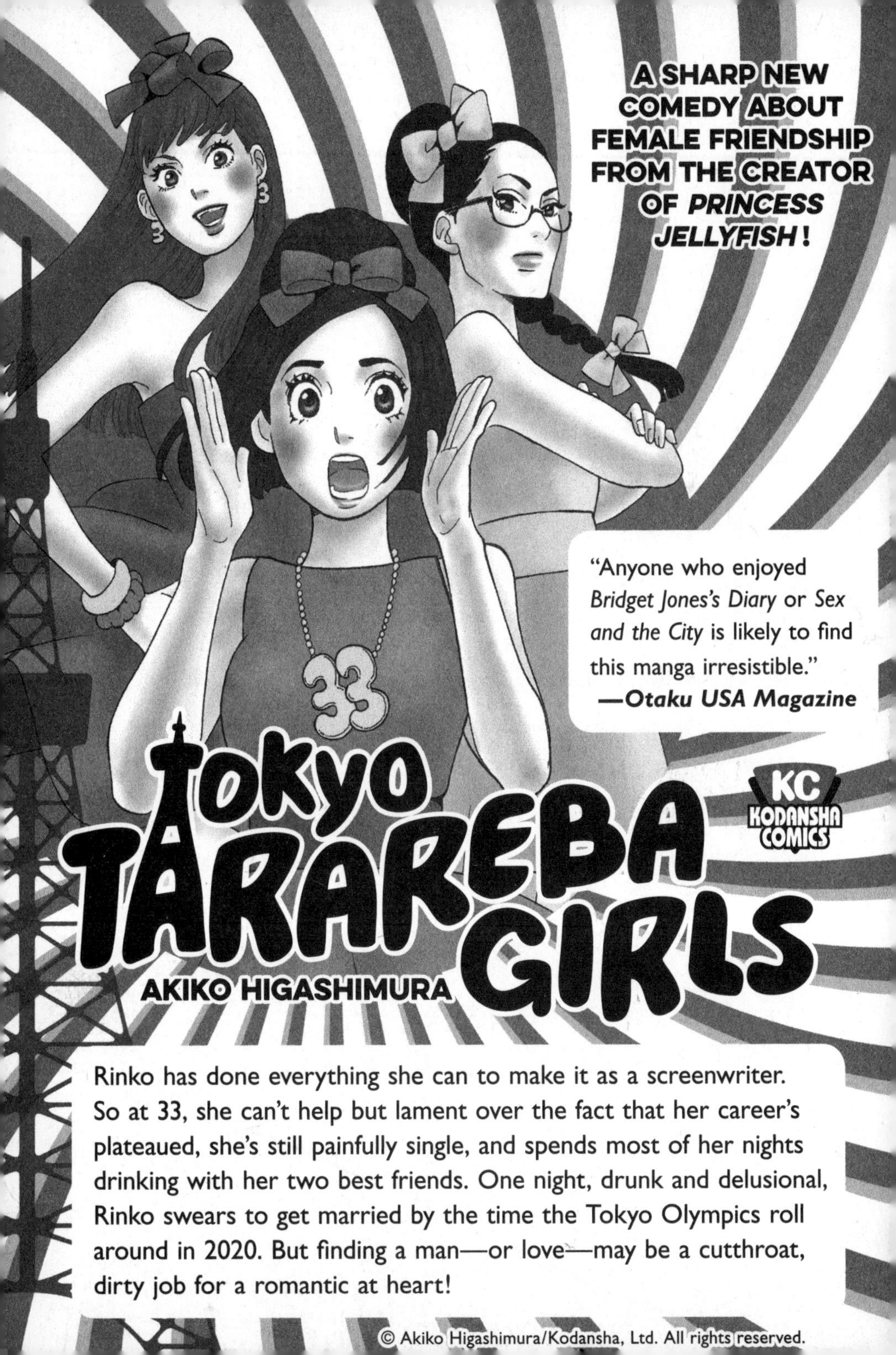
A SHARP NEW COMEDY ABOUT FEMALE FRIENDSHIP FROM THE CREATOR OF *PRINCESS JELLYFISH*!
"Anyone who enjoyed *Bridget Jones's Diary* or *Sex and the City* is likely to find this manga irresistible."
—*Otaku USA Magazine*
KC KODANSHA COMICS
TOKYO TARAREBA GIRLS
AKIKO HIGASHIMURA
Rinko has done everything she can to make it as a screenwriter. So at 33, she can't help but lament over the fact that her career's plateaued, she's still painfully single, and spends most of her nights drinking with her two best friends. One night, drunk and delusional, Rinko swears to get married by the time the Tokyo Olympics roll around in 2020. But finding a man—or love—may be a cutthroat, dirty job for a romantic at heart!
© Akiko Higashimura/Kodansha, Ltd. All rights reserved.

A Kodansha Comics Trade Paperback Original.

Aho-Girl volume 12 copyright © 2017 Hiroyuki
English translation copyright © 2019 Hiroyuki

Published in the United States by Kodansha Comics, an imprint of Kodansha USA Publishing, LLC, New York.

Publication rights for this English edition arranged through Kodansha Ltd., Tokyo.

First published in Japan in 2017 by Kodansha Ltd., Tokyo, as *Aho Gaaru* volume 12.

ISBN 978-1-63236-716-7

Printed in the United States of America.

www.kodanshacomics.com

9 8 7 6 5 4 3 2 1

Translator: Karen McGillicuddy
Lettering: S. Lee
Editing: Paul Starr
Kodansha Comics edition cover design by Phil Balsman